WHAT THIS BOOK WILL DO FOR YOU

1. It will show you how to use the greatest power in the universe to develop your abilities and attain your desires.

2. It will teach you how to use the strongest structure in the universe to build better memory and accelerated mind-power.

3. It will show you how to use Inner Ecology to improve your health, increase your longevity, and restore your body to youthfulness.

4. It will teach you how to use the feedback signals of Outer Psychology to remove emotional charge from your memory bank and free your energies for success and achievement.

5. It will show you how to use the Ecology Diet to build up your vitality and increase your energy and free yourself from disease and malfunction.

6. It will teach you a simple new way to quit smoking, stop drinking, and rid yourself of excess weight.

7. It will show you how to open the door to your subconscious mind and use its forces to win love and happiness.

8. It will teach you how to establish contact with your Master Mind and use its powers to expand your consciousness and experience astral travel.

9. It will show you how to meet and know your Master Self — the spiritual guide who controls your destiny.

10. It will give you techniques for recalling your past lives and teach you how to become free of your karma.

11. It will show you how to see into the future, perceive things at a distance, read the thoughts of others.

12. It will reveal to you your spiritual destiny — show you how to claim that destiny now — place in your hands the keys to immortality and power.

Printed in the United States of America

ISBN O-87980-339-8

⊖ ATLANTIS UNIVERSITY

The Greatest Power in the Universe

by U. S. ANDERSEN

Published by
Melvin Powers
WILSHIRE BOOK COMPANY
12015 Sherman Road
No. Hollywood, California 91605
Telephone: (213) 875-1711

THE FRONT COVER ARTIST

Though John J. Stancin is one of the most copied painters in the world, an authentic Stancin always carries an indelible impression of the immensity of the universe and the eternal question posed by the tiny figure who contemplates it. Born and raised in Chicago of Roumanian immigrant parents, Stancin was instructed by his father in the fine arts of self-defense and pool shooting and learned about life as a concessionaire on the carnival circuit and an unwilling steeplejack. His education in art began when he received a scholarship to the Chicago Art Institute, and he has been a Director of the American Academy of Fine Arts and an elected officer of the Santa Monica Art Association. Now residing on Maui, Stancin can be seen behind his easel at various locations around the island — capturing for posterity the landscapes of paradise.

CONTENTS

CHAPTER 5 — SPACE AND TIME UNVEILED

Dimensions of the mind. Gate to the root of the world. Dynamics of ecology. Notes on Space and Time. Insight into immortality. Measuring the intelligence quotient. A synthesis of Yoga. The alpha champ who was a failure. Mysticism and magic. The structure of the chakras. Exercises of Ecology Yoga. Counting the people who only count trees. Taking the intelligence test. Space and Time — the Forces of Balance. Dynamics of balance.

CHAPTER 6 — THE POWER TO CHANGE

An announcement worthy of Pavlov. People who believe they are ducks. A paper dagger. The power of suggestion. The horse and the rider. An experience with hypnosis. The king and the brilliant idiot. Good enough to bottle. A review of hypnosis. Path of saint or path of madman. Brainwaves and hypnosis. Another job for the electronic wizard. The wise man takes the middle path.

CHAPTER 7 — INNER ECOLOGY

The art of meditation. Instant yoga. The technique of concentration. The ladder of Kundalini. Building a god-like self-image. The yoga of ecology. The physical postures of ecology yoga. In the heart of the lotus. The dynamics of breath control. Breathing with the belly. Breathing with balanced rhythm. The secret of sound. The power of chanting. The ecology mantra. Color and cosmic consciousness. Three color exercises. Conditioning the spiritual athlete.

CHAPTER 8 — THE ECOLOGY DIET

Balance in both directions. Elements and brainwaves. Proteins, fats, and carbohydrates. Nature's carburetor. The appalling facts of the nation's health. The myth of man the meat-eater. The dangers in canned and processed foods. The Space-Time relationship of sodium and potassium. The bountiful table of Mother Nature. RNA and DNA. Natural foods. Diet and higher consciousness. The transition diet. The alpha balancer. High protein cereal. High energy salad. The booster and the calmer. Foods in order from Space to Time.

CHAPTER 9 — OUTER PSYCHOLOGY

The galvanometer. Measuring idea resistance. Removing emotional charge. A serious fall. An out-of-the-body experience. A battle with guilt. A brush with the hangman. A panel of experts. The wheel of balance. Ascent and descent. A meeting with the beloved. Physical, mental, emotional, and spiritual balance.

CHAPTER 10 — MALE AND FEMALE FORCES

Unknown journey. Members only. The ascent. The descent. Trapdoor into time. The rites of ancient Ephesus. Rose-colored glasses. The sentinel of sex. The Forces of Balance.

CHAPTER 11 — SEX ECOLOGY

The function of the orgasm. The genesis of life energy. The experiments of Wilhelm Reich. The Space-Time source of life energy. The sympathetic and parasympathetic systems. The engine of life. Channeling sexual power. The temptations of Satan. The rhythm and the tune. Some characteristics of ecologists. Some characteristics of sadists and masochists. The mating of ecologists. Living orgastically. The man in the mirror. Some advantages in being alive. The magic of creative power. Space-Time orgasm.

CHAPTER 12 — THE NEW ECOLOGISTS

Space-Time balance. Spontaneous remission. The love exercises of ecology. New life styles. The ethic of honesty. The psychology of love. The philosophy of beauty. The ecology diet. More on sodium and potassium. Sodium and fats. Proteins, vitamins, and minerals. Alcohol and drugs. Why ginseng and musk are aphrodisiacs. Nutrition and ecology. The health food movement. Dynamics of ecology.

CHAPTER 13 — PSYCHIC POWER

The marvelous money machine. The carrier wave of psychic power. A practice in black light. The astral body. Discovery of the energy body. How the energy body functions. The psychotronic generator. The energy of Time. Breakthrough in telepathy.

The Gates of Horn. Accelerated learning. Superman aborning. The power of imagination. The uses of conflict. The secret of magic. The Gates of Ivory.

CHAPTER 14 — THE BROTHERHOOD OF LIGHT

New Atlantis. Pyramid power. In the king's chamber. The missing caprock. The hidden arcanum. The philosophic death. The inscrutable answer. The greater self. The divine will. Pearl of great price. Seven rings to eternal light.

CHAPTER 15 — THE MASTER MIND

Vision in a cosmic mirror. The secret destiny of America. The expanding mind. The bio-chemistry of psychic power. The psychic poisons. The psychic energizers. The coming new age. The forces of darkness. The mission of Michael. Lucifer's last stand. The interplannetary confederation.

CHAPTER 16 — THE MASTER SELF

The strongest structure in the universe. The ascending masters. The Master Self. The secret being of the Master Self. The physical body of the Master Self. The psychic power of the Master Self. The seven centers of ascension. The power dynamics of the pyramid plan.

CHAPTER 17 — THE MASTER GAME

The Magic Theatre. The Cardinal's Ball. The arrival of the queen. The magician intervenes. The magician's warning. The Queen's Vision. Triumph of the magician. The Satanic Creed. The Fallen Prince.

CHAPTER 18 — THE MASTER PLAN

The scrolls of Atlantis. The standards of ecology. The Masters of Balance. The Pyramid of Atlantis. The earth's imbalance. Realigning the poles. The living truth.

ABOUT THE AUTHOR

U. S. Andersen is widely regarded as America's most challenging and original thinker in the field of human dynamics. His patriotic initials were selected by Norwegian parents grateful to their new homeland, and his first two names are Uell Stanley. He brings to his writing a broad experience in sports, the military, business, finance, science, religion, psychology and the arts, and he is the author of such books as Three Magic Words, the Secret of Secrets, the Magic in Your Mind, and Success Cybernetics. An articulate spokesman for mystical patriotism — the spiritual meaning of America — he is an unforgettable lecturer; and his insights into ecology have led to the founding of Atlantis University.

ATLANTIS RISING

The American Dream is the ancient dream of the prophets of Atlantis who sought union with God and thereby a measure of God's freedom and power.

Today, all that man remembers of Atlantis is "the gods who came out of the sea" — the glory of their golden ornaments, the transcendency of their wisdom, and the sanctity of their symbols. Wherever the Atlanteans roamed, they erected temples and pyramids patterned after the great sanctuary in their City of the Golden Gates, and so it was that they built the pyramids of Egypt, Mexico, and Central America.

In the midst of this program of colonization, the cataclysms began that sank Atlantis beneath the sea. The spiritually illumined withdrew from the doomed continent, carrying with them their Sacred Scrolls. Nearly all the cosmological myths that underlie the world's Great Religions are based on the Atlantean Sacred Scrolls, for they comprise the Great Way to spiritual illumination. There are many paths, but there is only one Great Way.

Now the cast of characters has assembled once again. Now the costumes and settings have been taken from memory's storage and refurbished anew. Now the orchestra strikes the first resounding chord of the overture. The curtain is about to go up. Atlantis is rising . . .

Discoveries of Cybernetics

1

Within a small and heavily wooded ravine in the Cascade Mountains on the Oregon coast nestles a tiny, jewel-like lake where human foot has seldom trod. In crystal depths swim giant trout, landlocked all the year except for spring when over-flowing waters carry them by creek down to the sea. Anglers greet this sudden bounty by renewing faith in the mysterious lake that not a single one has seen, though more than one has often searched. I, too, looked for the lake but never found it. I even wrote a story about a man and his son who looked. They didn't find it either. I realized then that the lake symbolized the Secret of Life.

I discovered that secret through cybernetics.

THE REAL AND
THE UNREAL

The word was coined in 1948 by Norbert Wiener, a mathematics professor at Massachusetts Institute of Technology, when he published under that name a book describing the functioning of the automatic feedback control devices that were being used in steering ships and flying planes and in the new computing machines. He derived the word from the Greek, meaning steersman, and much of the book was devoted to drawing analogies between the feedback control devices of machines and the feedback control devices of the human nervous system. The brain, illustrated Wiener, might best be likened to a complex computing machine.

Since his book was published by M.I.T., it was distributed to a restricted audience, but computer developments over the next decade made Wiener's utterances so prophetic that John Wiley published a 1961 edition for the general public. A copy fell into my hands.

It is difficult to describe my excitement. After having travelled fully around the world in my search for the essence of man's mind, now for the first time, I felt I had found something concrete and material, something demonstrable and repeatable, something I surely could learn to understand and control. Earlier I had published several books which developed the premise of an indwelling God, but mine was an intellectual vision only, and the full realization had eluded me.

Hard on the heels of the Wiley edition came a popularization of Wiener's work by the eminent plastic surgeon, Maxwell Maltz. His book, *Psycho-Cybernetics,* combined feedback control with positive thinking to provide a regime for self-improvement, and it became a best-seller. Overnight, thousands of Americans were introduced to the idea that the brain was a highly sophisticated machine. A few, like myself, were thus led to ask, "Who's operating it?"

THE GHOST IN THE SKULL

Dean Wooldridge thought that nobody was. The wealthy co-founder of Ramo-Wooldridge resigned his company position in 1962 to devote himself to scientific pursuits and to writing, and in 1963 he published *The Machinery of the Brain,* a schol-

12

arly compendium of correspondences between brain and computer functioning, an area which he felt offered unparalleled opportunity for scientific advancement.

Several other books carried the same theme. Among them were J. von Neumann's *The Computer and the Brain,* D. O. Hebb's *The Organization of Behavior,* and *Brain Mechanisms and Learning,* a compendium of papers edited by Fessard, Gerard, Konorski and Delafresnaye. Though I refused to concede the argument of the materialists and give up the idea of a "ghost" in the skull, nevertheless I had to admit that most behavior seemed automatic. The human machine had enormous potential, but it had to be trained to develop it. Training was "conditioning," a term used by Ivan Pavlov to describe the process by which he produced automatic reaction in dogs.

On a sultry afternoon in mid-August, I received a long distance phone call from a vice-president of a national firm, requesting that I run a series of training programs for his sales force. I had received such invitations before and had always declined since my primary concern was man's spiritual quest rather than his financial aspirations, and I simply felt that my brand of philosophy was not particularly suited to the rough-and-tumble world of competitive capitalism. But this time my caller was insistent. He had read three of my books, he said, and he knew that I was the man to do the job. He was positive that what his sales force needed was a spiritual anchor. The upshot was that I agreed to take on the task.

A SESSION WITH GOD

The first session was held in a resort hotel in upstate Illinois. One hundred salesmen were in attendance, together with their wives, and they had won this privilege with their sales records, so they were affluent and gregarious and hardnosed and fond of alcoholic beverages. The first time I mentioned the word "God" I could feel my audience stir, and after a bit a tall man with a large Adam's apple and wearing spectacles raised his hand and I called on him. He stood, removed his spectacles, polished them carefully with a handkerchief, placed them back on his nose, stared around at the audience, then fixed me with his gaze.

"G-O-D," he said, "spells dog backwards." He sat down

13

amid strained laughter.

I glanced at the vice-president who was on the stage with me. Beads of perspiration were popping on his forehead, but he managed a sickly grin. Well, I hadn't survived four and a half decades by persisting in unrewarding efforts. If my audience didn't want God, I'd give them cybernetics.

"Apparently we have a champion speller in the audience," I said. "Since he has demonstrated his proficiency with three letter words, perhaps he would like to try something longer. Would the gentleman please stand up?"

Tall and bespectacled, he arose from his seat, a confident smile on his face.

"Try cybernetics," I said.

He stared. "What?"

"Cybernetics. It's a new science of improving human performance by feedback control."

"Never heard of it."

"Take a crack at it anyway. Cybernetics."

"S-I-B-U-R-N-E-T-I-C-S," he spelled hesitantly.

I spelled it correctly on the blackboard, then said, "So, you see, we've both learned something. I learned how to spell dog backwards, and you learned that things are not always what they seem. Now we both can get down to learning something about improving our performance through feedback control. That way we'll make more money."

The subsequent three days were a roaring success.

THE INGREDIENTS OF GENIUS

I had to wing it, of course — make up much of it on the spot — but my head was crammed so full of the stuff that it just seemed to be there when I needed it, and fortunately somebody had a tape recorder turned on, so I emerged from the session with a complete new course for improving human performance. I called it *Success Cybernetics*.

I like to think that it was not simply a parroting of things I'd read, but rather a genuine creative effort, that all I'd learned about cybernetics was filtered through my experience in athletics, business, and writing, my years of study in philosophy and comparative religions, to produce something different from anything that had been done to that time. For fundamental to my understanding of cybernetics was awareness of the power of a well-drawn plan to become a self-fulfilling prophecy. This kind of control of the future was something that seers and soothsayers had been after for years without notable success, and I found myself excited about being on the verge of a breakthrough in mental power.

The automatic feedback control devices in the human nervous system were easy enough for most people to grasp. They could understand that you could never become a good automobile driver, a good typist, a good piano player, until you were able to perform all the necessary movements automatically, without thinking, responding to signals in much the same way as an electronic computer responds to signals. Nearly everyone had had the experience of driving five or ten miles to the office through heavily congested traffic, making all the appropriate moves, with his mind on something else, so that when he arrived at the office he couldn't remember a single event that had transpired en route. Thus nearly everyone understood that the nervous system usually performed automatically. The obvious corollary of this understanding was the principle that to achieve skills you must practice. And practice. And practice. Until the skills were ingrained in the nervous system and functioned automatically.

To most people this realization came as a shock. They had thought that Heifitz just walked out there and played the violin, that Bob Hope was born with that timing, that Einstein popped out of the womb clutching the Theory of Relativity. For a person by dint of sweat and diligence to be able to train himself to genius seemed heresy.

HEREDITY AND ENVIRONMENT

Was environment more important than heredity then? Or was heredity more important than environment?

I couldn't help thinking that the question was much like the one that had plagued me from the start. Was materialism more important than spirituality?

For example, among people who practiced the same amount, some would perform better than others. And among the people who practiced the least would be someone who could perform better than somebody who practiced the most.

So there was a mystical factor.

But was heredity so mystical? Hadn't we isolated the genetic structure? Didn't it carry a coded signal to other cells to tell them what kinds of cells to be, just like the master program of an electronic computer?

Oh, that coded signal could tell those cells what to be, all right, but could it tell them what to *do?*

It could not tell them what to do. It could only tell them what to be. They would have to learn what to do.

So in the seminars we concentrated on goals — all the things we wanted to get done or see done sometime in the future, whether it was two hours from now or twenty years from now. You can't imagine the consternation this produced. People sat for hours with lead pencils to their tongues. It turned out that the cause of this paralysis was their feeling that they were being required to predict the future rather than make it up. That anyone could possibly make it up was foreign to their thinking. When it was pointed out that a writer made up a story, and an artist made up a painting, and a composer made up a song, they thought that the comparison was unfair because they were being asked to make up something that was real.

"The future isn't real yet," I objected. "It has to be made up."

"But that isn't always true," they complained. "The future isn't always what we think it is going to be. It's usually a surprise."

The only people who are surprised by the future are the people who don't make it up.

GOAL ACHIEVEMENT

That got us into goal achievement. We were able to understand that the only way a person could learn a skill was to get a mental picture of himself performing that skill. That was a goal. The goal gave him a means of disciplining his actions. After he had practiced enough to learn the skill, he didn't need the mental picture anymore, because the appropriate reactions had been trained into his nervous system. That was cybernetics.

Goals and automatic reactions — what you wanted to accomplish and the steps that would accomplish it — practicing the steps, getting good at them, doing them, reaching the goal — a nice little system for getting things done. It used both the mind and body, but there seemed no place for the soul. I missed the soul, but apparently nobody else did. The program won immediate acceptance.

Soon people were acting as if they had mastered all the secrets. "It's really so simple!" they exclaimed. That worried me. But as time passed and more and more people embraced the program enthusiastically, I gradually put my fears aside. After all, the proof of a thing was in its performance, and everybody who took to getting things done the cybernetics way was getting things done better and faster. Demands on my time, however, began to accelerate, so it eventually occurred to me to put the course in book form, thus it could be taught by sales managers and personnel directors and athletic coaches and military officers and business executives and school teachers and whoever else had a stake in improving human performance.

About this time, a disconcerting thing happened. One of my prize pupils, a super-achiever, was stricken with a heart attack. A relatively young man of 42, he was forced into a life of semi-retirement, being told by his doctor that he had strained his resources beyond the breaking point and would need much time and rest to repair the damage. To the credit of my stricken friend, he never once suggested that his cybernetics program might have brought on his heart attack, but I couldn't help toying with the possibility myself, and I didn't much like what I saw.

MR. MIDAS

After some prompting, his wife revealed how he had set a goal to be president of his company and how he had worked day and night to achieve it. She confirmed that the resultant seven-day-a-week, 16-hour-a-day schedule had been too much for him. So, for the time being at least, his goal had been defeated.

I thought over this problem for a long time but could see no solution. Eventually, I shrugged it off as just one of those things — the exception, perhaps, that proved the rule — and turned again to happier areas where things were working fine.

Then another unusual thing happened. A young man who had set a goal of making a great deal of money had made over two million dollars during a hectic nine week period on the commodity market. Everybody who visited him brought back a strange report. He appeared downcast, not at all elated. Some even reported him despondent. That observation was apparently close to the point, for within a few weeks he attempted suicide, and his death was narrowly averted. His friends prevailed upon me to call on him, which I did with misgivings. One does not easily face up to the fact that his antagonist is death.

I found him tucked into a lounge chair on the balcony outside his apartment. Though it was a pleasant day, he was bundled up in blankets, and his face was pale and drawn. The autumn sun cast shadows on the street below, and in the distance, the shimmering haze of the ocean could be seen. He apologized for not rising to receive me, and explained that he had been overcome by such lethargy that the simplest movements were beyond him. I tried to bring the conversation around to the money he had made, but he seemed not to hear me, staring into the distance in a manner which made me uncomfortable. Finally I tried talking about all the things he could do with the money, all the places he could go, the things he could see, but this made no impression either. At last I arrived at my wit's end, and we sat on the balcony in silence.

When I rose to go, his liquid eyes stared at me. "Call me Mr. Midas," he said.

A STRANGE MEETING

The interview had depressed me, and I felt like being alone, so I let the car have its head and before long discovered that I was driving south from Santa Monica along the Southern California coast. Eventually, I reached a deserted beach where a jetty jutted into the sea. On impulse, I decided to park and walk out on the pier, there to look upon the ocean and feel the breeze and reflect upon my afternoon visit.

The night had settled down chill, and by the time I found a parking place, I was thankful that I had a sweater in the car. Donning it, I hiked across the sands and made my way out on the pier. Along the horizon hung a faint reddish glow from the starboard running lights of a ship. The sky was overcast. Not a star was to be seen. Breaking seas ran beneath the jetty with an exaggerated whoosh and roar.

I wandered out onto the pier, staring unseeingly at the sea

and night. Thus it was that I suddenly came upon a man sitting on a small bench toward the seaward end of the jetty. His presence startled me. Doubly so, his appearance.

He wore a violet jacket of old-fashioned cut, a white ruffled shirt, dark striped trousers, square-toed boots, and he rested his hands on a gold-crested walking stick. His hair was long, dark and abundant, and he wore a full mustache and neatly trimmed beard. Clear blue eyes were fixed on me quizzically, and he looked so elegant sitting there that I wondered if I was suffering an hallucination.

"You look like an educated man," he said. "Do you know Faust?"

The question took me aback, but I managed to admit that I was familiar with Goethe's work.

He nodded his head, as if in affirmation. "One must pay, of course. That is what makes a bargain."

I suppose that at any other time the obliqueness of the conversation would have irritated me and I would have demanded to know at once what was meant, but there was something so sophisticated about his appearance that I found myself weighing the various meanings that might be intended. My mind was drawn at once to the situation of Mr. Midas.

THE FANTASTIC BARGAIN

"Can one truly have anything in the world if he gives up his immortal soul?" I asked.

"That is apparently what Goethe was trying to say," answered my companion.

"Why would Goethe occupy himself with such a question?"

The walking stick was raised then thumped against the planking of the pier. Its owner gave vent to a melodious laugh and said in high good humor, "Tell me, truly now, is there anything else for man to be concerned with?"

"Assuming he has a soul, I suppose not."

"Do you assume that he has no soul?"

"It is a question to which I have been addressing myself most seriously. For a long time, I felt that man had a soul and I made every effort to discover it, but at last it seemed mere vanity, so I turned away from the abstract to the concrete, which has proven a great deal more useful to both myself and others."

"Then you've made the Faustian bargain."

"How do you mean?"

"You've given up the abstract for the concrete, which simply means that you've given up your soul in order to have things."

I stared at him. "I should not like to think that the bargain was irreversible."

His gaze seemed to discern my innermost thoughts. "The fact that you are here is proof that the bargain is not yet irreversible." He banged his stick against the pier in emphasis. "Not yet, at least." Then he stood and threw a cloak about him. "Well, I must be going. It has been an interesting chat." He started off along the pier and immediately disappeared from view. A light fog had risen, and I was left in the isolation of my thoughts.

A strange sensation of vertigo seized me, as if there was no place solid to stand. I felt that I was immersed in a dream, trying desperately to awaken. Staggering along the pier toward the shoreline, it seemed that I must walk this narrow way forever. Finally I reached the sand then found the car and managed to drive home. When I went to bed, my dreams were haunted by an elegant figure in a violet jacket, and I knew that some great change was about to enter my life.

TREADING THE
FAUSTIAN LINE

In the morning, I arrived at a decision. I would postpone my teaching. An invisible weight disappeared from my shoulders, and I sang boisterously in the shower. I hadn't felt so good for months. Now I understood that I had only half the truth, and until I had much more, I had best confine myself to being a student rather than a teacher.

The question was, how best to start? Should I circle again the perimeter of man's philosophical and religious thought, hoping to discern something that had escaped me the first time? Or should I pick up my search among the axioms and formulas of science, an area that at least had produced cybernetics? I was persuaded at once, because of the little I knew of science, that whatever was missing from my complete understanding existed in the area where I understood the least. I resolved to carry on my subsequent investigations in the area of science.

In high school and college, I had a terrible time with mathematics. It seemed to me that numbers were a waste of time because there were no ideas in them. Five years later I woke to the fact that not only were there ideas in them, but those ideas were *permanent*. In other words, they were *laws*. The way I came to see this was I became navigating officer of my ship during World War II. They gave me some tables so I could correlate my star sight (height above the horizon, compass direction and time) with my ship's position on the face of the ocean. I got to wondering how all this was done, and that launched me into spherical trigonometry. When I started drawing in my mind those great triangles of balancing pressures that extend throughout the universe, when I actually started seeing that those triangles existed evermore, when I began realizing that the relationship between them was immutable and unchanging, for the first time I felt I had touched the eternal heart of God.

Now, I was treading the Faustian line. Because, to really get into something, one had to get into it exclusively. To get into science exclusively, I had to exclude mysticism. That meant I had to become one-sided. That meant I must adopt a hard-headed, materialistic, show-me, I'm-from-Missouri type of practical realism about everything that crossed my path.

Oh, I could play the role. What, after all, is an actor but his quest? And I knew I could save myself from being permanently cast in the role. What, after all, is strong enough to stand against growth? And the objective was intriguing, indeed. What is the meaning of man's life? Or was there a meaning? And if so, where was that meaning to be found?

THE MIND CONTROLS EVERYTHING

When one takes on an area of knowledge as broad as science itself, and an arena as large as the universe, he is likely to find himself in the position of not knowing where to start. In such cases, the winds carry their own boding, and leaning ladders, and black cats, and most of all, well-meaning friends. Thus it was, on a Saturday night, in the midst of a party that was "high" if not drunken, a friendly fellow who had known me in college told me that he was now a professor at U.C.L.A. Though I didn't remember him, I acknowledged the past, then politely inquired what he taught. "Brain Sciences," he answered, and for the rest of the evening, he educated me.

It turned out that the University of California at Los Angeles had a Brain Research Laboratory that was doing extraordinary work in lifting the mystery that surrounded the working of the human brain. W. S. Adey had come up with some remarkable findings that indicated how little was known and understood about how the brain really functioned.

I acknowledged that I had heard of Dr. Adey.

"Brainwaves!" cried the professor. "That's the thing of the future! Adey is discovering all sorts of things. For example, right now I know you're in beta. You'd feel better if you were in alpha. You'd get better ideas if you were in theta. Well, whatever, somewhere along the way we're going to discover that the mind controls everything."

"Are you an M.D.?" I asked.

"Everything is chemical," he replied.

"Where do I find out about these brainwaves?"

"Try the Biomedical Library at U.C.L.A."

Brainwaves Made Simple

2

The University of California at Los Angeles lies just across Sunset Boulevard from luxurious Bel Air and is wedged in between posh Beverly Hills and wealthy Brentwood, giving it perhaps the most strategic financial position of any university in the world. Nor is the campus itself disappointing. Constructed upon a spacious tract of rolling hills, like ancient Jerusalem, the university buildings are large and imposing and reflect pleasing groupings of color against the rich green of a well-watered landscape. One can easily believe in such surroundings that all is well with the world simply because everything about it has been put into books.

The UCLA Medical Center overlooks the athletic fields, and its parking lot is as jammed as any in downtown Los Angeles. The huge, multi-floored

23

structure houses research laboratories, operating rooms, convalescent rooms, testing laboratories, outpatient clinics, emergency facilities, libraries, lecture halls, stores, cafeterias, and recreation rooms. Along wide and silent corridors glide rubber-soled nurses, as well as M.D.'s, interns, and orderlies, starched and clean in blue and white, while the antiseptic odor of Hippocrates' profession wafts along hallways and embeds itself in clothing, furniture, and food alike.

I was given a map which revealed that the Biomedical Library was in the northeast corner of the building, and as I walked what seemed a mile along the corridors, I couldn't help sensing that the center had the self-sustaining quality of an independent organism. Should all communication with the outside world suddenly cease, it seemed clear that within these isolated halls business would be carried on as usual.

SELF-REGULATING PEOPLE

My doctor friend had given me a card of introduction to the librarian, but as it turned out it wasn't necessary. I was informed that I could use all facilities, but I would not be allowed to take books off the premises. I was shown the reference catalogue for both books and periodicals, then I was left on my own. I found several books that looked interesting, and bearing them to a desk, made myself comfortable and began to read.

Almost at once I became deeply engrossed in the material, being taken by a quote of Lord Adrian, the well-known biologist: "New ideas in science are induced by new discoveries, and at the present time the most potent factor in promoting new discoveries is the introduction of some new technique, some new tool, that can be used for exploring natural phenomena."

The book went on to say that sophisticated computer techniques applied to psycho-physical research were almost certain to shed additional light on attention, consciousness, thought, and emotion. Perhaps it might even be possible to produce a society of self-regulating individuals who would no longer have to be governed by threats and penal systems, but who would take charge of regulating their own inner and outer lives so as to harmonize with society. Such persons, of course, would make it easier for others to lead stable and creative lives.

For over two centuries, British medical doctors on foreign service in India had been sending back reports of such self-regulating people. They claimed that these persons, called yogis, could control many usually involuntary physiological processes, such as heart rate or pain. This control was laid to long practice of mental, emotional, and physical disciplines.

AUTOGENIC TRAINING

In this connection, there was some material on Johannes Schultz of Germany who developed a western system of self-regulation around 1910. It appeared to combine hypnotic techniques with methods of yoga. Freud had given up the use of hypnotism in therapy because its results were unpredictable, but Schultz felt that this defect was caused by the patient not being in control of the situation and resisting instructions. He therefore used auto-hypnosis in combination with yoga and called his system Autogenic Training, meaning self-generated training. The system had a measure of success in Europe, but never caught on in America.

The principle involved was this: Every change in the physiological state must be accompanied by an appropriate change in the mental-emotional state, and every change in the mental-emotional state must be accompanied by an appropriate change in the physiological state. This principle of balance made possible psychosomatic self-regulation. The key to understanding it seemed likely to be brainwaves, the tiny voltages emitted by the human brain as it went about its tasks of processing data, responding to signals, and otherwise governing the internal and external life of the individual. Here reference was made to studies of the brainwaves of yogis and Zen masters, but despite my eagerness to pursue matters further, the concrete confines in which I sat were proving too much for me, so I resolved to get a little fresh air and something to eat.

The cafeteria was crowded and there was a long line, so I took myself to the drug store where I found several small packages of breaded onion rings. These I carried onto the patio and sat in the sunshine, eating and smoking cigarettes and indulging myself in reveries. Thus occupied, I failed to hear my name called until somebody clapped me on the shoulder. I looked up into the face of an acquaintance whom I hadn't seen in years.

"I thought it was you!" he exclaimed. "There you sat, fat as a pig and smoking cigarettes like a chimney, and I couldn't believe my eyes. Somehow, I never thought you were the type to get fat and become a chain smoker."

MONITORING MEDITATION

The greeting scarcely endeared him to me. I remembered him from an advertising agency whose services I once had used, and it seemed to me he was as outspoken then as now. I mumbled that I had put on a few pounds and was having difficulty kicking the cigarette habit. He was disgustingly lean.

"Man," he said, "don't you read the medical journals? Cigarettes will kill you. So will fat. Quit smoking and reduce, friend, or your time amongst us is limited."

Nothing to do but invite him to sit down, and he spent the next half hour on this theme. I left uneaten at least half my onion rings and never smoked another cigarette in his presence. By the time a half hour had passed I was squirming in my seat. I finally excused myself and made my way back to the bookstacks, sucking in my stomach and feeling the conspicuous bulge of the package of cigarettes in my pocket. I resolved to get a doctor's appointment and find out what kind of shape I was in.

Back in the bookstacks, I began a study on the brainwaves of Zen masters. It developed that zazen, which is Japanese for "sitting in meditation," attracted the interest of physiologists and psychologists as early as 1950, but only recently had scientists at Komazawa University in Tokyo began investigating it with the electroencephalograph, the famed EEG that measured brainwave amplitude and frequency. Forty-eight Zen priests and nuns had been tested, together with 100 ordinary people who served as a control group. With electrodes pasted to their heads, the subjects adopted the stiff-backed, cross-legged position of meditation. Their respiratory rate dropped off to four or five breaths per minute, as against the normal seventeen or eighteen, and their pulses fell ten or fifteen beats a minute below their normal rate. Body temperature dropped a few degrees in some cases. These effects were explained as being due mainly to the sitting position itself, which placed a strain on the diaphragm and affected the autonomic nervous system, causing a calming influence and a slowing down of body functions.

ZEN AND ALPHA

The brain wave record of the Zen masters revealed that they were neither in a hypnotic trance nor asleep while they were meditating. When one of the laymen heard an electric bell, the pattern of his brain waves was interrupted for about fifteen seconds, but when the sound was repeated, he became used to it and eventually stopped reacting. The priests also reacted to the bell, but only for two or three seconds, and they continued to respond in this manner each time the bell was rung.

Most surprising was the fact that the Zen masters produced great trains of alpha waves, while the meditating laymen produced little or no alpha at all. It appeared that something unusual transpired within the brains of those who had trained themselves in meditation. The question was, did the increased alpha waves cause unusual abilities or were they the result of unusual abilities? It certainly seemed, in the light of the balancing action between psyche and soma, that either could be the case.

Here there was mention of the work of Gardner Murphy and Kenneth Gaarder in the area of bio-feedback research which was an attempt to train patients into voluntary control of their involuntary functioning by having them hooked up to instrumentation which signalled the electrical activity caused by inner states. I resolved to look into this farther, but the sun was lowering in the sky now, and I felt I had had enough for one day. Just before leaving the medical building, I stopped at a phone booth and called my doctor. He was going out of town for two weeks, and I would have to postpone seeing him until his return. In a way, it was a reprieve. We set the appointment for three weeks in the future.

That night the violet-jacketed man with the gold-headed walking stick appeared in my dream. "Syzygy to serendipity," he said. "The putting together of opposites leads to the fortunate finding of things not looked for." I awoke in the morning with a feeling of excitement. There was something strangely reminiscent about that dream, a feeling of *deja vu* — that it had all happened before. Then I recalled another dream that had come to me earlier. There had been a terrible pain in my heart and I had felt I was surely going to die, when suddenly my chest burst open, and lying in the gaping wound was a gigantic, irridescent pearl. "When one discovers a pearl of great price," said a voice, "he gives all that he has to obtain it." Now it seemed to me that the voice had been that of the man in the violet jacket.

BRAINWAVE FREQUENCIES

The next three weeks passed rapidly. I scarcely had time to attend to earning a living, so great was my absorption in research. I learned that there was a Brain Information Center on the top floor of the bookstacks of the Biomedical Library, and those in charge were kind enough to run a computer search delineating all source material on brainwaves. Since several hundred references were involved, I no sooner finished one text before I was into another. There was a certain drama to them, read like this, like pieces of an enormous jigsaw puzzle, and as I began to find various pieces that fit and to see an emerging pattern, I felt I was witness to some gigantic stage play, the third act of which promised a cosmic climax.

My studies revealed that four principal brainwave patterns were known, and they were named alpha, beta, delta, and theta. Each was classified according to the number of cycles it made each second, and these cycles were called Hertz. The delta wave varied between 1-3 cycles per second, the theta between 4-7 cycles per second, the alpha between 8-13, and the beta between 14-26. Researchers were unanimous in concluding that the beta and alpha waves were associated with conscious processes, while the theta and delta waves were associated with unconscious processes. This prompted the following diagram:

Brainwave Frequencies

Normally Unconscious		Normally Conscious	
delta	theta	alpha	beta

0   4   8   13   26

Hertz (cycles per second)

Conscious and unconscious nervous processes might best be visualized as being divided by a continuously undulating boundary as attention shifts from one region to the other. For example, the peripheral nervous system is divided into the autonomic and the craniospinal systems. The former is regarded as the involuntary nervous system, the latter as the voluntary nervous system. That each works in conjunction with the other is illustrated by the fact that when one learns to drive a car many of the activities that were at first conscious and to which attention must be given gradually become unconscious, so that eventually it is possible when the mind is preoccupied to drive through miles of traffic without conscious awareness of other cars or traffic signals.

SECRETS OF THE ALPHA RHYTHM

The significant difference in controlling these two systems is a subtlety not often recognized. For control of the voluntary nervous system requires the use of active volition, while control of the involuntary nervous system requires the use of passive volition, that type of volition exhibited by Zen masters and yogis. Here lay a clue to developing mind and body control through brainwaves.

The literature described a number of subjects who had been trained to produce a high percentage of alpha brainwaves through feedback, and these had reported sensations of great pleasantness, a kind of electronic "high," a serenity, an alertness, a feeling of competence and well being. Since this sounded like the meditation experience of yogis and Zen masters, it certainly seemed as if training oneself to produce a high percentage of alpha waves might be a shortcut to happiness.

The alpha rhythm appeared to hold a secret. This brain rhythm appeared when the subject was in a relaxed state and disappeared when he became tense, at which time the beta rhythm took over. Also, the alpha rhythm usually only appeared when the subject's eyes were closed and disappeared when his eyes were opened. It also disappeared when he fell asleep, giving way to the slower theta and delta rhythms. The Meninger Foundation had produced evidence indicating that some subjects were natural alpha producers while others produced little or no alpha. Natural alpha producers, through bio-feedback devices, could be taught to produce a great amount of alpha, to slow their alpha frequencies, to increase the amplitude of their alpha waves, and even to produce alpha with their eyes open, just as Zen masters. Non-alpha producers, on the other hand, had difficulty learning to produce alpha and their percentage of increase was far less than the natural alpha producers. In a delayed recall test, subjects who produced the highest percentage of alpha rhythm in their EEG patterns remembered the most material. High alpha production thus significantly correlated with the ability to learn faster and remember more.

Moreover, there was considerable evidence linking brain-wave production with creativity. Here the theta frequency was correlated with reverie and hypnogogic imagery. Hypnogogic imagery might best be described as pictures or words which are not consciously generated or manipulated, but which spring into the mind "full blown." Such imagery is the warp and woof of new invention, new art forms, new enterprises.

FEEDBACK CONTROL
OF ALPHA WAVES

In a report by Kasamatsu and Hrai on their EEG experiment with Zen masters, it was found that the moment the subject began to turn inward continuous trains of alpha rhythm began to appear on his EEG record, that the frequency of the alpha pattern began to decrease toward the alpha-theta border, and that the subject in a state of reverie (satori) produced long trains of theta waves.

Anand and Singh in their EEG study of yoga masters found the alpha-theta border intimately associated with the inward-turned attention of samadhi. They also reported that the inward-turned attention of their yogi subjects was so intense that neither flashing lights, sounding gongs, or intense heat could disrupt their concentration and cause alpha blocking.

Creative people often have described the states of reverie, dream, or near-dream in which creative solutions have come to consciousness. Robert Louis Stevenson commanded his "brownies" to furnish him plots. Poincare described mathematical ideas rising in clouds, dancing, colliding and combining into the first Fuschian Functions. Nearly all of us have had the experience of worrying for days over the solution to a problem then suddenly receiving it, whole and complete, while we were shaving or driving to the office. That there was a relationship between such inspirations and the production of low frequency alpha waves seemed inescapable.

In addition, insofar as an individual could extend the voluntary control of his nervous system, he would also be enabled to liberate himself from conditioned responses. Voluntary control would move him in the direction of increased inner freedom, while conditioned control could only produce a loss of inner freedom.

In this last insight I found the reason for my feeling that the theory of cybernetics was incomplete. For conditioned responses, regardless of how effective and efficient they might be, were far too robot-like to satisfy my intuition of a divine nature in man.

Feedback control devices used in brainwave training were varied and interesting. Because EEG signals are of low amplitude (10 to 100 microvolts), it usually required highly sensitive amplifiers encased in laboratory-type machines to detect brainwaves. However, recent electronic developments had made it possible to produce low-cost portable alpha detectors which a subject could use at home. Such alpha meters could be modified to show the presence of both alpha and theta waves, either by the production of sounds of certain frequency and amplitude, or by the presence of a flashing light. The latter device was not desireable, however, because of the necessity of keeping the eyes closed for optimum alpha production. Some experimenters had attached a small flashing light to the rim of spectacles which were placed on the subject, enabling him to see the light flashes through closed eyelids. In any case, once feedback techniques for producing the specific physiological state had been mastered, mechanical devices could be dispensed with. Eight to sixteen training hours attached to an alpha meter was generally regarded as sufficient.

THE DOCTOR IS FAR OUT

Involved as I was in soaking up data on brain rhythms, I nevertheless found it possible during the three week period before my doctor's appointment to quit smoking four times and to go on two diets. The remarks of my well-meaning friend had wounded me deeper than I thought, and I spent a good deal of time in front of the mirror observing my sagging waistline. Also, I began to count the number of cigarettes I smoked. That number was now between fifty and sixty a day. With only the slightest mental calculation I could easily see that I spent very little time without something in my mouth. Since I could neither stay on a diet nor quit smoking, I began to feel that there was something terribly wrong with me, that I was burdened with some Freudian oral fixation springing out of guilts or fears buried in my subconscious. Finally, to save what little self-respect I had left I decided to forget about diets and not smoking. After all, the doctor might easily find that I was in tip-top shape and that the extra weight I was packing around was actually beneficial to a man of my particular bone structure.

Meanwhile, I had become familiar with the work of Barbara Brown, Joe Kamiya, and Thomas Mulholland. Dr. Kamiya operated from a little laboratory near the University of California at Berkeley, and his work was being done under the auspices of the Langley Porter Neuropsychiatric Institute. Reportedly, the sign on his door, rather than saying, "The doctor is in," said instead, "The doctor is *far out*." Word had gotten around the Bay Area that being hooked up to Joe Kamiya's electronic gadgets produced a "high" equivalent to grass or acid, and it didn't cost a cent. In fact, Dr. Kamiya might even pay you. That didn't last long. Volunteers became so plentiful that some of them even began suggesting that they pay Kamiya.

THE ONLY LIMIT
IS IMAGINATION

Across the country at the Veterans Hospital in Bedford, Massachussets, Thomas Mulholland, a research psychologist, had been conducting feedback studies in electroencephalography for nearly a decade. Dr. Mulholland stated, "What we've done is to attach a subject to the EEG, and the EEG switch to the switch of a slide projector. When the subject is relaxed, voltage from the alpha rhythm activates the switch, and the projector beams a picture on the screen. When he looks at the picture, he becomes alert, the alpha waves diminish and the switch is turned off."

He went on to say that this feedback principle was the same as that controlling the working of a thermostat. "When the temperature of a room falls below a certain point the thermostat turns the furnace on. When the heat from the furnace raises the temperature sufficiently, the thermostat turns the furnace off. Our thermostat is the EEG machine; temperature, the attention level; furnace, the slide projector. When the level of attention is low, the projector goes on. When the level of attention is high, the projector goes off."

The advantage of this system according to Dr. Mulholland was that the subject learned to control his own attention level. "At this point, we've only begun to scratch the surface," he continued. "When the potential sophistication of feedback EEG first occurred to us, some people taught themselves to send Morse code by controlling their alpha. Now we are facing more practical applications. For instance, a teaching machine, with feedback providing reward for continued viewing, might well improve learning. Also, it could be applied as an attention trainer, both to enhance a student's retentive abilities and to evaluate the effectiveness of various visual aids. A few subjects have, through increased voluntary control over their alpha rhythms, successfully achieved a state of controlled consciousness similar to that obtained in yoga. In other words, they were able to "turn on." So it may be possible to teach people how to increase their awareness of — and control over — all physiological processes associated with a relaxed mental state. Really, practical applications of feedback electroencephalography are limited only by the human imagination. However, not everybody is able to produce a recordable alpha. We don't know why, but we draw blanks on approximately eight percent of those we test. In addition, there is quite a variance in alphas. Some can barely be picked up on the EEG, while others — well, we have one woman whose alpha is so strong I swear I can almost hear it."

A COSMIC SYMPHONY

At the Veteran's Hospital in Sepulveda, California, Dr. Barbara Brown had put together an intricate and sophisticated feedback system. Her subjects could, for instance, witness a fascinating light show, the colors and designs of which were governed by their particular brainwave patterns. The moods and imagery of the individual mind thus were reflected by specific colors and rhythms, the pace and tempo of which could be conducted on a pre-conscious level by the person's deep seated emotions, desires, or anxieties. Dr. Brown described herself as "very enthusiastic" about feedback. She saw it being applied for relaxation, developing athletic skills, problem solving, preventative medicine, anxiety control, accelerated learning, and something even more startling.

"Personally," she stated, "I think feedback may be the great white hope for extra-sensory perception." She cautioned that nobody could be sure at this point, however. Nevertheless, the intriguing possibility remained. Vast powers of the mind might be opened up through brain wave control.

Man had been trying to learn about himself for centuries, and maybe what brain wave control indicated was that for the first time means were available for the individual to find out about himself. Carl Rogers had talked of the self-image conflict that many people had. Most of us did not really know what we were like nor did we know what we *should* be like. Now at last an instrument may have been acquired that could reflect our inner essence in the same way that a mirror reflected our outer behavior. It couldn't have happened at a better time, for self-hate seemed about to explode the world. If man could learn to know himself and control himself and improve himself, he might even learn to like himself.

With the help of a small camera and high speed film, I was able to bring home for study copies of many of the papers which caught my interest, thus my lights burned far into the night, giving me opportunity for reflection on the vast and unexplored area of human consciousness which I was entering. As I reviewed the history of human accomplishment, that familiar chronology of wars and repressions and exploitations seemed to be fading away, and what appeared to be growing on the face of the earth was a gigantic laboratory of mind.

A CHALLENGE
WORTHY OF MERLIN

Up to the moment, the history of the study of the mind had reflected little in the way of achievement. Freudian psychoanalysis had proven a long and costly business, and its glittering baubles of Success, Security, and Peace of Mind were attained mostly by the therapists themselves. Recently, there had been some hope in new forms of psycho-therapy, nearly all of which rejected or ignored the ideas of Sigmund Freud. Encounter (group) therapy, in all its many guises — Essalen, Elysium, Synanon — was a lot cheaper than analysis and a lot more fun. It even seemed to do some people some good. Behavior therapy, the Pavlovian punishment-reward system, made no attempt to determine a cause and went singlemindedly after the symptom itself. It wasn't as much fun as encounter therapy, but it was fast and had established an impressive record of effectiveness. Its more sophisticated counterpart, cybernetics, had proven most effective of all, but, as I had recently discovered, dealt with only half the individual and could not relieve his existential distress. How to put the two halves together? that was the question, for the subconscious had never been amenable to exploration. Mystical, shrouded, and unknown — in it the key to man's nature must surely lie.

Hypnosis seemed to demonstrate the workings of the unconscious better than any other mental technique. Freud is reported to have abandoned hypnosis when he saw the Pandora's box it opened in the subconscious. The subconscious seemed to be capable of acting as if *any* idea were true, regardless of how bizarre that idea might be. The extraordinary power of the subconscious to maintain a harmful belief despite all evidence to the contrary seemed just that mental area where light was most urgently needed. Positive thinking had not alleviated this problem, but rather had given wide spread endorsement to the premise that in order for something to be a certain way all one had to do was believe it was that way. It is difficult to imagine a more regressive development. Even the savage dancing around the campfire to bring rain couldn't be talked into that. He knew he had to *do* something.

Confidence and optimism, of course, were strong psychological precursors of effective action, but unless confidence and optimism were based upon a realistic appraisal of the facts, they were little more than wind. People who rushed into oncoming trains with the utmost confidence of demolishing the trains seldom were reported as demolishing the trains, though they, themselves, were unlikely to be heard from further. The man in a mental ward announcing he was Napoleon exhibited every bit as much confidence as the international industrialist announcing the building of a new factory. The real and the unreal, there was the conflict. I recalled the words of my dream: "Syzygy to serendipity. The putting together of opposites leads to the fortunate finding of things not looked for." But how could one put together the real and the unreal? That seemed a challenge worthy of Merlin.

LET US LEARN TO
DREAM, GENTLEMEN

McKellar and Simpson, in an investigation of hypnogogic imagery, reported that their subjects described images which seemed to differ from dreams in that they were "more vivid" and "more realistic." Also, "they come and go in a flash," and "resemble lantern slides," and "contained detailed material which I didn't know I knew." These subjects reported four main characteristics of hypnogogic images: (a) vividness, (b) independence of conscious control, (c) originality, (d) changefulness. The authors commented that "Hypnogogic images merit investigation in that they may represent an instance in which greater knowledge of the normal may illumine the abnormal."

Such hypnogogic images seemed remarkably similar to those described by Kekule as leading to his theory of molecular constitution. "One fine summer evening I was returning by the last omnibus, outside as usual, through the deserted streets of the metropolis, which are at other times so full of life. I fell into a reverie, and lo! the atoms were gamboling before my eyes. Whenever, hitherto, these diminutive beings had appeared to me, they had always been in motion; but up to that time I had never been able to discern the nature of their motion. Now, however, I saw how, frequently, two smaller atoms united to form a pair, how a larger one embraced two smaller ones; how still larger ones kept hold of three or even four of the smaller, whilst the whole kept whirling in a giddy dance. I saw how the larger ones formed a chain. I spent the greater part of the night putting on paper at least sketches of these dream forms."

Later he recorded the finale: "I turned my chair to the fire and dozed. Again the atoms were gamboling before my eyes. This time the smaller groups kept modestly in the background. My mental eye, rendered more acute by repeated visions of this kind, could now distinguish larger structures, of manifold conformation; long rows, sometimes closely fitted together, all turning and twisting in a snakelike motion. But look! what was that? One of the snakes had seized hold of its own tail, and the form whirled mockingly before my eyes. As if by a flash of lightning I awoke . . ."

With this dreamed symbol of the snake biting its tail, Kekule was enabled to make the discovery that some organic compounds occur in closed chains or rings. Small wonder he urged his contemporaries, "Let us learn to dream, gentlemen."

BEHIND THE
DOORWAY OF DREAMS

That statement plunged into my heart like a dagger, for I suddenly realized that for all of my adult life I had been trying to stifle my dreams.

Odd, how you can live with something so long that you no longer recognize it. Oh, you call its name, only it isn't that name, it's something different, and when it turns out to be part of you, you're a stranger to yourself.

Everyone had always told me that I was imaginative. I even thought so myself. After all, hadn't I written short stories and novels and screenplays and television dramas? Surely one had to be imaginative to do that.

Writing novels is just about as supressed as imagination can be, almost as suppressed as writing short stories, screenplays, and television dramas. It is possible to imagine ·ANY-THING.

At that moment, I knew for certain that the key that unlocked the mysteries of life lay behind the doorway of dreams.

I didn't know that I was stifling my dreams before Kekule, but I knew I was doing *something*. What I called it was, "Being a realist." I thought this meant, "dealing with things as they really are." I didn't realize it meant, "dealing with things as other people *think* they are."

If I really wanted to have imagination, I had to carry imagination to its limit. I had to remove every resistance against imagination having absolute freedom. I had to cease at once being a "realist."

How, then, could I be sure that I wouldn't be swallowed by imagination?

Why, I had to have balance.

I had to be so sure of what was real that I could be as unreal as I wanted to be and still keep my balance. I had to nail down some facts in the material world upon which I could absolutely depend and on which I could build support lines. I had to have such confidence in those facts and support lines that I could lower myself over the precipice of imagination and let myself down into the chasm of ignorance as far as I could go. If I could do that, sooner or later I was bound to discover what was hidden in the chasm.

Take those hypnogogic images — like dreaming that a pearl was born through my chest and seeing the violet-jacketed man on the pier. They were clear as reality, even clearer, yet I had persisted in thinking of them as mere imaginations, at best, inspirations. What if there was reality in those images, a reality as great, perhaps even greater than the physical world? What if truth lay somewhere between physical reality and imagination? What if there existed some point of balance between absolute reality and absolute fantasy that was a source of immeasurable power?

Such ideas were already making me uncomfortable, so far out did they seem, but the die was cast now, and I knew there was no retreat. However far my imagination carried me, I knew I had an anchor in the physical world and would not be engulfed. That anchor was reason.

Reason may seem an insubstantial anchor to some, but I knew it would hold in the shifting tides for me, because I'd been testing it all of my life. Before I could accept anything as real, it had to make "sense." That meant it had to be perceivable by the five senses, and it had to "add up." Imagination alone could never convince me that it was reality; my senses and logic were too well anchored in the physical. Realizing this gave me a sudden feeling of freedom and security, as of a child who had developed faith in his sense of direction and knew that no matter how far away he wandered he'd always be able to return home.

THE FOUR STAGES
OF SLEEP

First off, it was necessary to come to a better understanding of hypnogogic images, and the best place to explore these, or so it seemed, was in my own mind. I must begin paying close attention to my dreams and discovering those images that occupied my sleeping consciousness, what the significance of those images were, how I might best use them, alter them, and otherwise control them for a greater understanding of life.

Research into the nature of dreaming had been mostly a matter of correlation between the electroencephalogram (EEG) and rapid eye movement (REM). According to the EEG, there were four different stages of sleep. Stage One consisted of an irregular mixture of theta waves (4-7 cps), alpha-like activity (waves one to two cps slower than the subject's waking alpha), and occasional alpha waves (8-13 cps). Stage Two contained spindle activity (14 cps) in addition to the above, and Stages Three and Four contained increasingly larger proportions (up to 100%) of delta waves (1-3 cps) in addition to spindle activity. Exact divisions between Stages 2, 3, and 4 were arbitrary, based on the percentage of delta waves in each. The Stage One pattern was readily distinguishable from the other stages by its total lack of spindles and delta waves.

When subjects were in Stage One sleep, they unconsciously signaled the experimenter of this fact by rapid movement of their eyes under closed eyelids. Awakened, they unanimously reported that they were dreaming. When awakened from any other stage of sleep, they reported no dreams. It was therefore Stage One sleep with its rapid eye movement and dreams that was of principal interest.

The literature showed that Stage One sleep alternated with the other stages in a more or less regular fashion throughout the night, with a period of dreaming occurring approximately every 90 minutes and each dream period running somewhat longer than its predecessor. For example, the initial dream period ran about ten minutes for most subjects, while the fourth or fifth might run nearly an hour. Altogether, Stage One dreaming occupied between 20% and 30% of the total sleep time of most young adults, spread over three to six Stage One periods.

Of especial significance were experiments in which subjects had been deprived of dream time but not sleep time. They simply were awakened at the first sign of rapid eye movement and Stage One EEG signals, so that no dreaming could occur. After 72 hours of such dream deprivation, nearly all subjects were exhibiting psychotic symptoms ranging from paranoia to schizophrenia. Apparently, the dream mechanism of the human brain performed some powerful integrating function, and this was exactly the clue I was looking for. I resolved at once to devise some method for better recall of my own dreams.

A SIMPLE METHOD
OF INVESTIGATING DREAMS

I knew that when I fell asleep the magic lantern of my mind turned on at once. This is to say that when the first warm sensations of sleep began creeping over my body there was an accompanying increase in the vividness of the imagery occupying my inner attention, so that as falling asleep progressed entire scenes were cast up in complete detail. I had no need to "make up" anything. It was all there; I was simply observing it. Then, of a sudden, some strange alteration of identification would take place, and the dream no longer seemed a dream. Now it seemed real.

This was the borderline I was after, that fine line between reality and unreality where imagination brought to the physical world its most creative solutions. There was danger, of course, for hadn't Nietzche and Van Gogh plumbed these depths too, and hadn't they both gone mad? But I felt that the danger was simply that they had entered too far into the unconscious without an anchor in reality. This I hoped to circumvent by refusing to accept as real anything that was not physically demonstrable and repeatable. Thus resolved, I was left only with the necessity of devising a technique for exploring my dreams. The one I settled upon was simple.

From the very first moment of my contact with brainwave mechanics, I had been taken by the feeling that the unusual effects surrounding the production of alpha waves were due to some balancing influence being exerted over both body and brain. Through my familiarity with computer technology, I knew of the periodic synchronizing pulse which all computers had to employ in order that the firing potential of each storage cell be kept at optimum levels. Without that synchronizing pulse, cell potentials varied widely, and the computer would begin making errors.

Something of the same nature seemed to be going on in the brain through the medium of the alpha rhythm, for when sleepers were deprived of dreaming (in other words, deprived of alpha-theta time), they began making errors about what was real and unreal (exhibiting psychotic tendencies). The word which kept occurring to me, over and over, was "balance." The idea of balance gave me the methodology for investigating my dreams.

I simply fell asleep on my back with my right forearm pointing upward and resting on its elbow on the bed, in perfect balance. When sleep began to overtake me, the arm would lose balance and begin to fall toward the bed, and this sensation would awaken me with perfect recall of what I happened to be dreaming.

Door to the Subconscious Mind 3

Dr. Gene hadn't set eyes on me for five years, and he let me know that I'd changed. "You're fat," he said, "and you smell of tobacco. What are you trying to do? Kill yourself?"

I mumbled a dissent and tried to accustom myself to the plush decor. Dr. Gene had been moving up in the world, and I found myself struck by the notion that I would be paying part of the rent.

"Take off your clothes," he ordered, "and lie down on the table." He at once began a process of prodding, probing, squeezing, jabbing, peering, listening, measuring and weighing which eventually revealed to his practiced eye the kind of shape I was in. It wasn't so good. I was many pounds overweight, weighing 237, a figure I couldn't believe myself. My blood pressure was up, my pulse was too high, and I had difficulty getting my breath.

After I'd put on my clothes, he shook my hand warmly. "So many funerals to go to lately. If you don't mind, I'll say good-bye now." As he showed me to the door, he suggested that I probably could prolong my stay on the planet by taking off fifty pounds and giving up cigarettes. Before I knew it I was standing in the hallway, one hundred dollars poorer and far from serene. Right on the spot, I gave up smoking and went on a diet.

Four hours later, I ate a steak dinner and started smoking again.

AN ELECTRONIC WIZARD

Oh, I knew I should do something about my smoking and eating, but it seemed too much trouble. After all, I was fifty years old and couldn't be expected to look like a teen-ager. Besides, doctors were confirmed alarmists, and cigarette smoking probably wasn't nearly as bad as everybody said. I had to remember that Doctor Gene hadn't found anything *seriously* wrong, at least nothing that needed an operation. By the time I got through reconstructing the interview, I could almost believe he'd given me a clean bill of health.

Anyway, I was on a new tack now. Since then I'd bumped into an electronics wizard, and he was going to build me an EEG machine. Nothing fancy, of course. not like the giants found in neurological clinics. But my wizard felt that he could miniaturize the works and put them in a cigar box and make them go "beep" when they were picking up alpha. The whole thing would cost maybe four hundred dollars. That sounded cheap at the price. A regular EEG could cost over five thousand.

It took three weeks for him to fit the pieces together, and he demonstrated it on his own head. When I first saw him sitting there, wired for sound, electrodes leading from head to box, I couldn't help a feeling of ridiculousness. I consoled myself that plenty of people were already staring at boxes with shadows on them, so it shouldn't hurt to get hooked up to one.

The wizard was handy at producing alpha. He really made the box sing. I calculated offhand that, with his eyes closed, he was producing alpha about eighty percent of the time. He showed me how the switches and knobs worked, how the electrodes were pasted to the scalp, then he hooked me up, and we waited for the beep. There was an embarrassing silence.

He fooled with knobs, adjusting things, and I tried again. This time there were several lonely beeps, so we knew the machine was working all right. I wasn't about to lose face further, since the wizard was already looking at me oddly, so I paid him his money, picked up the alpha meter and took it home, all the while hoping that I wasn't in that eight percent that couldn't produce alpha.

EXPERIMENTING WITH
THE ALPHA METER

The alpha meter was powered by two radio batteries, so I took to carrying it around the house while hooked up to it, hoping thereby to get some clue as to how alpha was manufactured. Every now and then, the thing would let loose with a series of beeps, even though my eyes were open, but for the life of me I couldn't put my finger on what caused them. And much of the time, even with my eyes closed, I got no beep at all. The harder I tried, the greater the silence.

Much of this I expected, but as always, there was a vast difference between intellectual understanding and actual experience. Brainwave literature had been explicit about the fact that the production of alpha depended on one's ability to develop "passive volition," that kind of volition that "permitted" an event to transpire rather than "ordering" it to happen. This passive volition was as elusive as mercury. No matter how I placed my fingers on it, I soon started to squeeze, and the mercury scooted away. Since the permissive method of accomplishing something seemed so foreign to my nature, I was led to the conclusion that a good deal of my conditioning had been toward the end of holding back rather than letting go. In short, it was inhibitory rather than excitatory.

The physical picture of such a situation is that the firing threshold of each neuron in a circuit is excessively high, and it therefore takes an extraordinary stimulus to cause it to fire. Persons with such high firing thresholds appear inhibited, since they do not react to the ordinary events that transpire around them, seeming "wooden," "non-expressive," "apethetic," "disinterested." Those appelations are scarcely designed to win personality contests, though they might perhaps

45

be of service if one were undergoing torture and wanted to keep secrets. Since such exigencies seldom arise in our modern society, excessive inhibition produces no noticeable service either to the individual or his peers, and he does both himself and them a service by getting rid of it. Andrew Salter, a New York psychologist, practically founded a religión on this one point alone.

Cloistered with my machine, I sat for hours, trying to relax my mind and body so as to produce alpha "beeps," attempting every conceivable manner of mental gymnastics, from the "mindlessness" of Zen to the ecstatic visions of mysticism, and still I could not reach a consistent alpha baseline, which is to say that what alpha I produced was both sparse and sporadic. Much as I hate defeatist attitude, I finally accepted the conclusion that I was one of those cases that simply would never be a high alpha producer. I disconnected myself from my newly-acquired machine and ruefully wrote off the money I paid for it. Then an interesting thing happened.

THE VIBRATING UNIVERSE

I developed a muscular spasm in the lower part of my back and used a vibrator to dissolve it. I'd stumbled across this therapy several years before, after I'd become convinced that muscular spasms were unconsciously controlled and represented an extreme case of protective armoring against threat. The works of Wilhelm Reich had enlightened me in this regard, and they had taught me that while approaching such spasms in a psychological manner could be costly and time-consuming, those spasms yielded quickly before the soothing effects of heat and vibration. Experience itself had shown me that the worst of my backaches would dissolve under a half hour sessions with the vibrator, and this case proved no different. At the end of it, simply because I felt relaxed, I rehooked myself to the alpha meter. To my astonishment, I immediately began producing a strong alpha baseline.

For fifteen minutes, until my inner tensions began to reassert themselves, I was able to continue this strong alpha production and to experience sensations which I hadn't undergone since a child. These were so delightful that at the moment I could only describe them as joy. After the session was over, I was able to further refine them as being allied to feelings of freedom, security, and confidence. Through the medium of the vibrator, I not only had broken through the inhibitions producing the muscular spasm in my back, I had also broken through the inhibitions in my own brain structure which were preventing me from producing a strong alpha rhythm. Apparently, the mechanism of vibration was closely allied to brainwaves.

Though the effect was astonishing, once I stopped to analyze it, it came as no surprise. I had known for years that we live in a vibrating universe and that differences in rates of vibration account for all we know of matter, space, time, color, light, and sound. The senses, themselves, are little more than devices for picking up certain prescribed ranges of vibration and carrying these to the brain where they are translated into the images that we come to regard as the forms and events of life. In this rarified area, where physics and metaphysics blend, all is seen to be in an intense state of flux, matter appears to be non-existent, and energy seems but an attribute of a master intelligence.

DISSOLVING THE MUSCULAR ARMOR

After this experience, I resumed my alpha meter sessions, always preceding them by a session with the vibrator. Optimum times with each appeared to be thirty minutes with the vibrator, and thirty minutes with the alpha meter. While working with the vibrator, I concentrated on relaxing all parts of my body until not a single area of tension remained. Though in principle this sounds easy, I found it difficult to actually do. However, my acquaintance with Reichian therapy proved helpful.

It was Reich's theory that the individual unconsciously designed for himself a muscular armor around transverse sections of the backbone in order to prevent the free flow of life energy along the spine. These muscular armorings were all designed to prevent the occurence of the orgasm reflex, for in Reich's view all living functioning was the result of that reflex — that's the way the heart beat, the lungs and liver worked, the pancreas, stomach and intestines functioned, and that's the way life reproduced itself. Since most of the early training of the individual had to do with inhibiting the orgasm reflex, a muscular armor gradually was set up around his spine and began to function unconsciously, manifesting first as reduced energy, then as aches and pains, then as disease and malfunction. Since Reichian techniques for dissolving this muscular armoring took the form of stretching the musculature around each segment of the spine, I began preceding my vibrator session with about fifteen minutes of yoga postures. These are stretching exercises and are the opposite of the more traditional form of exercise which seeks to bunch muscles and to tire them. Stretching neither tires muscles nor drains their energy away. Conversely, it rejuvenates and activates, as witness the feeling of well-being that follows immediately after the natural stretching that one does on awakening in the morning.

I now began to develop a regimen for alpha training. On arising in the morning, I first would do fifteen minutes of yoga exercises. Then I would spend thirty minutes sitting with the length of my spine against the vibrator. Following this, I would spend thirty minutes hooked up to the alpha meter, working at increasing my alpha production as well as the amplitude of the waves themselves. In addition, I would try to slow my alpha rhythm, leading it downward from its normal range of about 12 cycles per second toward the alpha-theta border of eight cycles per second, for that was the hypnogogic area. After adopting this schedule, my progress was steady, if not spectacular.

CAUSE AND EFFECT

Meantime, a great number of ideas were circulating through my mind, and I was literally in an intellectual whirl at the many concepts that were now falling into place. For example, the close association of alpha waves with a relaxed mental and physical state, an association which I had now proven beyond doubt, was pregnant with deeper meaning.

Brainwaves are electrical currents and manifest as a pulse denoting a flow of energy from a positive pole to a negative pole, then from negative to positive. The rate at which electricity flows is determined by the pressure differential between polarities and the resistance which the flow of that electricity encounters in the conductor. So, as far as strengthening my alpha waves was concerned, two things were immediately apparent. I must try to establish widely differing pressures at opposite polarities of my inner electrical works, and I must lower my resistance to the flow of energy between them.

At first, I could see no way of increasing the pressure differential between polarities, but I thought I could perceive methods of lowering resistance to the flow of energy between them. My experience with the vibrator helped me here, and also some knowledge of the history of electricity. The first power plants employed direct current generators. So inefficient was this method of power transmission that a separate power plant would be needed for each square mile of the cities we know today and would be far beyond the bounds of economic feasibility. Interestingly, a well-known and respected inventor, Thomas Edison, was responsible for the development of the direct current system, while a little-known and not so respected inventor, Nikola Tesla, designed the alternating current system in world-wide use today. Tesla, as anyone knows who is familiar with the facts of his life, was a genius.

In the Edison-Tesla dispute lay a lesson. Electrical current was not most efficiently transmitted by pressure alone, but rather by *rhythm*, an alternating pulsation. Therefore, in the matter of increasing my own alpha output, I seemed least likely to achieve results by *trying* to achieve them (exerting pressure) and most likely to obtain them by getting into rhythm with whatever source was producing those brainwaves. Such a conclusion, seemingly simple enough to arrive at, nevertheless was to have the most revolutionary consequences for both my attitudes and life style.

Like most people, I had been brought up from earliest childhood to believe that I caused effects in my environment. That statement undoubtedly sounds like the a-b-c of reality, but now that I had started to question it, I suddenly saw that it was based on the flimsiest of assumptions. Simply because my consciousness happened to be the center of my environment was no reason at all to assume that it was responsible for the effects that existed there. Or even that it *could* be responsible, for that matter.

PARADISE LOST

I certainly didn't feel that I could alter the course of the celestial galaxies, or the earth's orbit around the sun, or the moon's around the earth, or stay the tides, or change the weather. Those things I lived in *accord* with, accustomed myself to the *rhythm* of, *attuned* myself to, worked in *conjunction* with. But when that environment drew in close enough, so that it became a nearby house or tree or animal or person, I at once was overtaken by the feeling that I could *affect* it, and what's more, affect it any way I chose. Just let the objects in my environment be small enough and close enough, and I was seized by the sensation that I was the determiner of their fate, that I was the cause of their future. Yet the simplest reflection on the matter revealed the inescapable fact that I myself was but an effect in that environment, produced by some unknown and mysterious cause.

I tried to remember the last time I had gone about doing anything with the idea of attuning myself to it rather than trying to control it, and I couldn't remember a single instance in my entire adult life. I searched my childhood memories, and finally came upon a day, a misty, overcast day which lighted the ponds and sloughs of rolling farmlands, an enchanted place where riverbank caves were inhabited by gnomes, and nymphs cavorted in the waters, and dew-laden air was riven by the flight of sylphs, and high above the clouds rode the sun drawn by a team of fiery salamanders. The world was magic, and I was an awed spectator. How had that bliss been lost?

Why, somehow I had divided myself from the world and then sought to control it.

THE EFFORT OF
MAKING NO EFFORT

So now when I sat down for my session of feedback training with the alpha meter, my entire effort was to make no effort, but rather to get into rhythm with the pulse beat of life, to permit rather than to control, to feel myself in contact with that very power that actuated the alpha waves themselves. No sooner had I managed to come close to this inner condition than I became conscious of tensions all over my body.

There was a spasm between my shoulder blades, another in the solar plexus, still another in the small of the back. What was unusual about these spasms is that they existed where formerly I had thought I was totally relaxed, so I knew at once that they were both chronic and below the level of consciousness. For years, perhaps nearly half a century, I had been maintaining a tightly-controlled muscular tension in certain parts of my body. Why?

To prevent something from happening.

But what?

Whatever might happen.

A gold-headed walking stick was raised in the air and then banged down on the boards of the jetty. "Not irreversible," intoned the violet-jacketed man. "Not yet, at least."

Forty-five years of muscular spasms in order to prevent spontaneity. And all I had to show for it was an aching back. Well, goodbye, aching back. Hello, spontaneity.

But it wasn't as easy as it sounded.

TAKING IN AND GIVING OUT

In the first place, those muscular spasms weren't anxious to dissolve. They'd lived there so long that no doubt they felt entitled to squatters rights. Sessions with the vibrator and yoga exercises were able to dissolve them temporarily, so at least I had a taste of what it felt like to be free and alive, but before many hours passed in the workaday world, I could sense that gremlins had crept back into customary spots and once more were gumming up the works.

Perhaps the primary contribution of Sigmund Freud to the understanding of man was his hypothesis that it is helpful in trying to change a psychological effect if one knows the cause of that effect. If I were subconsciously maintaining muscular tension in some parts of my body, that muscular tension had once served a purpose, and if I could determine what that purpose was, perhaps I could discover what I was doing internally to maintain the tension.

Now when something is made tense in the human body, it is either to prevent taking in or giving out. If my original purpose in creating that muscular tension was to prevent taking in, then I had maintained the tension to keep something out. If my original purpose in creating that muscular tension was to prevent giving out, then I had maintained the tension to keep something in. Of course, once the tension had become chronic, it naturally restricted both taking in and giving out. But which had I originally been afraid of? I tried to remember.

Right off it seemed difficult to believe that I could ever

have been afraid of taking in, no matter how buried in my subconscious such a memory might be. All my life I'd been avidly
taking in new knowledge, and I'd always taken in plenty of food,
and now I was even taking in smoke.

BALANCING THE TWO FORCES

I tried to picture a person whose muscular armor was arranged to prevent taking in. What would be his primary characteristics? Why, he would be defensive, suspicious, and
hostile would he not? He would tend to be unteachable and
would probably gravitate into police work or the military services where suspicion and hostility would be useful. It was
difficult to equate my past with such a person. I'd been a loner,
a do-it-yourself-er. Why had I been a loner? Because I felt I
could only *be* myself when I was *by* myself. Why did I feel
that way? Because when I was with other people I couldn't
express my real feelings. Why couldn't I express my real feelings? *Because people wouldn't understand them.* Clearly, my
muscular spasms had been created by long practice at keeping
my feelings inside. If there was a button that controlled the
human psyche, mine was set on Hold In.

All these years I'd been on the take, bent out of balance
because I couldn't give. And even my taking had been restricted
by the very same armor that prevented my giving. Oh, I'd tried
to give, no question about it. But such efforts had been awkward and tense and a deep emotional drain. Looking back on
them, I could see quite clearly how often I had exhausted
myself by trying to overcome my resistance to giving. Now
instead of overcoming it, I saw the possibility of dissolving it.
At this prospect of liberation from a life-long prison, I felt
profound excitement.

Now my sessions with the vibrator took on deeper purpose,
for I carefully applied heat and vibration to just those areas
where my subconscious mind was chronically holding my
muscles in spasm.

A GLIMPSE OF THE
PHILOSOPHER'S STONE

I set the vibrator at ten cycles per second while I worked
at the muscular spasms between my shoulder blades, in the

small of my back, and in my solar plexus. Following the first of these sessions, I hooked up the alpha sensor and immediately began producing an alpha baseline of eighty percent, high amplitude waves, gradually slowing from twelve cycles per second to the alpha-theta border of eight cycles per second. This slowing down of frequency and increase in amplitude I attributed to my inner state of mind, for I felt that my consciousness was flowing out from my body and diffusing through space. It was a heady feeling, one of high vibration and intense lucidity. I finished the alpha session feeling better than I'd ever felt in my life, and in a far different way than I had ever thought it was possible to feel — light, airy, clear, effervescent.

That evening I had a dream in which the man in the violet jacket visited me and showed me an unusual jewel. It was a large stone set in spun gold and apparently designed as a broach. Deep indigo in color, it was cut strangely and had the quality of lightening its hue into the upper ranges of violet, and this changefulness gave it a living quality, the moreso since the stone was highly polished. It resembled no gem I had ever seen before, so I asked the violet-jacketed man what it was called. "The Philosopher's Stone," he answered. I reached out to take it and woke up.

The experience left me vaguely distressed, and though it was three in the morning, nevertheless I arose and wandered about the apartment, smoking cigarettes and drinking coffee. I had a feeling of intense frustration, as if an opportunity had been given me and I had failed to measure up. Reviewing the dream, I could see no immediate place where I might have behaved differently, and to actually have seen the fabled Philosopher's Stone, even though only in a dream, should have been exciting, but my depression persisted. It was only when I decided to do some work with the vibrator and the alpha meter that I suddenly became aware of how I had failed in the dream. I had reached out to take, when I should have been seeking some way to give. The realization so upset me that I tried to fall asleep and once more pick up the dream, but the dream did not recur.

THE ALPHA-THETA BORDER

Now I was rapidly reaching the point in alpha training where

53

I was producing close to 100% baseline in the eyes-closed position and about 30% baseline with eyes open. Eyes-open alpha had been reported in the literature only by Zen masters and yogis, and I felt sure I was getting close to a mental breakthrough. During the sessions, as my brainwaves increased in strength and slowed in frequency, sliding down to the alpha-theta border, my consciousness focused on vivid mental images, as real as any in the actual world. I seemed able to hold a single image in mind indefinitely, entering into it, exploring a million ramifications, seeing within the image, however mundane it might be — whether of a tree, a flower, a street, a person — the whole kaleidescope of evolving and unfolding life. I knew I was reaching a point in meditation that formerly had been available to practitioners only after years of the most arduous and painstaking apprenticeship.

I now was able to start my alpha rhythm when I chose, to stop it, to increase or lower its amplitude, to speed it up or slow it down, to keep it on with eyes open, and I was satisfied that I had achieved conscious control over this formerly unconscious process of my brain. I knew that I would now need only occasional sessions with the alpha meter to reinforce my control. So my alpha conditioning was completed. How long had it taken me?

From the very start, I had kept a log, and this log revealed that I had spent eighteen and a half hours hooked up to the alpha meter. This figure was much higher than the average conditioning time reported by other experimenters, but then I had been one of that unfortunate eight percent that reported little or no alpha to begin with, so I felt that my progress had been satisfactory. Each alpha session was a half hour in length, and thirty-seven of them were recorded, spread out over a six week period.

THE LOG

June 22nd. First session with the alpha meter. Had some difficulty making the electrode connections. Grease or dirt on the skin is best removed with alcohol for a clean electrode contact. This contact must be bound by moisture. Regular EKG (electrocardiograph) paste excellent for this purpose. Optimum electrode placement is one terminal centered on the forehead and the other two inches above the posterior base of the skull. Care must be taken with this latter placement so that hair doesn't interfere with the contact. No problem in my case! Spent ten minutes adjusting sensor to pick up my alpha activity. Received nothing.

June 22nd. Tried another session the same day, with equally discouraging results. If I hadn't seen my electronic wizard make this thing hum, I'd think there was something wrong with it.

June 23rd. Spent fifteen minutes trying to produce alpha and couldn't. Turned up sensitivity and audio so I could pick up beta. It was reassuring to hear something going on inside my skull. That rapid, twenty-two cycle per minute pulse was almost a continuous sound and rather unnerving. Anyway, at least I know the machine is working. Resolved to work only for alpha from now on.

June 24th. Visualized peaceful images, tried to think of the times I'd been happiest, worked up excitement, tried feeling drowsy, generated feelings of fear, love, passion, hate, boredom, interest. Nothing. Just a few isolated beeps which I couldn't tie to anything — they just seemed to happen. Pretty discouraging. Will lay off for a couple of days.

June 27th. Couldn't face up to another half hour of just sitting there waiting for something to happen so hooked myself up to the alpha meter and carried it around the apartment, going about my usual activities. I read, sharpened pencils, wrote letters, paid bills, shaved, brushed teeth, went to the bathroom, always hoping to receive some kind of electronic signature for these mundane activities. But all I received were occasional alpha beeps occurring at the most unexpected times for no apparent reason and seemingly with no less frequency than in the eyes-closed position. Jim came by and saw me hooked up, asked in all seriousness, "You having heart trouble? Is that a Pacemaker?" I told him it was a pacemaker for the brain. Now he thinks I'm a real kook.

CHRONOLOGY OF A
BREAKTHROUGH

June 28th. Sat another half hour without making progress. I'm exactly where I started. Maybe it's about time I admitted I can't produce alpha. Just an eight percenter. Member of a minority group. Wonder if I'll be discriminated against?

June 29th. Another fruitless session. But I noticed one thing. I can't keep my mind from wandering. Hops all over the place, like a monkey playing with jumping beans.

June 30th. Very discouraged, and about ready to chuck the whole thing. Wish I had my four hundred bucks back.

July 5th. The most exciting thing happened. Went swimming at Malibu over the holidays and a wave caught me and strained my back. That, itself, wasn't so exciting, but when I got home first thing I did was plop myself down on the vibrator to get rid of the pain and the soreness. After I'd gotten relief, thought I'd give the alpha meter another try. To my surprise, I immediately began producing a strong alpha rhythm. Kept up for fifteen minutes before tailing off. Forced to conclude that the vibrator had something to do with it.

July 6th. Tried alpha meter without the vibrator. No results. Spent a half hour with the vibrator, then hooked up to the alpha meter again. Began producing powerful alpha at once. No coincidence this time. The vibrator is breaking down some inner resistance and allowing me to generate alpha.

July 7th. Experimented with using the vibrator and the alpha meter at the same time. Produced steady alpha from the start, though not as strong as when using the alpha meter after a vibrator session. Thought I could perceive some kind of synchronization between alpha production and the vibrations of the vibrator. Curious sensation.

July 8th. Half hour on the vibrator, and half hour on the alpha meter. Will be my regular routine from now on. Strong alpha throughout whole session, better than 50% baseline, good amplitude, tailing off a little at the end. Very encouraging. Several times it seemed as though I was establishing some sort of control, though what that control was and how it worked, I couldn't say.

CONTACT WITH THE FORCE FIELD

July 9th. Good alpha. Becoming aware of deep-lying areas of muscular tension. Reichian armoring? These seem chronic and subconsciously controlled. Cut alpha session short and went after these areas with the vibrator. No apparent effect.

July 10th. Decided to add yoga exercises to my regimen. Led to try this because a spasm bunches a muscle, while yoga postures stretch it. No apparent results on the first try, but alpha production seems to be progressing. Maintaining above a fifty percent baseline now.

July 14th. Short business trip left no time for alpha training, but did yoga exercises in my hotel room. Felt fine the whole trip. Had good energy. Returned to regimen and found alpha strengthened. Even managed some alpha with eyes open.

July 1th. Continued progress. Mind whirling with ideas. Many things seem about to fall into place. Intense significance in everything.

July 16th. Deep muscular spasms haven't yielded but have had an insight concerning them. Armor isn't always designed to prevent danger from coming in. It may also be designed to prevent danger from going out. Example: the lead shield used on nuclear fission devices.

July 17th. Becoming convinced that my muscular armoring established to keep my feelings in. Somehow I must have gotten the idea that they were as dangerous as radiation. Was I that concerned over the safety of others? Or did I think that expressing my feelings was dangerous to myself?

July 18th. Great session. Deep muscular spasms seem to be yielding. Some gigantic scale in the far reaches of the universe is gradually moving into balance.

July 19th. Hearing my alpha waves, the electrical functioning of my brain, I visualize emanations beamed from some gigantic force field which holds the universe together and contains within itself electricity, gravity, and magnetism. Sensation of I AM is very strong. Floating. Mindlessness of Zen.

A HIDDEN SPLENDOR

July 20th. Rhythm. The alpha rhythm. All is an exchange of energy between two polarities. And at the point of balanced interchange is light! Everything in the universe is a pulse, a cycle, a circle. Layers of complexity removing themselves like the skins from an onion. Underneath, simplicity.

July 21st. Control is the wrong word for alpha training. Attunement is the key. Get into the rhythm with the rhythm. The question is, have you got rhythm yet?

July 22nd. Heavy rap session with physicist. Weird guy. Thinks there's a soul in matter — consciousness, that is. Heavy, arrested, and dull, to be sure, but consciousness nonetheless. Said he could transmute base metals into gold. Followed him around the party for several hours, hoping for evidence. Only trick he pulled was transmuting alcohol into urine. This he did copiously.

July 24th. Took a day off and baked in the sun. Got a slight burn. Couldn't help wondering if sun worship didn't conceal a secret science. Alpha session today was an eye-opener. Gradually achieving some control at lowering frequency and increasing amplitude. At the alpha-theta border hypnogogic images intrude upon consciousness. On this knife-edge may lie the key to creative power, extrasensory perception and more, and beyond it may lie madness. Did Nietzche cross over? Those strange notes written from his cell, alternately signed Dionysus and The Crucified. Perhaps he couldn't reconcile the duality. So it engulfed him.

July 25th. The vibrator can be set to stimulate the alpha rhythm. Synchornization between the two produces the most extraordinary sensation.

July 26th. Unusual sensation of incipient power. Must be careful not to get into this too deeply. One could easily abdicate the world for the mind. Must be similar to the lure of drugs. Looking forward to each of my alpha sessions now. It's the high point of my day.

July 27th. Held the alpha-theta border for twenty minutes. Longest time ever. Frightened me a little though. Lost all sense of time and don't know how I came out of it. Had amnesia for all but a fragment of the experience but carried back into full consciousness a recollection of some hidden splendor.

SOLITUDE AND ALPHA TRAINING

July 28th. Have no way of knowing whether I can lower brainwave cycles below eight per second because at that point I cease hearing the beep and am totally focused on the images in my mind. Decided to enlist an observer. KF seemed just the right person, so brought her in. Dismal failure. Could scarcely produce any alpha at all. Still uptight around people, I guess.

July 29th. Good session conducted alone, so decided to have KF back. Some clue here. Perhaps alpha training shouldn't be conducted in the presence of another person, especially one who is in close relationship.

July 30th. KF observed session. Did better this time, but not so well as when alone. No doubt this obstacle could be overcome eventually, but offers strong evidence that alpha training is best conducted in solitude.

July 31st. Really with it now. 90% baseline alpha with eyes closed, 30% with eyes open. As good as some Zen masters and yogis.

August 1st. Dreaming very vividly. Saw Philosopher's Stone last night, brought by the man in the violet jacket. Wish he'd show up when I'm awake. Think our dialogue could get beyond Faust now.

August 2nd. Give and take, and the point of balance between. When one overcomes the other, imbalance results — decay and death. With a perfectly balanced interchange is there immortality? Perhaps a structure built on the earth, perfectly balanced between the poles, would never rust, rot, or decay. What shape should it be? A pyramid? Would human beings residing there live forever?

August 3rd. Pairs of opposites produce everything.

August 4th. Really getting control now. Getting it by *letting* it.

August 5th. Discovered I can immediately switch from alpha to beta and from beta to alpha. Could turn a light switch on and off with my brainwaves now or send morse code to a computer and have it type letters, just like in Air Force experiment.

August 6th. Growing a bit weary of hooking up each day. Nothing new.

August 7th. Held at alpha-theta border for full half hour. There are things within the mind that can never be imagined!

August 8th. Did all my tricks to be sure I'd mastered them, then packed up the alpha meter. From now on will use it only for reinforcement and experiment.

Turning on with Alpha Waves 4

Gently tapping his right forefinger against the outside of the small plastic container, he sprinkled a rich tobacco-like substance into cupped cigarette papers held between the thumb and forefinger of his left hand. "You can tell good grass by the smell," he said. "That's what it smells like, see? Like grass." He held the container under my nose. It smelled like grass, all right — like childhood memories of new-mown hay and freshly-cut lawns.

He put the container aside and finished rolling the cigarette, slender fingers moving expertly. "Grows wild all over the country. In some states, there are thousands of acres of it. Cops burn it, of course. Nothing good can ever be free."

He held the cigarette up to the light and studied it. It made a tiny, perfect cylinder. He struck a match and lit it, taking a drag and inhaling deeply, then holding his breath. With smoldering match in one hand and glowing cigarette in the other, with the electrodes of the alpha meter attached to his head, with his eyes widened with the effort of holding his breath, he looked like a man being hit with the first jolt of an electric chair.

GRASS AND ALPHA

What I wanted to find out was the effect psychedelic drugs had on the production of alpha waves. The widespread use of such drugs in our culture indicated that users were receiving some form of inner relaxation, and the hallucinatory visions reported seemed evidence of brainwave production at the alpha-theta border. If brainwave training could produce the same "high" without the dangers of drug use, it could prove a real benefit. Bob was my guinea pig. He was an artist who regularly smoked marijuana and occasionally took LSD or mescaline. I first hooked him up to the alpha meter and took a brainwave reading in his normal state, finding that he produced a strong thirty percent alpha baseline. Now he was smoking a marijuana cigarette. Afterwards, we would take another reading.

We sat in Bob's studio above the Sunset Strip. Walls were hung from floor to ceiling with unframed paintings, surrounding us with splashes of color. High intensity light beamed upon an easel from fluorescent bulbs overhead, illuminating a canvas with sketched horizon and the rest of the landscape languishing in limbo. Music played from a stereo tape deck, and a familiar voice chanted, "The English army had just won the war." A side table was littered with paint rags, multi-hued pallettes, crumpled paint tubes, and an abandoned painter's smock.

Bob finally emitted an exhalation of light blue smoke with an aroma as exotic as a Turkish coffee house. He grinned. "That's a hit. Now I'm feeling a warm flush between my shoulder blades, and a pleasant relaxation in my head. Pretty soon, after the next hit, or the next, the warm flush will move up into the back of my head, and I'll feel my whole brain open up. Then power will pour into it from above to meet the energy that has come up from below." He took another drag and stared at me, holding his breath. His eyes were taking on an inner excitement. The pupils were neither expanded nor contracted. Now and again, the alpha sensor gave out a few beeps, but we weren't ready for the test yet. The stereo wailed, "I'd love to t-u-r-n y-o-u o-n." I felt half turned on already.

After the fourth hit, Bob suddenly announced, "There she goes." His eyes focused inwardly. "Right up the brainstem, opening up the brain . . . and now energy pours in from above." He quivered slightly. Then his left eye closed in an exaggerated wink. "Wow! That makes all the difference. Just to feel this way, even once in a lifetime, makes everything worth while."

THE COLOR SPECTRUM
OF LIGHT

He put the cigarette out, though it still was not quite finished, and carefully recovered the remaining grains of marijuana, placing them in the plastic tube. "Stuff's getting to be like gold," he muttered. "Mustn't waste it." Then he settled back in his chair and closed his eyes. "Okay, professor. Let's go."

Immediately, the alpha meter began ringing with the continuous beeping of an extraordinarily strong alpha rhythm.

"What are you thinking about?" I asked.

"Nothing."

"How do you feel?"

"Floating. Light and airy."

"Are you relaxed?"

"Not a bone in my body."

"Open your eyes."

He opened them and the beeping stopped. But almost immediately it started again, sparser and more subdued, but still very strong. The whites of his eyes were slightly bloodshot. His attention seemed focused far away. Electroencephalographically, he was in a state of samadhi.

"Tell me what you're seeing," I urged.

"Colors. A kaleidescope of colors. One follows the other, all the seven colors of the spectrum. First red, then orange, then yellow, then green, then blue, then indigo, then violet, then back to red and it starts all over. Everything is in the cycle. Everything is a harmonic of a vibrating frequency. The wheel of color is the play of opposites, an interchange of electrical forces, very mysterious, very magical." He lapsed into silence.

"Do you know what you're saying?" I managed.

"Not saying. Just seeing."

The frequency of the beeping had lowered now, and the amplitude was growing stronger. The alpha-theta border had been reached.

"Now what are you seeing?"

"Construction of the universe. Made out of light. Everything is a level of consciousness. Lowest level is matter. That's red. Highest level is spirit. That's violet. Then there are levels of levels. Those are octaves, and they get higher and higher. Seven levels of seven levels." He chuckled, then suddenly sang, "Sweet violet, sweeter than all the roses." He laughed loudly.

A CREATIVE MIRACLE

"What level are you on?" I asked.

He made a face. "First level. Been here a long time. Can't seem to go beyond. I can see the other levels, though. They're like reflections in a mirror facing a mirror, and the images reflect back and forth, seven times seven. "Hey!" he cried. "I feel like painting."

"Wait a minute. Tell me about those levels."

But he had already risen to his feet. Now he moved to his easel, trailing wires. "Can't talk about it, professor. But maybe I can catch it in a painting." He studied the canvas on the easel, pursing his lips. Despite his obvious concentration, bursts of alpha and theta rhythms continued to occur on the alpha meter. Finally, he picked up a brush, daubed it full of blue and began painting the sky. He moved before the canvas like a boxer before an opponent, on the balls of his feet, lightly and warily, and his lips were pulled back in an expression of elation, as if he knew beyond all doubt that he would finally succeed.

I watched as a creative miracle transpired before my eyes, for in two hours he completed a masterpiece. Light seemed to originate at some point within the painting itself, and time was there, past, present, and future, and space was a stage for the display of diversity. Though the painting was only a land-scape, it seemed impregnated with some profound philosophy.

Gradually, over the two hour period, Bob's alpha slowly decreased, until at the very end, he was producing no eyes-open alpha at all. At that time, he began to adopt a significant procedure. He would stand back from the painting to survey his work, then he would close his eyes and stand motionless for several seconds. I asked him why he did this, and he answered, "Just to rest my eyes a bit." Each of these eye closures produced strong alpha bursts.

When the painting was finished, he sat down beside me and we studied it together. "It's good," I said.

He nodded without vanity. "It's always like that when it's right. Like someone else had painted it."

TURNING ON AND TUNING IN

He rolled another marijuana cigarette. This time I took a drag from it, after first transferring the alpha meter's electrodes from his head to mine. I was surprised how strong the smoke was. It bit sharply at the membranes of my throat and lungs and set me to coughing. Bob grinned. "Always happens the first time. You'll get used to it."

"Maybe I won't have to," I answered. "I think I may get the same high just by controlling my brainwaves."

"You're kidding. You mean, just by hooking yourself up to that box?" He jerked his thumb at the alpha meter.

"That's the way I learned how to do it. But I don't have to hook up anymore, except maybe to test something. Like observing the effect on my brainwaves of smoking this joint."

Bob studied the box. "You think I could train myself to turn on with that thing?"

"Why not? I did."

He searched my face. "If people could do that, it would save them a bundle and the risk of being busted. How much does the box cost?"

"This one cost four hundred, but they could be produced to sell for less and be small enough to fit in your pocket."

"Will you show me how to use it?"

"If you like."

He offered the joint again to show his gratitude, and I took several drags. "You see," he explained, "it's the *feeling* that everybody's after, that's all. Nobody cares how he gets it. He just wants to feel that he's in tune with things and everything's all right and that there's a purpose to living. Nothing ever did it for me until I ran into pot and acid. Oh, I boozed it up, but that just got the problem off my mind for an evening and left me with a headache the next day. Grass gives me new insights. And I can work under it. What's more, there's no hangover. On the other hand, acid really takes me on a trip. I get into things so deeply that they seem absolutely real. I can work under acid too, but sometimes the work doesn't hold up. But even then something good happens. A lot of things come out in the open that were hanging around the fringes of my mind. Some kind of house-cleaning takes place, and I usually come up with a new outlook. Acid is hard on me, though, so I don't use it often."

THE SECRET OF LIGHT

I was feeling the effects of the marijuana now. My body was warm and relaxed, my head clear and open. I took another drag and kept my eyes closed while I held my breath. The alpha meter began sounding, and Bob said, "Man, you can really make that thing hum." I was *feeling* passive volition, that centered willingness to let go that I had struggled so hard to learn while conditioning my alpha. I wondered if I might have come to it easier if I had used marijuana, but there was no way to tell now. Grass was certainly no hindrance, in any case. I had never been more productive of alpha.

Studying the painting, I felt as if I could enter it, that my consciousness was released to wander in the imaginary landscape. Suddenly, I knew that the illusion of space had been created by the play of opposites, as had time, and even light. I could sense some vibrating harmonic, somewhere, in another realm of consciousness, where an exact duplicate of the landscape on the easel existed in more subtle form, imperceptible to the gross physical eye, but into that enchanted realm the artist had reached with spiritual vision and brought forth the scene on the canvas.

"How did you manage such a perfect illusion of light?" I finally asked.

"Like this," he answered. He picked up a brush, daubed paint on it and made two quick strokes on the canvas. Light went out of the painting. Depth disappeared. Reality evaporated. Two brush strokes had reduced the canvas to worthlessness. It was incredible.

"Now come over here," he said, "and I'll show you the

secret of light." I peered over his shoulder at his palette. "See this color?" he asked. He pointed at an olive green, and I nodded. "This is the color of the window frame through which we're seeing the landscape." He showed me on the painting. "I had a lighter shade of the same color on two of the inner edges of that window a moment ago. When I painted them out with the same shade as the other two sides, the sunlight disappeared. Do you know what an octave is?"

"In music, but not in painting."

"Same thing is true with colors as with musical notes. By raising the vibration of the color sufficiently, you eventually cause it to vibrate an exact octave higher. This puts it in harmony with the darker, or lower vibrating color, and since it can only be raised to this higher vibration by the addition of white, which is light, when it reaches such harmony, it shows the presence of light. Like this."

AN APOINTMENT
WITH ACID

Quickly he added pure white to the olive green, mixing with swift deft strokes, until he had achieved a light gold color. Then he painted this color on two of the inside edges of the window, and the painting came alive with light. I knew where the sun was, even though it was hidden, and its brilliance and its temperature. And depth came into the painting, so that I could see for miles into the canvas.

"There has to be some law hidden there," I breathed. "Something universal. What you've done is God-like. You said, 'Let there be light,' and there was light. Everything became real."

He cleaned his brush and surveyed his work. "I've felt the same way many times. Sometimes I've even thought I held light in my hand and could unleash it like a thunderbolt to create anything I wanted. Painter's paranoia, I call it. Usually I get it when I've taken acid. It's a God-like feeling, all right. About the highest 'high' possible."

"When can we experiment with acid?"

"How about a week from today?"

"Okay. I'm sort of disappointed in marijuana. I thought there'd be more to it."

He grinned. "It's pretty subtle. You may not notice much for awhile yet, then all of a sudden you'll have a thought, only it won't be a thought, it will be an inward seeing, an experiencing of something in a new way, and you'll wonder why you've never noticed it before."

After that, he yawned and stretched and said it was time to hit the sack, and he added that pot usually made him sleepy but with acid he would be up all night and maybe the next night too. I packed up my gear, and when I left the studio, he turned out the lights behind me. I couldn't help wondering if the painting on the easel glowed in the dark, so magical had it become in my mind.

As I drove home, I had a sense of well-being. It even seemed as if the car were running better than usual, that I was driving exceptionally well, that I had the car under excellent control. But then I noticed that I was driving only thirty miles per hour, considerably under my normal speed, so I knew I had undergone some time and space distortion. That was something I had never noticed when getting "high" on alpha waves.

ALCOHOL AND ALPHA

I fell asleep with my right forearm resting on the elbow in a balanced position, and I was awakened when it fell to the mattress, which allowed me to recall my dream. The man in the violet jacket had been straddling the earth with his feet in the seas and his head towering into space, and he had been announcing in a stentorian voice, "Let there be light." Vainly, I tried to recapture the details of this dream, but my only recollection was of journeying endlessly through the spectrum of colors.

During the ensuing week I could almost believe I had become a dope fiend as I continued my experiments. Though I was resolved to conduct my grass and acid experiments on Bob, since increased alpha in myself might not be noticeable due to my already strong alpha patterns, other experiments, such as with alcohol, barbiturates, and amphetamines could be conducted on myself, since these drugs were nowhere accorded the hallucinogenic properties which were the prime indicator of brainwave frequency in the alpha-theta region. Though I didn't know what effect barbiturates, opiates, and stimulants would have on alpha production, I was fairly certain they would not increase it.

I started my experiments by buying and drinking a pint of Scotch whiskey. The first noticeable effect was that the Scotch didn't taste as good as I remembered, nor did my stomach greet its arrival with the customary appreciation. I wondered if I had lost my taste for it, and if so, whether my increased alpha might not be responsible. The literature on marijuana repeatedly stated that users lost their desire for alcoholic beverages, and since I had already seen how marijuana increased Bob's alpha, I was about ready to conclude that alpha production was antagonistic to alcohol. Such a conclusion, at least in my own case, proved to be true.

At first I experienced a small increase in alpha as the alcohol was converted to glucose in my blood stream and I experienced a sense of relaxation and euphoria. But then as I began to exhibit the first signs of drunkenness — i.e., blurring of vision and awkward balance — it became increasingly more difficult to produce alpha even in the eyes-closed position. There was a definite slowing of my beta rhythm into the 16-18 cycle per second range, but this rhythm seemed erratic, as if something fundamental to its symmetry had been withdrawn. Finally, as I began to get toward the bottom of the bottle and was having difficulty navigating, I could produce no alpha whatever. However, for the first time, I heard my own delta. A few bursts in the 1-4 cycle per second range are all I remember, however, for I had great difficulty staying awake. Sometime later, I fell asleep in the chair, electrodes still pasted to my head.

AMPHETAMINES AND ALPHA

When the maid came into the apartment in the morning, her scream awakened me. She said afterwards that she thought I'd electrocuted myself. That scream set off a headache that lasted eight hours, and even aspirin afforded no relief. As I switched from alcohol to pills, I couldn't help reflecting on the vicious circle most Americans found themselves trapped in — uptight and seeking relaxation in booze, only to wind up with a hangover and forced to take pills for surcease. No wonder that hospitals and mental institutions were overflowing.

Toward the end of the day, when the hangover still showed no signs of alleviating, I decided to try an alpha treatment. I hooked myself up to the meter — because I felt sure that the pain in my head would prevent my turning on alpha without some guideline. It was fortunate that I did, for turning on alpha proved to be difficult indeed. Right off I produced a low amplitude, high-frequency beta rhythm, and my efforts to slow it into alpha were at first fruitless. My head seemed gripped in a vise as its musculature contracted in spasm. Gradually, however, I was able to let go. Before long, alpha began appearing in my brainwave pattern. When finally I was able to let go altogether, the pain in my head disappeared. I kept up the session for a half hour longer, emerging highly elated. Not only had I cured my hangover, but I had replaced lassitude with energy, pain with pleasure, and dullness with excitement. It seemed to me that probably all headaches were caused by spasms in the vascular system and that this restriction of blood to the brain prevented the occurrence of alpha. Relaxing such spasms could bring an end to headaches, but only when one learned the trick of passive volition.

Next day I dosed myself with amphetamines and got as charged up as a whirling Dervish. My problem was to sit still long enough to get a reading from the alpha meter, because what I really wanted was plenty of action. It was easy to see how "speed freaks" became addicted and to understand how "speed kills." My body was so revved up that I thought it would never slow down, and my mind seemed to work like lightning. I had an overpowering sense of megalomania, as if I could do anything. Quite suddenly I had become psychotic and was experiencing first hand what it felt like to be "Napoleon," "Hitler", or even "Satan." I couldn't help thinking of that secret formula by which the law-abiding Dr. Jekyl had transformed himself into the criminal Mr. Hyde, for I found myself scurrying about the apartment with a kind of monstrous energy and had to exert the utmost will to prevent myself from going out in the streets where I would have been almost certain to provoke a disturbance.

I finally managed to get myself hooked up to the alpha meter, but try as I might I could produce no alpha. All that could be picked up was a high-frequency beta, so fast that the beeping was reduced to a continuous tone. My vaunted alpha control had completely disappeared. Eventually, fearing that further fruitless attempts might destroy the conditioning I had already achieved, I disconnected the meter and abandoned

70

further attempts. To work off the energy that gouged at me, I drove to the beach and joined a furious volley ball game. Afterwards, I swam in the ocean for two hours. Even this activity failed to tire me, and when I finally went to bed at two in the morning, it was to spend a sleepless night. Thinking of the thousands of people taking amphetamines for weight reduction, I couldn't help wondering if much of the attention on drug abuse wasn't focused in the wrong area.

BARBITURATES AND ALPHA

I needed three days to recover from this experience, but when I did, I was ready to test barbiturates. What fell into my hands were pills known as "red birds," a compound consisting primarily of phenobarbital, the basic ingredient of most sleeping tablets. I'd been cautioned that one of these "goof balls" would be plenty, so that's what I took, then I hooked up to the alpha meter and waited for results. They weren't long coming.

Soon, I became so sleepy I could barely keep my eyes open. When I closed them, the meter began picking up slow delta rhythms with occasional bursts of theta, but no alpha whatever. I tried to correlate the theta bursts with mental imagery, but my thought processes were so disrupted that it was difficult for me to keep track of anything. I felt wiped out, completely out of it. It was hard to imagine anyone taking barbiturates for "kicks."

Apparently, through sheer willpower, I carried my experiment to a conclusion, but I have no recollection of it. My notes, almost indecipherable, tell of the struggle. The main thing that I sought to learn — the effect of barbiturates on alpha production — seems abundantly clear.

8:07 p.m. Downer taking effect. Feeling groggy. Attempt at producing alpha with eyes closed proved erratic. Some production of low amplitude waves. Rapidly losing control.

8:22 p.m. Very sleepy now. Beta rhythm practically disappeared. Delta rhythm predominating, with occasional theta. Trying to correlate theta to mental imagery. Hard to think. Mind moving very slowly.

8:43 p.m. Feel like a sleepy vegetable. Do vegetables get sleepy ? Rather be a carrot than a turnip. Better still an onion. Better yet a clove of garlic. Best of all a radish. Slipping.

Wonder how long I can stay awake?

9:03 p.m. Barely holding on now. Only delta rhythm. Basic pulse upon which everything is built. Must originate on some far off island in space and activate the whole universe. (Writing now almost illegible) Synchronize! Investigate!

There were a few other notations that were completely indecipherable. I found the philosophical content of the final entry particularly intriguing, especially after the foolishness of the third entry. This seemed to indicate that there was much to be learned from the study of the subconscious. By now I was equating delta rhythms with the subconscious and beta rhythms with the conscious and the alpha-theta border as the balance between. Certain patterns were beginning to emerge, giving me glimpses of some grand design. It left me with a feeling of excitement, as if I were on the verge of a discovery.

ACID AND ALPHA

By the time the weekend rolled around bringing my "acid trip" appointment with Bob, I was in rare good humor, and this good humor was mostly attributable to my new reaction to drugs. Not that I had overcome my prejudice against them, but where before I had failed to find any redeeming feature, now I began to see that drugs could be a gateway to the study of the mind, for they could slow brain rhythms, speed them up, and even balance them. Brainwave control could do all these things more cheaply and with less risk, but now I saw that much of the drive to use drugs was not based merely on a desire to "escape" or to experience new "kicks" but to actually learn more about the self and the mind and the brain and imagination and creativity and spiritual realization. Seeing myself possessor of a method of achieving these results with none of the hazards of drug use, I was pleased.

Bob had company when I arrived, and I was introduced to a lovely young lady whom he described as a talented painter and designer. She had black eyes and hair and a classical Roman cast to her features. Her name was Kay. They were discussing marketing some jewelry which she had recently designed, and she held up various pieces to illustrate. Since most of them were cast in signs of the Zodiac, I asked if she believed in astrology. She answered that she had made a life-long study of it and felt that it answered more about the behavior of people than psychoanalysis, to which she had been subjected for two years.

"Astrology was devised before Copernicus," I said. "When men still thought the sun revolved around the earth."

She studied me. "You're a Virgo, with Leo rising."

A LOVELY NEW SUBJECT

I was startled. I knew I had been born under the sign of Virgo, but since I had never had a horoscope drawn, I did not know my rising sign. I told her as much, and she asked for the date and hour and place of my birth. These I gave her. "I'll work it out for you," she stated. "We'll see where your planets are. But I'm willing to bet that you have Leo rising. Over-thoughtful and overly-independent, doesn't that describe you?" I had to admit that it did. But I was far from sure that astrology had served her. More likely, it was a shrewd appraisal.

"She's going to take acid too," announced Bob. "We've been planning a session but have never made it yet. Are you going to drop with us?"

I said that I planned to, but would take it at least an hour after they did, just to be sure that I wasn't high when measuring their reactions. With that, Bob passed out tiny purple pills. He swallowed his with a gulp of water, and Kay followed suit. I placed mine in my pocket.

"Takes at least forty minutes before there's a reaction," said Bob. "I've got some finishing touches to put on this canvas, so if you'll excuse me, I'll get to work."

"Does Kay know about my alpha meter?" I asked him.

He said that she did.

I turned to her. "Maybe I could do your head before the acid takes effect. That would give me something to compare results with." She smiled and said that she'd be glad to try it because Bob had told her that you could "turn on" by learning to control your brainwaves and you didn't need acid or pot or anything. I said I wasn't completely sure yet, but it looked like it. We decided to go downstairs so as not to disturb Bob at his work.

We found a place in the study, a large room with bookcases, a desk, and several comfortable chairs. From above, we could hear the stereo hi-fi as Bob turned the music up, and I closed the study door. As I wired Kay to the alpha meter, she let me know that she had a friend who was interning at the UCLA Hospital and who intended to specialize in neurology and that she'd heard him mention brainwaves several times. When I finally got her hooked up and the alpha meter tuned, she immediately began producing a strong alpha baseline.

A BRUSH WITH ASTROLOGY

I couldn't help making a correlation between her and Bob — both artists, both highly creative, both producing good alpha. In addition, they were attractive people — slim, lithe, energetic. I had to admit a tinge of envy as I recalled my own hard struggle to gain alpha control, while these two, right off the bat, were farther ahead than I had been after a month of training. Putting my wounded vanity aside, I got on with the business of instructing Kay in feedback training. Then I found a seat beside her and watched.

I allowed her to experiment in this manner for five minutes, enough to satisfy her curiosity but not enough to give her any control, for I didn't want to interfere with the test I was about to make. When I turned off the device, she expressed regret, for she said she was getting the feeling of what an alpha "high" meant, and it was a great deal different than a drug "high," — clearer, more natural, as if regaining some lost way of seeing. I thought that described it very well and told her so, and she said she wanted to do my horoscope immediately. With that, she drew a book from her handbag and began thumbing through it, now and again pausing to jot down a notation.

It was cozy in the study. The many books, the filtered light, the attractive young lady, the thought that I might be on the verge of some breakthrough, all combined to give me a pleasant, relaxed feeling. When I looked at my wristwatch I saw that a half hour had passed since Bob and Kay had taken the acid, and I turned on the alpha meter and began to observe her closely for effects. As she concentrated on her work, the meter gave out the rapid sounds of beta, a natural response to concentration. Several times she emitted little gasps and stared at me, so I gathered she was running into something unusual. When she finally finished, she studied her work a last time and then announced, "You have Mercury in Leo, Mars in Leo, Saturn in Leo, Neptune in Leo, and just as I thought, you have Leo rising. These are all leadership signs."

74

"Tell that to the navy," I commented.

"Your leadership signs are in science, business, philosophy, and mysticism — a highly unusual, almost conflicting combination. Can your work resolve these?"

"I hope so."

A CREATIVE KEY

"Your Venus is in Libra, which means that your sex drive is gentle and easily repressed," she laughed. "Your Jupiter is in Gemini, which means that you see both sides of things. And your Uranus is in Aquarius which means that you bring secrets into the open."

"Surely there must be some negative aspects."

She studied her diagrams. "Your worst fault could be an asset. Both your sun and your moon are in Virgo, and there isn't a single water sign in your entire horoscope. This means that you are highly rational and disinclined to accept anything as fact that cannot be scientifically proven. That could make you a source of irritation to your more intuitive friends, especially those who are believers and accept things on faith. In addition, you often enjoy argument for argument's sake, that's Mars in Leo, you see, and some people might find you a trifle belligerent. Then too, you find it difficult to accept a subordinate role. You must either be the leader or operate on your own. This has made you something of a lone wolf."

"You couldn't be more accurate if you'd known me for twenty years," I admitted.

"Though these traits can be faults, they can also work for you," she answered. "You see, the energy of Leo and the rationality of Virgo and the lack of water signs mean that you can journey as deeply as you like into the world of fantasy without danger of believing that your fantasies are real. In short, you can really let your imagination go without losing contact with the real world. You could never freak out on acid, for example. You would always know that the images were only in your head. "Believe me," she emphasized, "there is great creative power in such a position."

I couldn't help but be impressed. "To tell you the truth, I never believed there was much to astrology, but you've really won me over. Are you sure you haven't picked up most of this from Bob?"

AN INTRODUCTION
TO THE DEVIL

She grinned. "There goes your Virgo rationality. No, Bob hasn't told me a thing. Except that you have a machine that can teach people how to turn on with brainwaves. I'm a Cancer, you see, and my horoscope is full of water signs. You and I will always be a bit of a mystery to each other, but then, that's what makes the world go around. Oh dear," she suddenly exclaimed, "I think I'm feeling the acid." She pointed to her abdomen. "It always hits me in the solar plexus first. I get a feeling of excitement right here." She placed her palm below her breasts. Her eyes were beginning to shine, and her inner excitement was obvious. I asked her to close her eyes, and the ensuing beeping showed increased alpha. But I preferred to get my principal reading when the session was farther along, so I asked her to reopen her eyes and tell me something about herself.

She said that she was an old soul who had been incarnated many times and that she once had been Queen Cleopatra of Egypt and had been entrusted with the secret teachings of the Egyptian priesthood, those rites conducted within the Great Pyramid of Giza and upon which the entire Mediterranean civilization had been based. But she said that she had misused the trust placed in her, choosing to gratify her own desires rather than enlighten her people, and now she had to live through the karma caused by that act, a very difficult karma because that act had caused abandonment of the feminine principle of mystery and its replacement by the masculine principle of authority. Now the age of the masculine principle of authority was ending too, and there would soon be a return to feminine mystery. Then the secret teachings of Cleopatra would rise again to seize the imaginations and the motivations of men and to launch a new age of peace and prosperity.

All this sounded quite fantastic, and I had in mind that it was the acid talking and not Kay, but it was interesting enough, and I didn't shrug it off entirely, because after all she had made astrology seem real, and if she could do that, maybe I shouldn't turn my back on reincarnation either.

By this time, over an hour had passed since she had taken the acid, so I ran a full scale test of her brainwaves. With eyes closed, she was producing a 90% alpha baseline, with frequencies mostly in the alpha-theta region and interspersed with long trains of theta. With eyes open, she was producing nearly a fifty percent alpha baseline as well as getting a noticeable amount of theta. Clearly, she was in an unusual state. When I disconnected her from the alpha meter, she found a mirror and began making faces in front of it.

"I am the Devil," she announced. "Did you know that the Devil is a woman?" She whirled on me with teeth bared and head thrown back, as if to mesmerize me on spot.

THE TRINITY IN DUALITY

It was an idea that had never occurred to me before, but I considered it carefully. If God were masculine, the Devil should be feminine, for there were only two forces at work in the universe, and by their intereaction all things were created. As she stood there, so perfectly posed as a female Devil, it seemed to me that there was something classic in her stance, and I visualized a masculine God in the sky on the right and a female Devil in the sky on the left, and down below, upon the earth, man between, the creation of the eternal forces of masculine and feminine.

"You see!" exclaimed Kay triumphantly. "You know that it's true!"

I withdrew the purple pill then and placed it in my mouth, washing it down with saliva. I had no idea what was about to happen, but I was sufficiently intrigued by what was going on in Kay's mind to look forward to similar events in mine.

"Add an O to God, and you get Good," she intoned. "Subtract a D from the devil, and you get Evil. Good works in the light. Evil works in the dark. Woman is the fallen angel, you see. Lucifer is female. By her creation out of light, life ensued and will continue until all mysteries are solved. Then everything will once again be light."

That was pretty heavy stuff. Indeed, she might have been Cleopatra presiding over some secret rite in a chamber of the pyramid, for the manner in which she stood there and pronounced the words. But this is only her trip, I thought. It's just a story that she lays on herself to give her life meaning and significance. Yet, somehow I was unconvinced. The duality and the resolution of the duality which she so graphically described made a deep impression on me. Now I saw this conflict and resolution stretching back into the beginning of time, casting up all forms, creating all philosophies, making all works of art, all governments and religions, all wars, diplomacies and dynasties. I sensed that at my fingertips lay a simple truth, a truth so profound that once I understood it I would comprehend all knowledge.

AN ILLUSTRATION OF
THOUGHT TRANSFERENCE

There was a clatter of footsteps on the stairs, and the door burst open. Bob stood there, clutching a canvas in one hand and waving the other excitedly. "I finished a painting in an hour!" he cried. "It just seemed to leap off the brush onto the canvas. I have no idea where it came from or even what it means, because I never saw a landscape like it before!" He held it up to our view, excited eyes showing the effects of LSD.

In the background of a golden landscape, a series of pyramids were silhouetted against the sky. Before them, marked by crosses and tombstones was a giant cemetery. In the immediate foreground lay a large rock. Something like human hair grew from the rock, and now I could see a face hidden there, peering out from the darkness, a feminine face, queen-like, watching and waiting. From this head extended a rope, snakelike over the sand, entwining around a giant needle and climbing to the top to penetrate the eye.

I could feel my hair stand on end. That's Cleopatra's Needle, I thought. And that's her in the rock, waiting. And beyond, in the graveyard before the pyramids, all her knowledge is buried. And soon somebody will pull the rope through the needle and hoist her on high to rule once again.

Bob had painted this picture in his studio above even as Kay had been discussing Cleopatra in the study below. It was a graphic illustration of thought transference.

Space and Time Unveiled

5

I had expected mind-blowing hallucinations from LSD, or at least some far-out visual effects, but all that happened was that I felt stimulated and had a sensation of drawing in on myself. This "drawn in" feeling was physically manifest by my unconsciously pulling in my stomach. I could feel a tautness in my muscles too, though it wasn't an "uptight" sensation but more an over-abundance of energy. For awhile, I thought that the acid had failed to affect me at all, but when I looked in the mirror my eyes shone like polished agates and my face was unusually pale. Here and there on the surface of the skin were faintly perceptible blotches. I'd seen myself in this condition before. It was immediately following a night-long naval battle off the Philippine coast during

World War II, and my system had been full of adrenalin.

DIMENSIONS OF THE MIND

Adrenalin and I were old friends. We'd played football together, fought the war together, and taken plenty of financial risks together. Never once had adrenalin betrayed me. But I knew lots of people who adrenalin had destroyed. Adrenalin simply turned to adrenoxin or adrenochrome in their bloodstreams, and since these substances were toxic and affected the brain in such a manner that things could be seen that weren't there and things could be heard that weren't said, such persons were regarded as schizophrenics. As I peered at myself in the mirror, I couldn't help wondering if the much-vaunted hallucinatory drug, LSD, was after all only a stimulant of the adrenal glands, and people who couldn't handle adrenalin were thrown into temporary schizophrenia. But then I remembered the high alpha readings I had gotten from Kay, and the startling example of thought transference between her and Bob, so I knew there was more to it. The problem was that LSD was a strain on the body, and if you couldn't handle that strain, you went temporarily crazy.

But adrenalin was friendly with Kay and Bob too, so we had a good trip. Yet it was a far cry from anything I'd expected. Bob went back to his easel and continued painting. Kay pulled out some wax and a Bunsen burner and began making molds for jewelry. And I cloistered myself in the study with pencil and paper and began jotting down notes on "Space and Time — the source of the ten thousand things." Somebody looking in the window at the three of us at work would have difficulty believing we were all on "dope." Now and again we gathered in the kitchen for coffee and shared our problems and insights, but for the most part each of us was content with solitary exploration of his inner world.

I departed at dawn, leaving behind the alpha meter so Bob and Kay could train their own brainwaves, then I drove up into the Hollywood Hills and watched the sun rise over the Sierra Madre Mountains and cast its first rays on the city. Later, I motored to the beach and spent the day on the sand. Sometime in the afternoon, I fell asleep by the ocean and didn't awaken until nightfall. I felt tired and drained, so I went home and to bed.

As it turned out, it was the last acid trip for Kay and Bob. Using the alpha meter, both were able to condition their alpha waves. Kay gave up marijuana too, finding the alpha "high" more satisfying, but Bob continued to smoke grass occasionally, explaining that it allowed him to get into his work more deeply.

GATE TO THE ROOT
OF THE WORLD

Meanwhile, my beginning flirtation with Space and Time had blossomed into a romance, and this love affair could be traced to my increased understanding of brainwaves. The polarities that seemed to exist between the various brainwaves had become a source of deep fascination. For example, two of the brainwaves, the delta and theta rhythms, could be identified with the subconscious mind as exemplified by the autonomic nervous system, while the other two brainwaves, alpha and beta, could be identified with the conscious mind as exemplified by the central nervous system.

Within the autonomic nervous system, the delta rhythm seemed synonymous with the parasympathetic division, while the theta rhythm seemed synonymous with the sympathetic division. Within the central nervous system, the alpha rhythm seemed representative of the afferent or receptor nerves, while the beta rhythm seemed representative of the efferent or motor nerves. These groupings appeared to be neatly divided into stimulus-response patterns.

On the unconscious level, delta seemed to indicate reception of the stimulus while theta seemed to indicate response to the stimulus. On the conscious level, alpha appeared to represent reception of the stimulus while beta appeared to represent response to the stimulus. These polarities themselves seemed to be contained with the larger polarities of conscious and unconscious minds, the unconscious governing reception of stimuli and the conscious governing response.

With a little speculation, this structure of polarities within polarities could be carried even further, for a universal mind might govern all stimuli while the individual mind might govern all response. For the first time, I glimpsed a resolution of the apparent contradiction between free will and predestination, and there welled up in me the feeling that I was onto some

profound but simple truth. I recalled the words of Lao Tzu:
> These two come paired but distinct
> By their names.
> Of all things profound
> Say that their pairing is deepest,
> The gate to the root of the world.

DYNAMICS OF ECOLOGY

The philosophical system thus described is based on dualism and the resolution of that dualism. For the most part literature concerning it has disappeared, and little is known except Lao Tzu's tiny book of twenty-five pages called the Tao, in which the two forces are referred to as Yin and Yang. The emblem of the system has been left us and consists of black and red teardrop shapes combined in such fashion as to make a half-red and half-black circle known as a syzygy, meaning "the putting together of opposites." Since in deepest essence, Yang represents the male force of light, heat, and activity, while Yin represents the female force of darkness, coldness, and passivity, any study of the methods by which these two forces combine is naturally tinged with eroticism.

There may be difficulties with this conception, since popular usage associates eroticism almost exclusively with human sexual arousal, but this shallow interpretation surely will yield in the face of overwhelming evidence that male and female polarities conceal a key to life's mysteries. The dancing, playful flow of life is sexual — forms merging, spinning together, reproducing Eros in countless manifestations. All living organisms are throbbing together in a billion-year-old electric sexual dance. Inanimate matter too consists of multitudinous combinations of two fundamental polarities, and there seems to be nothing under the sun, or even beyond the sun, that does not follow this basic law. The creative power of the universe is thus made manifest as a dynamic point of balance. Therefore I proposed to define this particular philosophy as ecology.

While the symmetrical polarities of brain rhythms turned me onto this line of reasoning, what launched me on a full scale quest was the sudden awareness that the structure of the atom appeared to be identical with the structure of the solar system. In each case, there was a sun (proton) around which planets (electrons) revolved, and the centripetal force (gravity) of the sun balanced the centrifugal force (velocity) of the planets, creating a structure held together by vast electromagnetic forces. For example, forcing an electron out of or into the tiny atomic system unleashes the awesome power of the fission and fusion bombs.

It was to this point that my mind had taken the problem when I underwent the acid trip with Bob and Kay, and the hours spent making notes in Bob's study now proved most fruitful. Those notes follow as originally transcribed.

NOTES ON SPACE AND TIME

1. Space and Time are both antagonistic and complimentary, like night and day, woman and man, winter and summer. They combine to create and destroy everything that exists in the universe.

2. Space and Time are always limited and always relative. Nothing exists that is altogether Space or altogether Time. Each thing is either more Space than Time or more Time than Space.

3. All things follow a cycle, a pulse beat, a sine wave. Therefore Space changes into Time and Time changes into Space.

4. Centripetal Time is constrictive. It produces heat, density, heaviness, sound, and the tendency to go downward. Centrifugal Space is expansive. It produces cold, dilation, lightness, silence, and the tendency to go upward.

5. Whatever contains more water than solids is Space. Whatever contains more solids than water is Time.

6. A broad form represents Time. A tall form represents Space.

7. The seven colors of the spectrum range from Time (red) to Space (violet).

8. Beauty is the proper proportion of Time to Space. Love, too, is the proper proportion of Space to Time. What is the proper proportion? It is that proportion which leads to the balanced interchange of energy between polarities. Aesthetics holds it to be 1:1.618 — The Divine Proportion.

9. A man is Time — centripetal, strong, active. When too Time, he is violent, cruel, and destructive. A woman is Space — centrifugal, yielding, and passive. When too Space, she is

lethargic, weak, and escapist.

10. Men and women are antagonistic and complimentary. Their fate is to play tag forever. That is what makes life so interesting, amusing, and dramatic.

11. Time is alkaline. Space is acid. Preparing the uterine tract with an alkaline may result in the conception of male children, while preparing it with an acid may result in the conception of female children.

12. Foods that grow above the ground are more Space than Time while those that grow below the ground are more Time than Space.

AN INSIGHT INTO IMMORTALITY

13. Nowhere are the forces of Space and Time better illustrated than in the pulse beat of life itself — in the expansion and contraction of the living heart. Systolic is Time. Diastolic is Space. Systolic pressure is created when the heart contracts, pumping blood through the arteries. The flow of this blood through the arteries is Space, since it is expansive, thus illustrating how Time creates Space. Diastolic pressure is created when the heart expands, sucking blood back through the veins. The flow of this blood through the veins is Time, since it is moving toward the center, thus illustrating how Space creates Time. Moreover, the Space flow of blood through the arteries is colored Time (red), while the Time flow of blood back through the veins is colored Space (blue). People with high blood pressure are too Time. People with low blood pressure are too Space. These conditions probably are correctible by the appropriate eating of Space or Time foods to offset the imbalanced condition.

14. The balanced interchange of energy between Time and Space always creates something other than Time or Space. The Time proton and the Space electron create the balanced structure of the atom. The Time sun and the Space planets create the balanced structure of the solar system. The Time positive pole and the Space negative pole create the balanced power of alternating electrical current. The Time male and the Space female create the balanced structure of the family. Time oxygen and Space hydrogen create the water which results in life.

15. Time gives or sends. Space receives or takes. Once Space has received extra energy, it then turns into Time and sends that energy, and once Time has sent energy, it then turns into Space and receives energy. This pulsation, this balanced shifting of polarities, this pulsing alternation of giving and receiving, keeps all structures intact and makes them relatively immortal. When imbalance creeps into the system, however, and one polarity continues to take while the other continues to give, then decay sets in and the mortality and eventual demise of the system are established. "Not irreversible," said the man in the violet jacket. Is this what he meant?

Now as I examined the diagram which represented the simple workings of ecology, for the first time I realized that there had been a profound change in the way my mind worked. The many diversities of life had suddenly, it seemed, arranged themselves in such a fashion as to be easily dealt with and quickly understood. I couldn't help feeling that I was now much wiser than I had been only a few months before.

I saw that excessive Time in the human being produced sadism, while excessive Space produced masochism, and that social institutions were as prone to such imbalanced conditions as individuals. For the first time I began to understand that love was a power resulting from the balanced interchange of energy between individuals, and that any imbalance in this interchange could only produce exaggerated cruelty or dependent suffering. Seeing this, it seemed to me that understanding the principles of ecology should increase man's ability to cope with his environment and his fellows, and such increased ability should be evidenced by a higher intelligence quotient.

MEASURING THE INTELLIGENCE QUOTIENT

For years, it had been assumed that one's I.Q. was something he was born with, that it was mostly a matter of the genetic structure of the original 23 chromosomes that made up the embryonic human being, that if a person had an I.Q. of 100 when he was ten years old, that's the same I.Q. he would have when he was twenty, or thirty, or forty. However, nearly all testers agreed that a grasp of the tools of thought, such as language, arithmetic, and basic mechanics was necessary before a person's intelligence could be tested. Now I had stumbled across a new tool for thought, one that could break down every problem into two basic components and find the point of balance where the solution lay. The possession of such knowledge should provide a substantial rise in an individual's I.Q.

I had taken several intelligence tests over the years, and the highest score which the testers had given me was 124 on the Cattell scale. Now I wanted to take another test to see if my alpha conditioning and recent insights had brought about a verifiable increase in intelligence. While I shopped around for a place to take a supervised test, I ran into a man who said he was a member of Mensa, a high I.Q. club which restricted membership to those who could score in the upper 2% of the population on a supervised intelligence test. I inquired as to what that score might be, and was told, "At least 147." I sent in my application and in a few days received notification of my testing date. As it happened the test was to be administered at my old stomping ground, the Medical Center of U.C.L.A., and the date was three weeks in the future. Meanwhile, I became involved with Kundalini Yoga.

A SYNTHESIS OF YOGA

I had been doing yoga postures for some weeks now, and the sense of well being that followed these exercises prompted me to look into the discipline further. Much of my early writing and research had been inspired by the works of Sri Aurobindo, and among his books was one entitled, *"The Synthesis of Yoga,"* in which he extracted from the numerous yoga disciplines that which he considered to be the heart of the training.

"Yoga," stated Aurobindo, "is a turning of the human soul from the egoistic state of consciousness absorbed in outward appearances and attractions of things to a higher state in which the Transcendent and Universal can pour itself into the individual mold and transform it. When the human ego realizes that its will is a tool, its wisdom ignorance and childishness, its power an infant's gropings, its virtue a pretentious impurity, and learns to trust itself to that which transcends it, that is its salvation. This is the decisive movement, the turning of the ego to That which is infinitely greater than itself, its self-giving and indispensible surrender."

I had read this passage many times, but now it suddenly awakened new reverberations. The word "surrender" did it. Now I saw that it was synonymous with the passive volition necessary for the production of alpha brain rhythms. The polarities of Space and Time had provided new insight into the mind, and I perceived that the way into the unconscious and loss of ego lay through passivity and surrender, while the way to greater self-consciousness and larger ego lay in the exercise of active volition, or willpower.

Suddenly the eternal duality of God and the Devil flashed before my eyes, and I saw that God, ruler of the subconscious, required subordination and passivity, while the Devil, ruler of the conscious, required the exercise of will, and I knew that the man in the violet jacket, on the ocean pier in the darkness, real or unreal, had been the point of balanced interchange between these eternal opposites, and so had confronted me with the Faustian bargain. It was as if my consciousness suddenly leaped over the centuries and I sat down in the presence of Johann Wolfgang von Goethe, he in wig and greatcoat and moving a quilled pen over foolscap, its scratching the only sound in the silence of the house, and I said, "One need not sell his soul to the Devil, for neither the will nor the imagination rules, but rather a balance between." And Goethe smiled, though he did not look up, for my statement was only a thought in his mind.

THE ALPHA CHAMP
WHO WAS A FAILURE

Now polarities were clearly drawn. There was mysticism, which sought the answer to man's condition by surrender to the forces of the unconscious, and there was magic, which sought the answer to man's condition by the exercise of will-power. Carried to extremes, the mystic was reduced to worldly ineffectiveness, while the magician destroyed himself by opposing universal law.

It often happens that when we are prepared to see something that we find it transpiring under our noses. So it was that a recent acquaintance, having heard of my alpha meter, called me and asked for a training session because he was convinced that alpha production was the gateway to the development of psychic powers. Over the years, he had been involved in just about every psychic activity on the face of the earth, and he didn't intend to miss this new opportunity. When he showed up for the first session, and I hooked him up to the alpha meter, he began producing a 100% alpha baseline. He could even produce alpha with his eyes open.

I couldn't believe it. I sat there with my mouth open and gaped, because here, right before my eyes, was a man who had achieved the ultimate. He could produce alpha with the best of them. But his life was a mess.

He couldn't make money, couldn't hold a job, couldn't sustain a relationship, was overweight, hypochondriachal, and totally impractical. Yet he was a champion at producing alpha. As I sat there and stared at him it finally dawned on me that I had fallen victim to the very trap that I sought to extricate myself from. Simply because I myself had been hung up in the conscious world of logic and willpower and had been greatly benefitted by learning to mesh this world with the subconscious world of passivity and imagination, I had assumed that everyone else suffered from the same malady and that the cure for all ailments was learning how to produce alpha. Now I saw that it was possible for a person to become imbalanced in the opposite direction, by producing too much alpha, by becoming too passive, by coming to believe that the world of the imagination was the only reality. To test my theory, I asked my friend to try producing beta. He couldn't produce a lick.

MYSTICISM AND MAGIC

During the next two hours, I learned that it is even more difficult for a person who is too passive to become more aggressive than it is for a person who is too aggressive to become more passive, for once a person has built a habit pattern of passivity, it requires aggressiveness to change it, and since he cannot find this aggressiveness within himself, he must depend on someone else to change the pattern for him. On the other hand, the person who is too aggressive is at least able to muster the action-energy needed to change some of his aggression to passivity. To further complicate matters, few counselors knew how to turn passivity to aggressiveness, and even fewer had the courage to do so. In the case of my friend, I simply disconnected him from the alpha meter and told him that he was a miserable failure because he was more female than male and would never amount to anything because he let everybody push him around and I didn't have any time to waste on people who had no spunk so it would please me if he just left. He left all right, but when he did, he was showing plenty of aggressiveness.

Now I had to resolve the conflict between mysticism and magic. Sri Aurobindo's yoga was too passive for this purpose. Was there another yoga that combined aggressiveness with passivity in such a fashion as to achieve both serenity and power? There was indeed. It was Kundalini Yoga.

The theory behind this ancient discipline was that of serpent power, the fire of Kundalini (goddess of nature), which lay coiled up at the base of the spine and which by exercise, meditation, and concentration could be moved up through the seven ganglionic centers of the body (known as chakras) until it entered the pineal gland at the top of the head and there merged with divine power (solar energy). Two forces, one emerging from the earth, the other emerging from the sun, and in their balanced interchange lay both peace and power. Kundalini Yoga, it seemed to me, provided a mental and physical discipline which applied the principles of Space and Time and the balanced interchange of the energies of ecology.

Here, then, was a discipline aimed at achieving balance between the will and the imagination — a discipline which sought the point of equilibrium between the subconscious and conscious minds indicated in brainwave technology by activity at the alpha-theta border. Here, it seemed, was the point of innovation, the place of greater awareness, the region of increased power. With a firm anchor here, one could move as deeply into the imagination as he liked, or absorb himself in the material world as much as he liked, and always return to balance. Seeing this, I began the practice of Kundalini Yoga.

THE YOGA OF ECOLOGY

What struck me at once was that the seven chakras (ganglionic centers) corresponded to the seven colors of the spectrum, and since the ascent of consciousness through the seven colors led to revelation of the ultimate, I couldn't help thinking that the legendary pot of gold at the end of the rainbow (the seven colors of the spectrum) was really not at the *end* of the rainbow, but rather *across* it.

The seven chakras were arranged in the following order: 1. The seat of Kundalini in the coccyx, the lowest vertebra of the spine. 2. The sexual organs. 3. The adrenal glands, behind the naval. 4. The heart. 5. The thyroid gland, in the throat. 6. The pituitary gland, behind the forehead. 7. The seat of Vishnu (the sun), in the pineal gland below the top of the skull.

Colors corresponding to the various chakras were as follows: 1. Red, for the coccyx. 2. Orange, for the gonads. 3. Yellow, for the adrenals. 4. Green, for the heart. 5. Blue, for the thyroid. 6. Indigo, for the pituitary. 7. Violet, for the pineal.

The seven notes of the musical scale also correspond to the various chakras, beginning with note F in the key of C for the coccyx and continuing up to the note E for the pineal gland. Certain vowel sounds also corresponded to the chakras, and these were as follows: 1. *Ih,* for the coccyx. 2. *Uh,* for the gonads. 3. *Eh,* for the adrenals. 4. *Ah,* for the heart. 5. *Oh,* for the thyroid. 6. *Ooh,* for the pituitary. 7. And *Eee,* for the pineal.

Chanting these vowels together with masculine or feminine consonants could provide selected stimulation for any of the chakras. Masculine consonants of action and aggression were those that were hard or growling, such as d, k and r, while feminine consonants of serenity and passivity were those that were soft or yielding, such as m, n, and y.

According to Kundalini Yoga, the spine with its 33 segments including the uppermost vertebra, the skull, is the carrier of life. At the top of the uppermost vertebra is the positive pole while at the bottom of the lowest vertebra is the negative pole. Tension between the two produces life. This philosophy, thousands of years old, calls the positive pole the residence of Vishnu (Spirit) while the negative pole is the seat of Kundalini (Nature). These two poles might as easily be referred to as Time and Space, Time being the beaming fire of the uppermost or positive pole whose brilliance constantly attracts Space, the negative pole. Kundalini, coiled up like a snake in the lowest vertebra, waits for the moment when she can climb up through the channel of the spine and unite with her master, Vishnu. This condition represents the highest fulfillment of consciousness, the most perfect realization of happiness and power, for the individual then experiences the supreme measure of perfection. The name Kundalini means "the coiled one."

EXERCISES OF ECOLOGY YOGA

The exercises designed to create this equilibrium include physical postures, chants, breathing exercises, color visualization, meditation, and concentration, all of which are designed to move Kundalini up through the various chakras to eventual union with Vishnu in the pineal gland. When the energy of Kundalini advances upward step by step, this always means a new level of consciousness on the way to finding one's true self, for the chakras are simply batteries for storing energy. Most of these centers are dormant in the average person. The gradual elevation of consciousness awakens them one at a time in order that at the moment of fulfillment they are not overpowered.

Occasionally, someone with no understanding of the chakras suffers an accident that liberates Kundalini and causes it to race up the spinal column. His unprepared consciousness is overwhelmed, and he falls in a faint. Certain drugs may also liberate Kundalini, and an unready consciousness may be shocked into madness. But whoever reaches this highest level through conscious effort will experience it ecstatically, in perfect awareness and peace. He comes into possession of clear vision, the art of seeing the truth, for on this highest plane his consciousness fuses and becomes one with the cosmic consciousness. The secret of every religion lies in this esoteric fact.

Now I began experimenting with chanting, postures, breathing exercises, color visualization, meditation, and concentration, and it seemed to me that I quickly experienced a noticeable increase in energy. Though it would be some time before I would be able to synthesize the various exercises into a quick and efficient daily routine, already I was astonished at the progress I had made since I first decided to obtain an alpha meter and see if I could train my brainwaves.

COUNTING THE PEOPLE
WHO ONLY COUNT TREES

The day of my Mensa examination dawned smoggy and warm, and by the time I arrived at UCLA and parked my car, I already was beginning to perspire. I found the examination room on the ground floor, a small auditorium occupied by approximately forty people scattered about in such a fashion as to indicate that they hoped to avoid contact. The resulting silence made the atmosphere oppressive, and when the test administrator failed to put in an appearance at the appointed time, I stepped out into the hall to stretch my legs. There I ran into a man on an identical mission.

"Did you get a good look at that bunch?" he groaned. "Computer programmers, mathematicians, research engineers — ivory-tower specialists, the whole bunch. Give 'em puzzles, and they burn up the course, but when something fights back, it spooks them!"

That surprised me. I had thought the group somewhat withdrawn, but I had attributed this to the tension created by the forthcoming examination. Altogether, they had seemed much like any other group selected at random from the general population — short, tall, skinny, fat, young, old, male, female, neither rich nor poor — though there was about them a bit more of the studious look than one might expect in his next door neighbor. But that seemed natural in people who suspected that their intelligence might be high. It was difficult to account for my companion's disdain.

"Professional employees!" he expostulated, nearly shouting now. "I've had hundreds of them work for me. They can name all the trees and can't see the woods. Never knew one who could run his own business or take charge of anything, including himself!"

I thought for a moment that he expected an answer and began searching about for something to say, but he drew a deep breath and labored on.

"Now you look like a man who hasn't been sucking tit his whole life like the rest of those birds in there. So what in hell are you doing here?"

I said that I wanted to see if I could pass the test.

"What gives you the idea that you might be able to?" he demanded.

I told him that I'd recently been conditioning my brainwaves and had reason to believe that this had made me smarter.

He fell back a step and looked me over carefully. "You've been conditioning your *what*?" he wanted to know.

"My brainwaves," I repeated firmly.

"Brainwaves!" he exclaimed and rolled his eyes. "Oh, brother!" He staggered into the auditorium.

TAKING THE INTELLIGENCE TEST

After that, a psychologist arrived, carrying an armload of tests. I followed him into the auditorium and took a seat, and he explained that we would be required to take two examinations, each of which would be an hour in length and there would be a fifteen minute break between them. The tests would be against time, and they were divided into segments which tested verbal ability, mechanical ability, and reasoning ability. Since each segment had a particular amount of time allotted to it, we were not to look at the tests until he told us to begin and we were to stop immediately when he told us to stop. With that, he passed out the first test, face down so nobody could see it, and all over the room tension was spreading as runners took their marks and the starter's gun was raised, and my explosive friend who didn't like people who could see only trees had his jaw clenched and sweat was breaking out on his forehead.

"Begin!" cried the psychologist. We all began.

When time was called on the first test, I hadn't quite finished, but I calmed down during intermission and finished the second test all right. Several weeks later, I was notified that I had passed the admission requirements and had been admitted to Mensa. I attended a number of meetings, but I never saw the man who didn't like people who could see only trees.

Ecology

SPACE AND TIME

The Forces of Balance

SPACE	TIME
Expansion	Constriction
Outward	Inward
Ascent	Descent
Violet	Red
Cold	Hot
Light	Heavy
Water	Fire
Negative	Positive
Electron	Proton
Potassium	Sodium
Vegetable	Animal
Salad	Cereal
Female	Male
Sympathetic Nerves	Parasympathetic Nerves
Hot, sour-sweet	Salty, bitter

Ecology

Dynamics of Balance

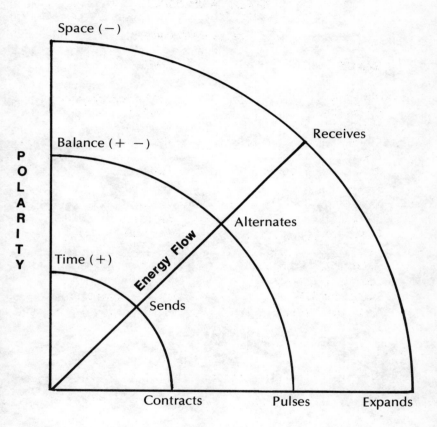

Space (−)

Balance (+ −)

Receives

P
O
L
A
R
I
T
Y

Alternates

Energy Flow

Time (+)

Sends

Contracts

Pulses

Expands

BEHAVIOR

The Power to Change

6

T he sign on the marquee announced, "Oliver, the Hypnotist," and seemed strangely out of place on the plush resort hotel at the edge of Mission Bay in San Diego. In the late afternoon sunshine, seagulls swooped low over the rooftops, and to the west, the waters of the bay were blue and serene. A friend named George had dragged me down here. "Oliver," he said, "is no ordinary stage hypnotist. Oh, he does all the stunts, but the man knows something. I'm convinced that he has deep insight into how the mind functions, but he won't open up. I got to thinking about it and decided that you're just the fellow to draw him out, because when you hit him with that brainwave stuff of yours, he's bound to turn on."

I'd resisted at first. Over the years, I'd had a lengthy skirmish with hypnotism,

97

and I'd found the area as full of charlatans as a carnival side-show. It was difficult to believe that a man who plied the trade of stage hypnotist could be anything other than a con-man, but George, who once sold $20,000,000 of life insurance in a single year, was mighty persuasive. He picked me up, took me to lunch, drove me to San Diego, and promised the world's finest dinner. I figured I'd be lucky if I got out of the evening without buying insurance.

AN UNCONSCIOUS DECISION

We parked the car, entered the hotel and found the bar where we took seats at a table and ordered cocktails. While waiting, George offered me a cigarette. "No, thanks," I said.

He removed one from the pack and tapped it thoughtfully, then he lit it and peered at me through the smoke. "When did you quit?" he asked.

"Quit what?"

"Smoking, of course."

"What makes you think I've quit?"

"Listen, since I picked you up before lunch I've offered you a cigarette a half dozen times. You never accepted and never smoked any of your own. I remember you, buddy. You used to smoke like a furnace. What's the matter with confessing you've quit? Is that supposed to put a hex on it?"

I tried to remember when I'd last had a cigarette. It must have been over twenty-four hours. I'd lit one after breakfast the day before, which was usually the only cigarette that I truly enjoyed, but it had tasted so vile that I'd ground it out after a single puff. Later, after I'd left the house, my hand had moved unconsciously for the pack, and I discovered I'd left it at home. I'd thought I would buy another, but I hadn't, and when I returned home I'd left the open pack on the desk, un-disturbed. What's more, I hadn't taken it with me when I left the house this morning. Strange, how it had never occurred to me that I'd quit. All these actions seemed to have been done unconsciously, so that I hadn't actually noticed, though now it was easy enough to remember.

"Hey!" I said, "I think I've stopped smoking!"

"Do tell," answered George.

I could smell the aroma of his cigarette clearly. It was an aroma that had always been an automatic signal for me to light up one of my own. I smelled it deeply now, waiting for a reaction. None came. I hadn't the slightest desire to smoke.

AN ANNOUNCEMENT
WORTHY OF PAVLOV

"I can't believe it," I said. "I think I'm cured."

"Well, clue me onto it, boy. I'm sick to death of this filthy habit."

"I don't know what to tell you. I don't seem to have done anything. I just seem to have quit."

"Oh, come now. I've seen you quit twice in the same day. There was always some method you were trying to follow."

"Not this time, George. What seems to have left me of its own accord is the desire to smoke itself."

He thought about this and then he said that maybe it had something to do with my brainwave training. I told him I'd been thinking the same thing myself. Maybe the desire to smoke was the result of imbalance, and since I was beginning to achieve balance, maybe the desire had simply left me.

He considered this, but thought there was more to it. "We both know that smoking is primarily a conditioned reflex. A whole host of people have claimed that you can erase conditioned reflexes by brainwashing techniques, or even by retraining those reflexes, but a reflex is a reflex and the only other way it has been known to disappear is through disuse."

It was an announcement worthy of Pavlov, but the logic failed to dissuade me. "I don't have any desire to smoke," I repeated. "Two days ago I was smoking. That's certainly not long enough to erase a conditioned reflex, and I haven't been brainwashed, and I haven't been hypnotized."

The word rang between us.

"Are we thinking the same thing?" asked George.

"Self-hypnosis," I murmured. It certainly was possible.

The waitress brought the drinks, and we clicked our glasses together. "To our meeting with Oliver," George said.

PEOPLE WHO BELIEVE
THEY ARE DUCKS

Before long, we moved into the restaurant and ordered dinner. George proved to be right, the food was delicious. Afterwards, we lingered over coffee until the first show came on. Oliver turned out to be a handsome, athletic man of middle years who wore a dark beard and had a commanding presence. He warmed up the audience with the customary patter, then began selecting his subjects, constantly making suggestions and carefully observing whether they were followed. He was very polished. His rapid delivery and fast stream of jokes kept the audience attentive and in good humor, and he seemed to accomplish his ends without effort. Finally, he had a half dozen subjects chosen, and these were seated on chairs arranged in a row on the stage.

There were four women and two men, and as he continued bantering with them, he established that he had never seen any of them before and none of them had ever seen him, that no one in the group had ever been hypnotized, that they were attending the show with boy friends, husbands, wives and girl friends who were seated at tables in the audience and whose reactions varied from daring them to volunteer to being apprehensive about it. Finally, he asked his subjects to close their eyes and gave them suggestions for relaxation which he shortly changed into suggestions for sleep and finally into suggestions that they would obey him implicitly.

After this, he told them that they were attending a sad movie, and they all cried. Then he told them that they were attending a comedy, and they all laughed. Then he told them that they were all ducks, and they quacked and waddled around the stage. Then he told them that they were all dogs, and they began barking and growling. One of the males even raised his leg as if urinating on an imaginary lamp post. By this time, the audience was roaring with laughter. I glanced at George and raised an eyebrow, but he winked back, as if to say, "Just wait and see."

A PAPER DAGGER

Now Oliver gave each subject a different suggestion, and the resultant slapstick had the comedy overtones of a Mack Sennett movie about the Keystone Kops. One man was told that he had an irresistible urge to kiss every woman he saw, and one woman was told that she could only be kissed on the fanny. When these two ran into each other, the house came down. Another woman was told that her raised middle finger

100

was the peace sign, and she walked around giving everybody the finger. Still another woman was told to go around asking everybody, "Who?" while the second of the two men was instructed to go around asking everybody, "What?" The last woman was told that whenever she heard the word, "Who?" she would freeze, and whenever she heard the word, "What?" she would unfreeze. She was run like a robot by the Who'er and What'er, and some of her poses were hilarious.

When the laughter seemed to have reached its peak, Oliver reassembled his subjects and turned serious. Choosing the younger of the two men, he presented him with a paper dagger and told him it was real. Then he said that there was a man in the audience who intended to destroy the world, and the only way that the world could be saved was for the man to be assassinated. He instructed his subject to sneak up on this man because the man was dangerous, and to stab him to death with the dagger because it was silent and wouldn't bring the man's bodyguard. When he described the man, he described me. I glanced at George and saw that he was in on it. I didn't like it at all.

Oliver told the man to start, and the audience fell into a hush, and out into the crowd the man stealthily crept with his paper dagger poised in his hand. A feeling of uneasiness gathered in my stomach. I would have liked reassurance that the dagger was paper. Down the aisles and between the tables the man prowled, once passing close enough so I could see his eyes. They were fixed and glassy. His path now became marked by ever-shortening circles as some unerring instinct seemed to guide him in my direction. When he finally caught sight of me, I looked him in the eye, and he hid behind a table. Then, despite the fact that I continued to stare at him, he slithered forward, glaring.

THE POWER OF SUGGESTION

Frankly, I was unnerved. Even though I could now see that the dagger was only paper, I had no doubt that the man would throw himself upon me, and I didn't know whether to defend myself or run. It certainly seemed foolhardy to stand there and do nothing. I silently appealed to George for help, but he only smiled. I was growing irritated and angry.

Suddenly, with a bloodcurdling yell the man leaped to his

feet and charged, paper dagger aloft and eyes lighted with fury. I braced myself for the impact. Then Oliver's voice cracked through the room. "Freeze!" he cried. The man froze on the spot.

After that, Oliver came over and talked to him soothingly and led him away and awakened all the subjects from their trances and made a little speech about the power of suggestion, how it could cause murders and riots and robberies and arsons just as easily as it could cause brotherhood and love and justice and abundance. Then he left the stage to applause, but I wasn't paying much attention. My old friend adrenalin had come to my aid and I hadn't used him and now he was complaining. I felt sick to my stomach.

I let off steam by telling George how little I appreciated being involved in this stunt, but his composure remained unshaken as he assured me that there was a point and I would know what it was soon. With that, he took me by the elbow and steered me through the crowd. Here and there people shied away in apprehension, so I pasted on a smile in hopes they would perceive that I wasn't intending to destroy the world after all.

Oliver was waiting for us in his dressing room. He had changed into a loose white shirt and dark slacks and looked the picture of magnetic health. When George introduced us, he shook hands searchingly. "If that had been a real dagger, you could have been killed," he said. "Even as it was, you could have been hurt."

I told him I was aware of that fact.

"Are you satisfied that the whole thing was authentic?" he asked.

I answered that I thought it was authentic.

"Good," he said. "Sit down and tell me about brainwaves. We may be able to help each other."

THE HORSE AND THE RIDER

I sat down and considered where to begin. We obviously didn't have all night, since he had another show in two hours, so I tried to cut through extraneous matter and get right to the point. "I think I've stumbled onto the brainwave key to the subconscious," I said. "When people learn how to use it, they can put themselves into highly suggestible states. They

102

may even believe that what they imagine is real."

He leaned forward in his chair. "Carry on," he said.

I told him how delta and theta brain rhythms were aligned with the subconscious mind and alpha and beta rhythms with the conscious mind, and I told him how alpha showed the passive portion of the conscious mind and beta the active, while delta indicated the passive portion of the subconscious mind and theta the active. Then I pointed out how the subconscious mind itself was passive while the conscious mind was active, and I remarked that everything indicated the existence of some delicate balancing mechanism between the passive and active portions of man's mind.

Oliver kept nodding all through this, and when I finished he said, "Man has two minds, that's clear enough. He's dual-natured, dual-minded, and oriented to a world of duality. The subconscious mind is the horse, and the conscious mind is the rider, and the horse does what the rider tells it to, and any rider can take over the horse, but without a rider, the horse acts crazy. You saw me take over several horses tonight, so you know that riders are replaceable. And if you've ever visited a mental hospital, you've seen plenty of horses without riders."

I liked the metaphor and told him so. Then I described the dynamics of ecology and how it was my idea that a perfectly balanced interchange between conscious and subconscious minds produced the mental power described as genius. He reflected on that and then he said he thought it was true because in his experience the subconscious mind had all of the powers of imagination, but little, if any, of the powers of reason. On the other hand, the conscious mind seemed to have all of the powers of reason, but little, if any, of the powers of imagination. Genius, he had to admit, seemed the result of a classical marriage between reason and imagination. We were hitting it off fine. George sat there and beamed.

AN EXPERIENCE WITH HYPNOSIS

Now Oliver apologized for sending the man with the paper dagger after me, but he explained that he wanted to illustrate dramatically the dangers of hypnotism. "You wouldn't give an atom bomb to a child or a maniac," he said, "and neither would I. But from what you tell me, many people soon will be gaining access to their subconscious minds through brainwave feedback training. If that is so, it is important that they know the dangers involved. It's a pity that this knowledge can't be kept out of the hands of the selfish and greedy. That would lessen the danger considerably."

I said that I planned to publish a book, but I hoped to veil the most powerful facts in such a manner that the selfish would be unable to use them. Oliver brightened. I further explained that hypnotism would be an important part of the book, and while I had had some experience with it both as subject and practitioner, my experience as a subject had been unrewarding because I couldn't be hypnotized. Oliver then offered to hypnotize me, and I gave him permission. Within a few minutes, he placed me in a light trance and produced anesthesia in my left arm. Pins could be stuck in it, and I could feel nothing. I observed this effect with misgivings, but when he gave me the suggestion that all feeling had returned, I winced at the touch of a pin.

"You're not a difficult subject now," he said. "Perhaps your brainwave training had something to do with it."

George interrupted then and told Oliver how I had suddenly quit smoking without even trying where before I had quit dozens of time only to begin again.

THE KING AND
THE BRILLIANT IDIOT

Oliver studied me. "What's the name of that passive brain rhythm?"

"Alpha."

"Did you have trouble producing it?"

"So much trouble that I thought I'd never learn."

"Then the theory you hold seems to be right. The subconscious won't accept a suggestion unless the conscious mind is passive. Your conscious mind had difficulty being passive, so your desire to quit smoking had no effect. As soon as you trained your conscious mind to be passive, the desire to quit smoking, which you continued to have, impressed the subconscious and was turned into fact."

I was pleased with how perfectly this explanation dovetailed with both theory and events.

Oliver leaned forward searchingly. "I can see that you are

onto something profound and true, and I thank you for sharing it with me. First thing in the morning, I intend to launch a study of brainwaves. Now let me share with you what I know of hypnosis. It is only two things. First, the subconscious mind is a brilliant idiot. It will try its best to do or be whatever it is told to do or be, and it has vast and powerful resources. Second, the conscious mind is a child become king. It cries when things go against it because it does not yet know its power. Let the brilliant idiot find a wise king, and the genius of man is established."

The words set up echoes in my mind and I tried to think where I'd heard them. Oliver smiled and opened a drawer of his dressing table. He withdrew a battered book and tossed it to me. "Those sentiments were written fifteen years ago. Strange, how the wheel comes full circle." The book in my lap was my own *Three Magic Words*.

GOOD ENOUGH TO BOTTLE

George got into the act then and confessed how he and Oliver had hatched up this plot after Oliver had learned that he knew me. George had thought I needed a "shock treatment" because I'd lost sight of the principles in my own books, thus the man with the paper dagger. I had to admit that the shock had been successful, but I maintained that I'd never lost sight of the principles in my books because I'd never truly had them in view. It was one thing, I explained, to reason things out, and quite another to experience them. Now I felt I was experiencing them.

Somebody rapped on the door and called, "Ten minutes!" and Oliver began dressing. He asked if we were staying for the second show, but we had a two and a half hour drive back to Los Angeles, so we begged off. We shook hands and told him goodbye, promising to keep him posted. When George sought out the waiter and asked for the dinner check, he found that Oliver had paid it.

For most of the drive back to Los Angeles, we were silent, each absorbed in his own thoughts. Halfway back, George announced, "Now that you've become suggestible, I think you should buy an insurance policy."

"Sorry," I replied. "I've got my beta rhythm on."

When he dropped me off, I stood under the streetlight,

thanking him. "You know," he said, "I think you've lost weight too. Whatever you've got, you should bottle it."

As I entered the apartment, I checked my belt. It was taken in a notch, and my pants felt looser. I didn't own a scale, but I promised to weigh myself at the first opportunity. That opportunity came two days later. I'd taken off fifteen pounds.

A REVIEW OF HYPNOSIS

The meeting with Oliver had left strange repercussions in my mind, and I now found myself drawn to the pages of *Three Magic Words* and to try to discern, if possible, what had prompted a man of obviously superior intellect and knowledge to keep this book throughout the years and to find in it help and guidance. I was pleased to discover how well the book accorded with my present positions, even after the lapse of fifteen years, and I could see that what had once been primarily an intellectual perception had now filtered down into my subconscious and I become an experience as well. In truth, it delighted me that I had written this book so long ago, for I could not remember having either the resources or the skill. It seemed to me that my pen had been guided by a hand other than my own.

The conclusions drawn concerning the conscious and subconscious minds and the use of hypnotism seemed worth repeating:

1. The conscious mind is an instrument for the recording of pain and pleasure. It measures these experiences, files them for recall, analyzes the circumstances that produced them, and plans escape from pain and flight into pleasure.

2. The conscious mind is a finely-tuned instrument with the sole aim of physical survival of the organism.

3. The conscious mind is as destructible as the body of which it is a part.

4. The conscious mind has no memory of its own but has the ability to call up memories from the subconscious.

5. The memory of the subconscious mind is perfect.

6. The subconscious mind is the infinite substance of which all things are made. It has no beginning and no end and everything exists within it.

7. The subconscious mind *is* everything and knows everything. It is everywhere at all times and all of it is anywhere at

any time, for Space and Time cannot exist in the Infinite.

8. Inductive reasoning attempts to arrive at law through circumstance and is the type of reasoning primarily done by the conscious mind which can also reason deductively.

9. Deductive reasoning attempts to arrive at circumstances through law and is the *only* type of reasoning done by the sub-conscious mind.

10. Hypnotism exposes the essence of the subconscious mind and allows us to see that it responds only to suggestion.

11. We cannot order our lives through hypnotism but only through consciously exercising control of the subconscious mind, which means consciously exercising control over our thoughts.

12. Meditation is the tool with which we seek to control our thoughts and thus to control our world through the sub-conscious mind.

13. Thought transference is proof that all life exists within one intelligence — Universal Subconscious Mind.

14. Intuition is proof that Universal Subconscious Mind contains all knowledge and will reveal it to the conscious mind of man when the proper rapport is established.

15. Subconscious mind has the power to heal the body and to create physical form and physical circumstance, but acute ill health still must be dealt with by the doctor, and acute mental distress still must be dealt with by the psychiatrist, for we have not come far enough in faith and conception to be able to always treat cause and not symptoms.

16. First cause of every object and circumstance is its creation on the plane of mind.

PATH OF SAINT OR PATH OF MADMAN

Then there were the three magic words themselves — *you are God.* Path of saint or path of madman, depending on balance or imbalance.

A few nights later a man called me from across the country. He was drunk. "So you're the Andersen who wrote Three Magic Words!" he cried. "Boy, what a salesman you are! I just finished reading Success Cybernetics. I couldn't believe the same man wrote both books. You must be the world's greatest conman!"

I tried to tell him that each book was an opposite side of the same coin and the truth lay in putting them together, but he was well into monomania by this time and didn't want to think. I finally told him that my royalty on each book was five cents and if he'd give me his address I'd send him his dime back. Surprisingly, he gave me his address. Unflinchingly, I sent him his dime.

Not long afterwards I had a call from George who said that Oliver would be in Los Angeles in a few days and wondered if we could all get together. The prospect excited me because I wanted to run brainwave tests on someone who was under hypnosis, so I asked George if he'd ever been hypnotized and he said he hadn't and I told him what I had in mind and asked if he was willing to be the subject, and he said he'd do it, just for me, and wondered if I'd like to buy some insurance. I said I'd think about it.

It doesn't often rain in Los Angeles, but when it does it's usually a downpour. On the day that Oliver arrived, I was considering building an ark. The streets were rivers, the freeways jammed with stalled traffic, and here and there, hills were sliding into the sea. By the time the three of us had gathered, we were all thankful for a haven.

First off, I ran a brainwave test on Oliver. He could produce alpha, all right, but he wasn't very good at it, and I let him know that he had something to learn. That's when he told me that he'd never been hypnotized, that he'd gone to the best professionals in the business and nobody could put him under. Since this had been my own problem, I felt immediate camaradarie and suggested that it wasn't so bad learning to be passive because you didn't have to be unless you wanted to be and it could often be useful. He said that he'd been reading enough about brainwaves to realize he could help himself by undergoing brainwave training, so I gave him the address of the electronic wizard and he resolved to pick up an alpha meter.

BRAINWAVES AND HYPNOSIS

After that, we both worked on George. I hooked him up to the alpha meter and ran a test, and he produced strong beta with eyes open and relatively sparse alpha with eyes closed, so if the theory held true he wouldn't be a particularly good hypnotic subject. He wasn't.

First, Oliver used a simple eye-closure technique, suggesting to George that his eyelids were growing heavier and he wouldn't be able to keep them open. Everything seemed to be going fine, but when George got his eyes closed the alpha meter didn't pick up any change in brain rhythms, and right in the middle of everything Oliver broke off. "You're trying too hard to cooperate," he told George. "Resist a little."

He began again by dangling a ring before George's eyes and asking him to concentrate on the to and fro movement, at the same time suggesting again that his eyes were growing tired and that is was difficult to keep them open. As soon as George's eyes closed, Oliver put the ring away and began suggesting that George's right hand was growing lighter and beginning to float. He kept up these suggestions patiently and pretty soon George's hand rose from the table. I checked the brainwave patterns. George was producing alpha, though not profusely.

Now Oliver began suggesting that George's hand was rising higher and pretty soon would come to rest on top of his head, and when it did, George would fall into deep trance — he would be able to hear only what Oliver said, and he would obey it. Higher and higher George's hand floated until at last it came to rest on top of his head, and when it did, there was an abrupt change in his brain rhythms. He immediately began producing a powerful alpha in the 8-10 cycle per second range, large amplitude, and these rhythms were nearly continuous. I pointed this out to Oliver, and he nodded thoughtfully.

Now George was informed that he was an excellent tennis player who was engaged in a hard match with a skillful opponent and would have to call upon all his resources to win. He began making small, simulated tennis movements in his chair, sometimes grunting aloud, so I expected the alpha meter to be producing beta, but it began producing theta instead.

ANOTHER JOB FOR THE ELECTRONIC WIZARD

After this, Oliver told George that he was lying beside his favorite trout stream on a beautiful day and had just caught his limit and the soft spring breeze carried the scent of wildflowers and pine needles, and he was going to take a nap and fall fast asleep. I expected the alpha meter to begin producing delta rhythms, but again we heard theta.

Intrigued now, Oliver led George through a half dozen other imaginary situations. Never once did we hear a beta or delta rhythm. There would be a powerful alpha while George was just sitting there without imagining anything, and the moment he became involved in an imaginary situation, the meter gave out with theta rhythms. For the better part of an hour, Oliver continued in this fashion, and there was never a deviation from the pattern. At last he brought George back out of his deep hypnosis by suggesting to him that he count backward from ten and when he reached one he would emerge into full consciousness and feel fresh and energetic and remember everything he'd experienced.

When he woke up, he was astonished. For a moment he had trouble orienting himself. As far as he was concerned, he had just finished playing tennis, going fishing, attending a stage play, giving a lecture, and selling a million dollar insurance policy.

Gradually, it came back to him. And when it did, he wasn't so sure that he liked it. Never before had he surrendered his volition to anyone else, and the thought that he had been unable to tell dream from reality distressed him. But when I told him of the strong alpha and theta rhythms he had produced in his hypnotic state and how, in my opinion, he could learn to take these imaginary excursions anytime he chose, without any danger and with highly creative results, simply by learning to control his brainwaves, he too asked for the address of the electronic wizard and vowed to obtain an alpha meter.

Altogether, it had been an interesting afternoon. When the three of us said goodbye, we all felt we had learned something. Alpha unquestionably was aligned with the passivity of the conscious mind and was a highly suggestible state. We had further shown that when imaginary images became so vivid that they seemed to be real, the brain was producing theta. And we had discovered that hypnosis lowered brainwave frequencies into the alpha-theta region.

It now became clear why I had finally quit smoking. While producing alpha, I had placed my conscious mind in a passive state so the subconscious could be reached by suggestion. My desire to quit smoking then had impressed itself on the subconscious which had turned the desire into fact. Brainwave training had enabled me to use self-hypnosis.

It was easy to see, however, that this technique was a

double-edged sword. Some people were already too passive. Their subconscious minds would take suggestion, all right — the trouble was that they would take suggestion from everybody and everything. If such a person managed to resolve to quit smoking, the first whiff of somebody's ciagarette gave him a new suggestion and he was back to smoking again. Such a person needed willpower training, not alpha training. Willpower was concentration.

My own willpower had been fine, but the moment I relaxed it, I began smoking again because my will hadn't impressed my subconscious. The gateway to the subconscious was through the alpha rhythm, and I hadn't been able to turn on alpha. As soon as I learned how, my subconscious was reached, and I quit smoking without even trying. The brilliant idiot had received his orders.

Something of the same nature seemed to be happening concerning my weight. Already I had dropped fifteen pounds without going on a diet or making specific efforts. I thought back over the past few weeks and tried to remember if there'd been any change in my eating habits. There had been a change, all right.

THE WISE MAN TAKES
THE MIDDLE PATH

I'd always been a meat and potatoes man, and now I couldn't remember the last time I'd had meat. I'd been eating raw fruits and vegetables, unsalted nuts, whole grain cereals, dairy products and shellfish, and taking very little alcohol. These were drastic changes and it was difficult to believe that I had made them all without being aware of it. Not that I'd ever had anything against such a diet; it was just that it was generally second choice to my meat and potatoes diet, which also had been liberally sprinkled with ice cream, soft drinks, pies and cakes, lots of processed foods and plenty of liquor. All these things I seemed to have eliminated. I couldn't help wondering what powerful change had taken place in my appestat to so drastically alter my preference in foods, but I had little doubt that it had something to do with balance. As the days went by and my pants grew looser, I was driven to the drugstore to measure my avoirdupois on fortune-te'ling scales. I dropped my penny in the slot, and a little card came out with my weight printed on it: 212 pounds. The opposite side of the card was interesting also. "The wise man takes the middle path," it said.

Inner Ecology

7

O ver the next few months, my weight continued to drop at the rate of two pounds per week. When it reached 187, it stabilized. Altogether, fifty pounds had melted away. As I watched them disappear, I became aware of two causes. Fundamental, of course, was my ability to produce alpha, but there was the balancing mechanism of ecology as well.

For example, the legacy left us by Einstein is that matter becomes energy and energy becomes matter. In ecological terms this might be stated — Space becomes Time and Time becomes Space. When a person took in more energy than he expended, that surplus energy turned into matter, and he became fat. On the other hand, when a person expended more energy than he took in, some of his substance turned into energy, and he became thin. At just the right weight he was perfectly balanced. Since the regimen I was following had restored balance to my body, I chose to call it Inner Ecology. That regimen consisted of the following procedures:

1) Meditation;   2) Concentration;   3) Physical postures;
4) Breath control;   5) Chanting;   6) Color imagery;   7) Diet.

THE ART OF MEDITATION

Meditation is the art of producing alpha brain rhythms. For those who had conditioned their alpha rhythms with feedback training devices, this technique involved little more than closing the eyes and relaxing. For those who had not had this training, the technique became more complex. Main thing to be striven for was a perfectly passive state of mind, without thought, without images, without concentration — just an alert, aware, receptiveness. Yogis and Zen masters adopted the lotus position for meditation, and this had a double benefit. The muscle stretching attracted energy, and the straight back provided the most direct path for Kundalini to move up the spine. One need not necessarily take this posture to attain benefits, however. Simply sitting in a chair with feet flat on the floor and back straight would do nicely. Eyes must be closed naturally, as the propogation of alpha waves with eyes open was practically impossible for the novice.

Meditation — doing nothing — had long been known in yoga and Zen as a powerful state of consciousness. It's culmination in yoga was the experience of samadhi; in Zen, satori. In both, the consciousness of the meditator was united with the consciousness of God.

Letting go was the difficult thing — surrendering all aims and desires and agitations and concerns and worries. "The mind is like a monkey," the Zen masters said. It must quiet itself until it became a crystal clear pool. In this state, as we knew from brainwave technology, alpha rhythms were produced, and the gate to the subconscious opened.

INSTANT YOGA

Seemingly childlike in simplicity, meditation nevertheless remained a difficult technique to master. Yogis and Zen Buddhists often spent lifetimes without achieving satori or samadhi. Now the new brainwave training devices shortened the period of training to just a few weeks. Western technology thus bridged the gap between East and West by developing an "Instant Yoga."

With a trained alpha rhythm, meditation could be conducted a number of times each day, with no more than five minutes needed per session, and the meditator always emerged refreshed and ready to tackle his problems. With an untrained alpha rhythm, however, meditation should be practiced for at least an hour, even if this could only be arranged once a week. The longer period of time allowed the meditator to see how restless and uncontrollable his conscious mind was and revealed the difficulty of making it passive. That difficulty yielded swiftly to feedback training, but it was most difficult to master by mental discipline alone, for the monkey-like conscious mind carried on an incessant dialogue.

To tire out the monkey and make him relax his grip on consciousness, Zen masters used unsolvable riddles called koans, such as, "What is the sound of one hand clapping?" or "Show me your original face before you were born." The mind worked itself into a spasm attempting to produce an answer. When suddenly that spasm relaxed, the door to the subconscious opened, and the apprentice saw that there was never a riddle at all. This was the experience of satori. It could be produced in austere meditation halls after years of arduous effort, or in the privacy of one's home by electronic means after a few hours of feedback training.

THE ECOLOGY
OF CONCENTRATION

Concentration was focused attention and was applied to three different objectives. Those were: 1) The elevation of consciousness. 2). A god-like self image. 3). A major goal.

Focusing attention on one thing to the exclusion of all other things was an extraordinarily creative act. It enabled the percipient to "get into" the object of his contemplation in ways that were beyond the ken of the casual observer. When attention was pinpointed, sharply concentrated on one spot, it was as though a magnifying glass had focused the sun's rays into creative fire. Depth upon depth opened up to the observer.

Concentration developed the power of resolution between extremes which was the source of genius. That power was best illustrated by the functioning of the human eyes. Each eye produced a separate image, and these images differed slightly from each other due to the distance between the two eyes. The mind resolved these two images into one, and because it had done so, there emerged the dimension known as depth. Depth perception was the power of ecology. The farther apart the two viewpoints which were resolved into a single image, the greater the perception of depth. Concentration developed the power of resolution. It enabled the person to make a single balanced image out of increasingly divergent viewpoints, and thus he penetrated deeper and deeper into the meaning of life.

Concentrating on the levels of consciousness meant concentrating on the chakras and placing one's awareness there. In the average person, the sense of consciousness seemed to be centered about four inches behind the eyes. This present technique was aimed at moving that center of consciousness at will, placing it first in the coccyx, then in the sexual organs, then in the naval, then in the heart, then in the throat, then in the forehead, and finally below the top of the head. In this fashion, consciousness elevated Kundalini, guiding her up through the chakras to union with Vishnu in the pineal gland.

Moving the center of consciousness could at first seem difficult, but there was nervous sensation in each of the chakras and becoming aware of that sensation was the first step in mastering the technique. For example, by moving the tongue in the mouth, one could become aware of every nook and cranny. Focusing attention upon this experience and maintaining that attention for a few minutes could cause one to feel that he actually was inside his mouth.

THE LADDER OF ECOLOGY

To begin with, then, attention was focused on the coccyx, the lowest vertebra of the spine — one's "tailbone." It was helpful to place a finger upon it and exert a little pressure. Surprisingly, the coccyx was quite sensitive. The reason that this sensitivity was generally not perceived was simply because attention was directed elsewhere. Now the coccyx must receive full attention, and this attention must be kept focused there, unwaveringly, until awareness seemed centered in the coccyx itself.

You could not accomplish this the first time you tried it, or even the second or third, but each effort increased your ability, and once you had successfully shifted consciousness to the coccyx, you also had prepared yourself to approach the next highest chakra. In this manner, step by step, Kundalini was led up the ladder.

There was, of course, a temptation to run the ladder at one fell swoop, the very first session. You could try this, if you liked; no harm would come from it. But no benefits would result either. The act of concentration meant continuous focused attention on only one chakra until you were certain that you had succeeded in placing your consciousness there.

The second objective was the creation of a god-like self-image. This could not be done by thinking of personality or character attributes, no matter how attractive some of these might seem, for they were only physical prototypes and were subject to limitation. One must become aware of the quest that was fundamental to yoga and Zen in order to realize what the true nature of his self-image must be. For if union with God was possible, then in essence one must actually be God, and that was the only self-image that would serve for the attainment of samadhi.

Of course, one mustn't fall into the trap of visualizing himself as an old man with a long white beard presiding over all from a throne in the clouds. We couldn't know what the *form* of God was like, but we could know his *attributes*. He was the principle of absolute being and absolute power and absolute freedom. And that principle was within us.

THE ECOLOGIST SELF-IMAGE

How to realize this was the question. It sounded so grandiose that many people were frightened. But it was actually far from grandiose. The person trying to live up to a principle did not insist that he was greater than the principle, but instead recognized that the principle was greater than he was.

Building a god-like self-image was not complex. For the principle of absolute being realized itself by saying, "I am." And the principle of absolute power realized itself by saying, "I can." And the principle of absolute freedom realized itself by saying, "I don't have to."

Desire was the power that accomplished all things. Not willpower. *Want* power. Desire opened up the pineal gland and allowed pure energy through. A man who wanted something badly developed the power of ten. And the only reason he didn't want something badly was because his desire had been locked up in prison. The bars of that prison were always named, "I am not," I can't," and "I have to."

If you thought, "I am not," you couldn't choose a goal. If you thought, "I can't," you didn't try to achieve it. If you thought, "I have to," you only went through the motions. In any case, you were a loser. The simple self-image that brought success, whether building bridges or seeking God was "I am," "I can," and "I don't have to." These enabled you to "want to."

By repeating these three affirmations, you could cure yourself of headaches, tiredness, indigestion, irritability, and insomnia. If you fell asleep at night repeating them to yourself, you could get things done that you never thought possible. Only eight little words, but they made a world of difference.

The third use of concentration lay in choosing a goal and keeping it constantly in mind. That goal had to be major. It had to be the objective that you would rather attain above all others. It had to attract and excite you. Just the mere striving to attain it had to be sufficient to make you happy. Once you had settled on this goal, you visualized it clearly, becoming as familiar with what it looked like as you were with the face of your wife or husband or children or best friend. Then you put it in the back of your mind, moving it forward into consciousness at least once each day and concentrating upon it, then putting it in the back of your mind again. *You never let it out of your mind*.

THE PHYSICAL POSTURES
OF ECOLOGY YOGA

The third technique — physical postures — was the yoga exercises which increased health, energy and mental clarity, and aided the movement of Kundalini up the chakras to unite with Vishnu. These were muscle-stretching exercises as opposed to muscle-bunching exercises such as those used in weight-lifting. Muscle bunching exercises produced fatigue, while muscle-stretching exercises increased energy. The reason for this resided in the nature of Space and Time. Muscle-bunching was a Time action and required Time fuel (food). Since stored food energy easily depleted itself, a feeling of fatigue was produced by muscle-bunching, and when such exercises were finished, the person found himself hungry. Such exercises had a Time effect — they made a person broader and more massive.

On the other hand, muscle-stretching was a Space action and required Space fuel (air). Since providing such fuel was only a matter of breathing, no depletion of energy took place, and no fatigue was produced. On the contrary, Space exercises developed the pineal, allowing it to admit more psychic energy, and the person felt refreshed. What's more, since Time energy had not been used, there was no subsequent feeling of hunger. Such exercises had a Space effect; they made a person slender and supple. Not only that, they elevated consciousness.

Twelve physical postures follow. Each should stretch your muscles as far as they can go. Each should be held for the count of twenty. In between, take three deep breaths. If a posture cannot be fully taken, come as close as possible.

The Arm Flex: Seated on the floor with your legs stretched in front of you, extend your arms to the side and flex them against the elbow joint, spreading your fingers as far as they will go and bending your hands backward at the wrists. Next, holding the same position, bend your hands forward at the wrists.

The Ankle Grasp: Still seated on the floor with legs stretched in front of you, bend your toes toward yourself, moving your feet at the ankles. Next, bend them away from yourself. Then lean forward without bending your knees and grasp your ankles. Then lean farther forward and grasp your toes. After that, bend down until your forehead touches your knees.

IN THE HEART
OF THE LOTUS

The Lotus: From a sitting position, place your right foot atop your left thigh and your left foot atop your right thigh.

If this is too difficult, try the half-lotus, placing your right foot atop your left thigh and your left foot *under* your right thigh. Then reverse foot positions.

The Twist: From a sitting position, put your left foot under your right thigh with your left thigh flat on the floor, then place your right foot to the left of your left thigh, twisting to the right and bracing yourself on the floor with your fingertips. Next, reverse leg positions and twist to the left.

The Sitting Kneel: Kneel on the floor with toes pointed behind you, then sit on the backs of your ankles and bend backward at the waist as far as you can go, bracing yourself with your hands. Objective here is to lie flat with your legs bent under you at the knees.

The Rocking Horse: Lying on your stomach, raise your torso off the floor by pushing down with your hands until your arms are fully extended. Next, lie flat on your stomach and bend your legs up at the knees, reaching back with your hands to graps your ankles, then rock back and forth on your stomach.

The Shoulder Stand: Lying on your back, raise your legs with the knees straight and continue back over your head until your toes touch the floor behind you. Next, raise your legs over your head keeping your weight on your shoulders and bracing your torso with hands on back and elbows on the floor. Next, spread your legs as far as they will go and rotate your hips to the left, then rotate them to the right. Next, put your legs together and roll slowly off your shoulders onto your back, jacknifing to maintain balance. Slowly lower your legs until your heels are just off the floor and hold that position for twenty counts.

The Bends: From a standing position and with arms extended, bend to the right and touch the floor. Next, repeat to the left. Next, place your hands in the small of your back and bend backward as far as you can.

The Reverse Handclasp: From a standing position, reach behind you and interlock the fingers of your hands with the palms facing your back, then bend forward and raise your hands as high as possible, keeping the elbows straight.

The Hammerlock: Lead your left hand under your right elbow and grasp your right wrist, pulling down to the right. Reverse hands and repeat to the opposite side.

The Headroll: Lean your head toward your right shoulder,

then rotate it around your neck to the right. Repeat in the opposite direction. Ten times each way.

The Headstand: Put your forearms on the floor and interlock your fingers, palms up, then place your head on the floor and brace it with your palms, elevating yourself into a headstand. The triangular brace of the elbows, forearms, and head make this position fairly easy to maintain, but if you find it difficult, try it against a wall.

ECOLOGICAL BREATH CONTROL

In summary, the foregoing physical postures are designed to build up energy, make the body slim and supple, and move consciousness up the chakras. The Shoulder Stand and the Head Stand may seem a duplication, but the Headstand keeps the spine aligned while the Shoulder Stand does not. In both cases, reversing the order of the chakras subjects them to opposite polarities and has a beneficial balancing action.

Our fourth technique is breath control. Breathing is a visible representation of the rhythmic pulsation of life. We inhale and exhale, and we cannot do one without doing the other. These actions are not entirely automatic as the heart's are — they can be consciously interfered with. Nor does breathing maintain a steady tempo as the heart does — one can hold his breath. Holding the breath promotes an exhalation of impurities. Hyperventilation promotes elevation of consciousness.

The fundamental law of all correct breathing is: *One must breathe through the nose.* The nasal passages serve something of the function of a set of lungs, drawing the highest elements from the air for direct stimulation of the highest chakras — the thyroid, the pituitary, and the pineal glands. Mouth breathing tends to lower consciousness, while nose breathing tends to raise it. Also, sluggish thyroid and pituitary glands may result from protracted mouth breathing, so that the person becomes lethargic, tends to put on weight, and may even become mentally deficient. Adenoids often develop. Illness, too, may ensue, for the nasal passages act as a defense against impurities.

At the entrance of the nose, a screen of hairs block the way for dust, tiny insects and other matter which might injure the lungs. There follows a winding passageway lined with mucous membranes where cool air is warmed and tiny dust particles precipitated. Such dust can be instantly blown out through the nose, expelling millions of baccilli. The inner nose is guarded by another team of gatekeepers. Glands fight off any bacilli, while the olfactory organ identifies smells and immediately sounds the alarm when putrifying substances menace. The olfactory organ not only detects scents and odors but also absorbs Space elements of the air into the bloodstream. Test this for yourself by breathing fresh air through the nose. You will feel a "lift". Now breathe that same fresh air through the mouth, and you will find that the "lift" is missing. Mouth breathing is for emergencies only. An organ should serve the function for which it was designed, and the nose was meant to be breathed through.

The second most important element in correct breathing is: *Breathe with your belly.* This means, of course, to breathe with your diaphragm rather than simply expanding and contracting the rib cage. For a clear grasp of what this means, let us divide correct breathing into three separate actions, each of which follows the other in a continuous flow. The first action is abdominal breathing; the second, middle breathing; the third, upper breathing.

BREATHING WITH THE BELLY

Abdominal breathing is deep breathing or diaphragmal breathing. Everybody breathes this way when he is sleeping, for the delta rhythms of the subconscious take over and correctly employ the diaphragm — a strong set of muscles separating the chest and abdomen. At rest, the diaphragm arches upward toward the thoracic cavity. When functioning it flattens out, pressing the abdominal organs downward and arching the abdomen outward. The proper rise and fall of the diaphragm provides a surprisingly beneficial biological effect through gently massaging the abdominal organs. A mild pressure is exerted on the stomach, gall bladder, pancreas, kidneys, liver, adrenals, and intestines, stimulating blood circulation and increasing metabolism. In deep breathing, one simply pushes his stomach outward to inhale, and pulls in his stomach to exhale. The muscles of the abdomen also benefit from this exercise.

Middle breathing is the spreading out of the lower rib cage so that air can stream into the middle lungs. Upper breathing is the full arching of the chest so that the upper lungs can be filled with air. These latter two methods of breathing are used by ninety percent of Americans to the exclusion of deep breathing, which seriously impairs the intake of air and robs the abdominal organs of exercise, resulting in a lowered state of consciousness and a tendency to disease and malfunction.

Correct breathing employs all three methods of inhalation and exhalation in a continuous flow that seems but a single movement. The stomach is pushed out and the diaphragm swings downward, filling the lower lungs with air, and this movement flows into the spreading out of the lower rib cage, filling the middle lungs with air, and this action in turn flows into the arching-out of the chest, filling the upper lungs with air. Now the stomach is pulled in, forcing the diaphragm upward and pushing the entire column of air out of the lungs. As the rib cage and chest contract, the last bit of air is expelled. This rhythmic pulsation of inhalation and exhalation, best seen in a person who is sleeping, exactly parallel's brainwave pulsation and the beat of the human heart, illustrating the operation of a fundamental law of life.

BREATHING WITH
BALANCED RHYTHM

The third element of correct breathing is *rhythm,* for by controlling rhythm, one takes charge of balance. First, there is slow, deep breathing, with exactly as much time spent on inhalation as exhalation and with exactly the same pauses between. This not only establishes balance, but conscious attention to the act conditions the nervous system to automatic correct breathing. It also produces an awareness that one's life must follow the natural rhythm of the universe.

Secondly, there is holding the breath, which promotes the gathering and expelling of impurities through the lungs. Thirdly, there is fast deep breathing (hyperventilation) which tends to drive Kundalini up the ladder of consciousness. Breathe through the nose; breathe with your belly; breathe with rhythm — these are the elements of correct breathing, and they are resolved into the following simple exercise: 1)

Take ten deep and slow rhythmical breaths, followed by; 2) holding your breath as long as you can, followed by;   3) twenty rapid deep breaths. This exercise takes less than five minutes and has profound health-giving and consciousness-elevating effects.

You may experiment with breath-holding and hyperventilation as much as you please, as long as you don't overdo them at any one time. Excess of either can cause you to lose consciousness. Each of these activities tends to produce a "high". It seems to me that the breath-holding high is a bit like that produced by marijuana, indicating that carbon dioxide narcosis may lay behind the effect produced by this drug. It also seems to me that the "high" generated by hyperventilation is a bit like the "high" caused by LSD, indicating that nitrous oxide narcosis may lie behind the effect produced by that drug. How much better to obtain such "highs" by simple breathing exercises rather than by introducing chemical fractions into the body which may develop undesirable side-effects.

THE SECRET OF SOUND

The fifth technique — chanting — is the setting up of sound vibrations to stimulate the various chakras and aid in the ascension of consciousness. The well-known fact of physics — that we live in a vibrating universe — is perhaps best exemplified by the powerful effects which sound has on the living organism. Silence, which is Space, tends to produce a Time reaction — the desire for noise and activity. On the other hand, noise, which is Time, tends to produce a Space reaction — the desire for silence and inactivity. Of all forms of sound which affect men most deeply, music is undoubtedly paramount. Wrote William Congreve, "Music hath charms to soothe the savage beast / To soften rocks, or bend a knotted oak." And men are marched to war with martial tunes, led to the altar by those that inspire, and dragged off to funerals by mournful dirges.

There is Time music, and Space music. Time music emphasizes rhythm and tends to be loud. Space music stresses melody and is quiet. Time music produces activity, while Space music creates thoughtfulness. Time is rhythm, and Space is melody. It always takes both to make music.

Since eating is a Space activity, dinner music is quiet and

melodic. Dancing is a Time activity, so dance music is rhythmic and loud. The music that accompanies a motion picture is carefully scored with Space-Time in mind. Love is a Space activity, so we never hear a march while the hero proposes to his lady. Fist-fighting is a Time activity, so we never hear a hymn while the hero knocks out the villain. Comedy effects can be achieved in this manner, however.

A musical library can be accumulated that will promote the ascension of consciousness, and these selections can be played on the new stereo equipment with powerful effects. Such selections, of course, are always a matter of personal preference, for music is most effective when it awakens an emotional response in the listener. Since reactions to even a single piece of music vary from person to person, it would be impossible to devise a list which would elevate the consciousness of more than a small fraction of people. But it is a far different thing with chanting.

ECOLOGY CHANTING

Earlier, we discovered that certain vowel sounds stimulated various chakras, and we also learned that particular consonants produced an active or passive reaction. To review, the vowel sounds corresponding to the various chakras are: 1) *Ih*, for the coccyx. 2) *Uh*, for the gonads. 3) *Eh*, for the adrenals. 4) *Ah*, for the heart. 5) *Oh*, for the thyroid. 6) *Ooh*, for the pituitary, 7) *Eeeh*, for the pineal.

Time consonants of action and aggression are those that are hard or growling, such as d, k and r. Space consonants of serenity and passivity are those that are soft and yielding, such as m, n, and y. Combining those consonants with the various vowels in such a manner as to obtain specific stimulation of certain chakras in a particular order is the art of creating a mantra.

Lately there have been two noteworthy developments of mantra chanting in the West, and in both cases they were imported from the East. The first is the Transcendental Meditation of Maharishi Mahesh Yogi who dispenses the mantra in secret, and the second is the publicly disseminated "Nam myo ho renge kyo" chant of Nicheren Shoshu, a Buddhist sect. Many thousands of people have chanted these mantras with beneficial effects, but it seems a fundamental error of the

East that one can achieve enlightenment without a rational grasp of structure, just as it seems a fundamental error of the West that one can achieve mastery over life without recourse to mystical intuition. Hopefully, ecology will provide a balancing action between these opposing viewpoints.

In any case, a mantra is usually composed of words that tell of an aspirant's desire for enlightenment. Such meaning is not necessary, however, for sounds alone are sufficient to provide an effect. Most of the people chanting the mantras of Transcendental Meditation and Nicheren Shoshu have little, if any, idea what the words mean, since in the first case they are in the Indian language and in the second in Japanese.

Ideally, however, a mantra should have a meaning which is clearly understood by the chanter. This results in a "pinpointing" of consciousness to achieve the objective. The objective of the mantra presented here is union with God.

THE ECOLOGY MANTRA

A balance between Space and Time consonants is the aim, with only the higher chakras stimulated in order to attract Kundalini up the ladder of consciousness. The following mantra satisfies these requirements. It is a love mantra and speaks of the balanced union between Space and Time which leads to cosmic consciousness.

A mantra must be chanted with rhythm, for in the end its effectiveness depends on attunement with the pulsation of life. In order to attain this rhythm, the mantra must be broken down into syllables that can be chanted over and over. This makes the words unintelligible to anyone unfamiliar with their meaning. The syllables of our mantra break down as follows:

"Oom stu gah dyu ahn dye ahr."

These syllables comprise simple English words which are eventually understood as they are chanted. A group of people chanting them can practically raise the roof with their vibrations. Passersby enjoy the rhythm but don't have the vaguest idea what is being chanted. Group chanting is exceptionally powerful for achieving goals. A vast amount of energy is generated and can be directed toward health, achievement, relationships, supply, or enlightenment, whatever seems indicated. Even when chanting alone, a person leaves the exercise with his eyes clear and sparkling and full of energy. Beneficial effects can even be achieved by chanting silently, after one has grown accustomed to chanting aloud. Minimum time to chant is fifteen minutes. There seems to be no maximum.

COLOR AND
COSMIC CONSCIOUSNESS

The sixth technique for raising consciousness is color imagery. The spectrum is the main thing that interests us here — the alignment of the seven colors with the seven chakras, and how we can best use our knowledge of color combinations to elevate consciousness. As stated earlier, the colors of the pigment spectrum align with the chakras in the following manner: 1) Red, for the coccyx. 2) Orange, for the genitals. 3) Yellow, for the adrenals. 4) Green, for the heart. 5) Blue, for the thyroid. 6) Purple, for the pituitary. 7) Violet, for the pineal gland.

Primary colors are red, yellow, and blue. Complimentary colors are orange and green. Red and yellow combine to make orange, and yellow and blue combine to make green. Neither purple or violet is regarded as primary or complimentary, but in a very deep sense both are complimentary, for purple is made by adding red to blue, and violet is made by adding white to purple. The understanding of this fact is of deep significance.

Not only do primary colors create complimentary colors, but each color has an antagonist what may weaken it and which it may weaken. For example, green makes red more Space, and red makes green more Time; blue makes orange more Space, and orange makes blue more Time; and purple makes yellow more Space while yellow makes purple more Time.

When white combines with purple in the pineal gland, creating violet, the result is cosmic consciousness.

With color imagery, we adopt the same basic objective as with chanting, and that is stimulation of the higher chakras with balanced Space and Time energies in such a fashion as to aid the elevation of consciousness. What we are after is enlightenment, and since white is the color of light, its use is fundamental to our efforts. Three other colors are also important — the Space color of purple, the Time color of red, and the middle range color of yellow. With these, we can develop the proper color combinations to achieve our purposes.

THE ECOLOGY COLOR EXERCISES

It would be dangerous to use red in the higher chakras since it is too Time, so we reduce its value by adding white and wind up with pink. Yellow, also, is somewhat too Time, but in this case we darken its hue by adding purple and wind up with gold. And finally, we know that by adding white to purple we will produce violet, the color of enlightenment. With this information we are prepared to go to work. The color imagery exercises follow:

First, place your consciousness in the chakra of your heart and visualize it as a great cathedral with vast, high-ceilinged halls and long passageways. Stroll among these halls and see them permeated with pink energy. Next, place your consciouness in the chakra of your thyroid and visualize it as a powerful generating station. Stroll through this station, taking note of the many humming motors, and see everything surrounded by a vitalizing pink. Next, place your consciousness in your pituitary gland and there see the earth and its many people upon which you project a love colored pink. And finally, place your consciousness in your pineal gland and see there a throne and yourself upon it, sustained by the color of pink.

Now return again to the cathedral of the heart, and this time see it permeated with golden energy. Then to the generating station of the thyroid which you now see colored gold. Then to the pituitary and its earth covered with humanity upon which you project a golden love. And then to the throne room and yourself on the throne and everything surrounded with the energy of gold.

Again to the cathedral of the heart, and now all is sustained by royal purple. Then to the generating station of the thyroid, with purple permeating all. Then to the pituitary and its earth carrying humanity upon which you project a purple love. And then to the throne room with yourself upon the throne and purple surrounding all. Now the ceiling above dissolves to admit a soft white light which turns the purple to violet, and you rise from your throne with outstretched arms and raise your face to the light.

Pink for vitality. Gold for wisdom. Purple for power. Violet for enlightenment.

ECOLOGICAL CONDITIONING

This exercise can be performed in a very short period of time and has the great convenience of not disturbing others. In addition, it produces a rewarding feeling of power and peace. It should not be performed for more than fifteen minutes at a time, however, for protracted repetition tends to weaken its effect.

These then are the first six exercises for elevating consciousness: Meditation, concentration, physical postures, breath control, chanting, and color imagery. The seventh exercise — diet — is not properly an exercise but rather a way of life, and the entire next chapter will be devoted to it.

How much time should be devoted to the first six exercises? One hour each day. Just consider yourself a spiritual athlete and one hour daily the time required to put you in proper condition. That hour is best divided as follows: Fifteen minutes for meditation, five minutes for concentration, fifteen minutes for physical postures, five minutes for breath control, fifteen minutes for chanting, five minutes for color imagery.

Performing these exercises in a group can be a highly rewarding experience, not only for the additional power it develops, which can be used by the group for beneficial ends, but also for the relationships developed with brothers and sisters on the path. By this means you will come to understand the depth of the saying, "Those who love the same ideas are truly enabled to love each other." By this means, also, you will come into balance, achieving an inner ecology.

The Ecology Diet 8

For some time now I had been working out the Space-Time balance in nature according to ecology principles, and a good deal of my time had been spent consulting the *Handbook of Chemistry and Physics* as to the combining qualities of elements and the composition of foods, for it seemed to me that it was important to understand why I had been drawn to a diet of natural foods. Right in the middle of this research, I once again met the man in the violet jacket.

He was walking the fence of a schoolyard at midnight, waving his gold-headed stick for balance, and I found the sight most astonishing. I had taken this shortcut home on impulse, a way I had never traveled before, and the darkened windows of the schoolhouse reflected the dim lights of the neighborhood.

Streets were deserted, and from beyond a row of darkened houses, the sounds of traffic could be heard. The man in the violet jacket suddenly reversed himself and walked the fence in the opposite direction. Then his teeth flashed and he leaped lightly to the ground, strolling off into the darkness. I sensed it was useless to follow.

BALANCE IN
BOTH DIRECTIONS

I walked home slowly, thinking about the incident. I had once heard of a man snowbound in the winter storms of the Himalayas. To keep himself company during the long winter months, he imagined a companion — a young Chinese boy, quick-witted and lively — and they passed the long days in enjoyable conversation. When spring came and the man made his way back to civilization, he found that the young Chinese had accompanied him. When he finally arrived back in the United States, the Chinese boy was right by his side. He had created an idea and given it life, and now it wouldn't go away. Somehow I felt that I was in the same predicament with the man in the violet jacket. Only I didn't particularly want him to go away. Anybody who understood Faust and could walk a fence both ways was somebody I wanted to know better.

"Balance is the key," he seemed to be saying, "and it's balance in both directions." With this clue, I renewed my search.

What I ran into right off was a case of seeming imbalance. Of the nearly 100 elements, only four at the lightest end of the scale were capable of sustaining life — hydrogen, carbon, nitrogen, and oxygen — though one would expect life to exist somewhere between the heaviest element, uranium, and one of the lightest elements, hydrogen, according to the rules of balance. This was disappointing, but I couldn't help noting that the atom bomb sprang from the heaviest element, while a bomb many times more powerful had sprung from a combination of the heaviest element with one of the lightest. You could split off an electron from uranium and set up an explosion that fused two atoms of hydrogen thus turning loose the most awesome bomb of all. No question about it, a balanced interchange of energy between Space and Time produced power, so why didn't it apply to the phenomenon of life?

Then it came to me — it's balance both ways. Life wasn't just a matter of physical elements — it was consciousness as well. While the only consciousness we were able to see was that involved in four of the lightest elements, the rules of balance dictated the existence of as many levels of consciousness extending above the four lighter elements as there were heavier elements below. Consciousness was Space and matter was Time, and the most Time part of consciousness had descended into the most Space part of matter, and this point of balance produced life.

ELEMENTS AND BRAINWAVES

This perception unleashed an entire new area of speculation. If there was a whole range of consciousness above matter, what was this consciousness like? Since it was conscious, it clearly would have to be aware of itself. Would it then be spirit? That seemed likely. Would this spirit have a tangible form? That seemed likely too. After all, form was only an energy field, and consciousness was certainly energy. Also, a higher consciousness seemed likely to have a greater energy field, just as lighter hydrogen released more energy than heavier uranium. When this thought hit me, I saw man's dilemma. Only two ways to go — descent into matter or ascent into spirit — for matter was in process of devolving — compacting, growing heavier — subject to the forces of Time. And spirit was in process of evolving — expanding, growing lighter, subject to the forces of Space. This gave me a whole new perspective on the idea of reincarnation, for it seemed to me that a Time consciousness would be forced to cycle into and out of matter which would be continually devolving away from it, while a Space consciousness would eventually ascend out of matter into higher spheres of awareness.

That, I thought, was getting a little far afield for the moment, since my present problem was the matter-bound one of ascertaining the kind of diet that would produce health and vigor and promote the elevation of consciousness. Interestingly, it was a return to brainwave technology that provided a clue.

I got to thinking that there were four principal brainwaves and four principal elements which supported life, and it seemed to me that this coincidence was worth investigation.

133

So I lined up the four elements from Space to Time — hydrogen, carbon, nitrogen, and oxygen — and I lined up the four brain-waves from Time to Space — beta, alpha, theta, and delta. Since elements and brainwaves were opposite polarities, Space would attract Time, and Time would attract Space. That meant that the most Time element, oxygen, would match the most Space brainwave, delta, and this would align nitrogen with theta, carbon with alpha, and hydrogen with beta. These alignments seemed reasonable, since it already had been indicated that nitrous oxide could induce theta and carbon dioxide could induce alpha in my experiments with marijuana and LSD.

PROTEINS, FATS, AND CARBOHYDRATES

Next step was to determine the Space-Time order of proteins, fats, and carbohydrates. A chemical analysis wasn't necessary, for the body contained an excellent yardstick. Carbohydrates were digested in the mouth and therefore were Space foods. Fats were digested in the intestines and therefore were Time foods. And proteins were digested in the stomach and thus were a balance between. It so happened that atomic weights bore out this simple observation.

Carbohydrates, the simplest food chemically, consisted of chains of carbon atoms with attached water. Their origin was a process called photosynthesis, which occurred in the leaves of plants and combined water from the earth with carbon dioxide from the atmosphere in such a way as to imprison energy from the sun. Carbohydrates were the most basic and abundant food on earth. From their energy, all fats and proteins were formed. Each ounce of water-free carbohydrate contained approximately 130 calories per ounce.

Fats were only slightly more complex chemically. They consisted of chains of carbon atoms with attached hydrogen atoms. Though not nearly as abundant as carbohydrates, each ounce of fat contained approximately 280 calories of energy. Fats occurred naturally in a water-free state, whereas both carbohydrates and proteins were usually found with large quantities of water. Thus fat was a very concentrated form of energy.

Proteins consisted of chains of carbon atoms with attached oxygen and hydrogen and an occasional atom of nitrogen. The presence of nitrogen gave proteins their unique properties, for they were the essence of the life processes, the fundamental constituents of living body cells. Cell function occurred largely through the action of enzymes, which were themselves proteins. Food with high protein content was present in limited quantities and thus was expensive and unavailable to many people in various areas of the world. Each ounce of water-free protein contained approximately the same amount of energy as water-free carbohydrates, about 130 calories per ounce.

The muscles contained large quantities of protein. Thus meat, which was only animal muscle, was a very high protein food. But in order to produce meat, a steer or any other food animal had to eat grain containing protein to obtain the nitrogen necessary to build muscles. This was a very inefficient process, for the steer would consume many times as much grain protein as was retained in his body as muscle protein. To eat animal protein was to eat second-hand protein.

NATURE'S CARBURETOR

Grant Gwinup of the University of California at Irvine had cited a number of studies which revealed that it was a popular misconception that fat people ate foods of high carbohydrate content while thin people ate foods of high protein content. Given a choice of anything they wanted to eat, fat people selected exactly the same proportion of carbohydrates, fats, and proteins as thin people. In fact, the proportion of carbohydrates, fats, and proteins selected by any person from any culture, whether he was fat, lean, or somewhere between, was about the same when he was offered all types of foods in unlimited quantities. He would eat about 40 percent of the total calories in the form of carbohydrates, 45 percent as fats, and 15 percent as proteins, and this proportion applied to children as well as adults. Apparently, it was part of the life sustaining process itself.

This seemed to explain the limited success of any of the various reducing diets which allowed one or two foods in unlimited quantity, as for example the so-called Mayo diet which permitted all the steak one could eat but nothing else.

Anyone who stuck with this for any length of time lost weight, all right, simply because he had no desire for any more steak, so was practically fasting. Same thing applied to the rice diet or the egg diet. Even when men who had suffered severe heart attacks were cautioned not to eat fat, they refused to stay with a diet that varied even slightly from the normal proportion of fats, proteins, and carbohydrates. Heart attacks were usually blamed on carbohydrates and fats, yet the fact was that the number of heart attacks in any country corresponded more closely to the amount of meat and processed foods in the diet. The United States, home of the supermarket and the steak dinner, had the highest incidence of heart attacks in the world.

THE APPALLING FACTS OF
THE NATION'S HEALTH

The facts presented to the President by his Special Commission on the Nation's Health in December of 1964 were staggering. In 1963, heart-artery disease caused 55 percent of all U.S. deaths, and cancer 16 percent. Strokes killed 201,000; diseases of arteries outside the brain combined with diseases of the heart to kill 793,000. Cancer killed 285,000. Allergic disorders afflicted an estimated 20 million Americans. Diseases of the nervous system afflicted over 16 million. Arteriosclerosis and heart disease were chronic with 10 million. Ulcers plagued more than 8 million. Over ten million suffered from defective vision. Another ten million suffered from deafness. An estimated 15 million were sterile. Over four million were chronic alcoholics. Untold thousands were addicted to drugs and barbiturates. Some forty million — one out of every five persons — suffered from chronic obesity and overweight. Sixty million were undermining their health with cigarette smoking.

Every American spent an average of $300 a year for direct medication — more than the total income of the heads of families in some countries. Americans spent more than $100 million each year for pills to make them sleep, more millions for pills to wake them up. Some 15 million tons of aspirin alone were consumed each year. Pills by the ton to alleviate constipation, to reduce weight, pills to improve the appetite, pills to cut down the appetite, pills to pep you up, pills to calm you down, pills to break the habit of taking pills.

Not only had American medicine degenerated into a state of "pill prescribing," but it had become so fragmented with so many specialists in so many areas of the human body that a patient no longer could find his way through the maze, and hospital and medical services were pricing themselves out of reach. Why this chaos in a country of such brilliant materialistic and technological achievement? Blame was usually placed on the way we smoke and the way we drink, but it should include the way we eat and the way we think.

THE MYTH OF MAN
THE MEAT-EATER

Quantity not quality prompted most thought processes in our consumer-oriented society, so the fruits, vegetables, and grains of nature were sprayed, cooked, mashed, mixed, injected with preservatives, boxed, canned, frozen, tinned, and moved out to the consumer by the ton. Not only was their nutritional value thus put in question but their freedom from poisons as well. Then, too, the habit of eating the dead and decaying flesh of animals had become part of the American way of life to the degree that nearly every meal had its component of meat. A bloody and gigantic industry, slaughtering millions of animals and contaminating entire cities, had grown up around this habit. Slabs of decaying and putrifying flesh were placed on counters and eager hands were attracted with the pied-piper cry of "Steak!"

Meat and processed foods. These were the items I unconsciously had begun omitting from my diet when alpha training had brought my head into balance. Not only had my weight reverted to normal, but I felt like a new person. Had I eliminated poisons?

Where had the notion come from that we should eat meat and processed foods? For years I had heard people say, "Animal protein is essential in the diet of man," yet chemically there was no difference in the amino acids of vegetable protein and the amino acids of animal protein. Arguments for animal protein seemed mostly to be based on the length of man's intestine — it was neither as long as the herbivores nor as short as the carnivores, proving that nature designed man to be an omnivore and that he must eat meat to survive. These same people claimed that man could exist indefinitely on meat but would soon expire on vegetables and fruits, but all over the world thousands of people were existing on vegetables and fruits and scarcely anyone was living solely on meat.

THE DANGERS IN CANNED AND PROCESSED FOODS

Then there was the matter of canned and processed foods. Convenience and laziness were generally given as the main reasons why people found these items attractive, but even supermarkets had produce departments where one could find all the raw fruits and vegetables he wanted and even eat them right on the spot if he wished, so it wasn't just convenience and laziness. Some other force was drawing people to these foods. Then it came to me — advertising.

Hardly anybody advertising an apple or a head of lettuce, simply because there was no way to put your own brand name on it and claim it was remarkably different. But when you walked down the aisles of processed foods, brand names were all over the place, representing billions of dollars spent urging you to buy this particular brand because it was easy to fix and oh, so good and even would make you healthier.

About this time, I learned that the Agricultural Research Service of the United States Department of Agriculture published Agricultural Handbook No. 8, entitled, "Composition of Foods— Raw, Processed, and Prepared." I obtained the book and discovered that it ought to be in every home, because it flat out explains why people are fat, sick, taking too many pills, smoking and drinking, taking dope and in general feeling miserable.

The whole incredible story was unfolded by the sodium-potassium content of natural foods as against canned, processed, or cooked foods. The way these two elements naturally occurred in raw foods was a perfect illustration of the balance between Space and Time and was obviously designed by nature to provide maximum benefit for animal life, since all animal life fed on natural fruits, vegetables, and cereals and was never fat and never sick. Canning foods drastically increased the sodium content and just as drastically reduced the potassium content. Processing foods increased the sodium content, and cooking foods reduced the potassium content. If you ate canned, processed, or cooked foods, you were putting into your stomach a product that was greatly altered from the way it was originally produced by nature.

Take beets. Canning them increased the sodium content from

60 milligrams per 100 grams to 236 milligrams and decreased the potassium content from 335 milligrams to 167 milligrams. With asparagus, sodium increased from 2 to 236 milligrams, and potassium decreased from 335 to 166. Carrots went from 47 sodium to 236 while potassium decreased from 341 to 120. Corn went from a trace of sodium to 236 and fell in potassium from 280 to 97. Mushrooms increased from 15 to 400 sodium, and fell from 414 to 197 potassium. Peas moved from 2 to 236 sodium, and from 316 to 96 potassium. Spinach jumped from 71 to 236 sodium, and fell from 470 to 250 potassium. Tomatoes moved from 3 to 130 sodium, and decreased from 255 to 217 potassium.

THE SPACE-TIME RELATIONSHIP OF SODIUM AND POTASSIUM

To really understand the disastrous consequences attached to these facts, it was important to understand the Space-Time relationship of sodium and potassium. Sodium was the most Time of the elements used in nutrition, while potassium was one of the most Space. Space elements in food convert to energy, while the Time elements convert to substance. Thus canned, processed, and cooked foods had decreased ability to produce energy and increased ability to produce substance. In other words, they tended to make a person both sluggish and fat. And this was only part of the story, for their vitamin content was reduced and their enzymes partially destroyed. Altogether, they were a far cry from the balanced product turned out by nature and might as easily be considered poison as food.

Canning reduced the potassium content of fruits by as much as 100%. Cooking completely reversed some sodium-potassium ratios, such as brown rice, which before cooking had 9 parts of sodium to 214 of potassium, and after cooking had 282 parts of sodium to 70 of potassium. Processing produced incredibly high sodium contents in some foods, as for example, baking powder, which had 10,953 parts of sodium to 150 potassium. Biscuits had 1300 sodium to 80 potassium; bread stuffing 1331 sodium to 172 potassium; cavier 2,200 to 180; processed cheeses 625 to 240; corn flakes 1,005 to 120; cornmeal 1,380 to 109; crackers 1100 to 120; mustard 1307 to 130; Italian dressing 2,092 to 15; canned soup 875 to 86; soya sauce 7,325 to 366; catsup 1,042 to 370; waffle mix 1433 to 162. Cakes, pies, macaroni, spaghetti, breads — all the same story — high in sodium, low in potassium. And then there was salt itself, with 38,758 parts of sodium to 4 of potassium. When it was realized that the ratio between potassium and sodium in natural foods was at least 25 to 1 in favor of potassium, it could easily be seen that anyone using the above foods in abundance was throwing his body so far out of balance that there had to be disease and malfunction sooner or later.

THE BOUNTIFUL TABLE
OF MOTHER NATURE

And then there was meat. In general, sodium-potassium ratios were absent from most surveys and indeed were absent from the Department of Agriculture book, but a test on hamburger revealed a 4 to 1 ratio of sodium to potassium. This alone would be tolerable with a properly weighted potassium intake, but uric acid and bacteria, artificial preservatives and enzyme destruction through decay and cooking, and the disastrous consequences of ingesting animal fats made meat the most dangerous food of all.

How different the picture was when one looked at natural foods. Almonds, 4 parts of sodium to 773 of potassium. Apples, 1 sodium to 110 potassium; apricots, 1 to 281; avocados, 4 to 604; bananas, 1 to 370; green beans, 7 to 243; buckwheat 18 to 448; cherries 2 to 191; figs, 2 to 194; grapes, 3 to 158; grapefruit, 1 to 162; horseradish, 8 to 564; lemons, 2 to 138; onion, 10 to 157; garlic, 19 to 520; radishes, 18 to 322; oranges, 1 to 200; peaches, 1 to 202; pears, 2 to 130; peppers, 13 to 213; plums, 2 to 299; pumpkin, 1 to 340; raisins, 27 to 763; walnuts, 3 to 460; waterchestnuts, 20 to 450; brewer's yeast, 16 to 610; and wheatgerm, 3 to 827.

It was glaringly apparent that Mother Nature was preparing one table for man, while he himself was preparing a far different one. That this alteration of his chemical input was responsible for much of the disease and malfunction from which he suffered seemed a proper inference from the following statements. First, by W. Grey Walter in his book, *The Living Brain;* "We know that living tissue has the capacity to concentrate potassium and distinguish it from sodium, and that neural electricity results from the differential permeability of an inter-face or cell-partition, to these elements, the inside of a cell being negatively charged, the outside positively." And second, by Dean Wooldridge in his book, *The Machinery of the Brain,* as he speaks of the changes taking place in a nerve cell when it discharges its electrical potential: "This change is such as to allow sodium ions from the outside, which previously had not been able to penetrate the membrane, to surge into the axon, while a smaller excess of potassium ions move out." Thus an imbalance in the sodium-potassium ratio could disturb the electrical potential of nerve cells, and since the reproduction of cells seemed dependent on that electrical potential, disturbance of it might well produce diseased or deformed cells, leading to a whole host of illnesses, including cancer.

RNA AND DNA

The reproduction of cells, of course, was bound to another Space-Time relationship, this one between deoxyribonucleic acid (DNA) and ribonucleic acid (RNA). DNA, the genetic code imprinted within living cells, was Time, and RNA, the messenger that left the cell carrying the code for construction of a new cell, was Space. Because the code was electro-chemically imprinted in each cell, an alteration of the sodium-potassium ratio might well cause blurring or even obliteration of certain parts of that imprinting, and since the code was transmitted from each cell by an electro-chemical impulse, distortion of the sodium-potassium ratio could weaken this impulse to the point where it would take place ineffectually or even fail to take place at all. These Space-Time relationships carried on in the darker recesses of the human body concealed glimmerings of the causes of death and the gateway to immortality.

In addition to the sodium-potassium relationship, two other factors were at work determining the Space-Time balance in foods. The first of these was the ratio of proteins, fats, and carbohydrates. Those foods high in carbohydrates were generally more Space than those which were low, and those high in fats were generally more Time than those which were low in fats. Foods high in protein were generally more Time than those high in carbohydrates, and generally more Space than those foods high in fats. Proper balance was achieved automatically by a person's appestat, and that balance was 45% fats, 40% carbohydrates, and 15% protein. It therefore seemed impossible to err as long as one dined from Mother Nature's table, but as soon as he began eating from the table of man, he had to contend with the poisonous side-effects of animal fats and proteins, the high sodium content of processed and canned foods, and the low potassium content of cooked foods, so that even though his intake of proteins, fats, and carbohydrates was adequately balanced, his body suffered from malnutrition, or even worse, slow poisoning. Nearly every case of obesity and disease appeared to fall into this category.

NATURAL FOODS

Then there was the pH factor, alkalinity-acidity, the third part of the Space-Time relationship in foodstuffs. Acids were substances with a large number of hydrogen ions and a low number of hydroxide ions, while alkalines were substances with a low number of hydrogen ions and a high number of hydroxide ions. Since hydrogen was lighter than hydroxide, acids were Space and alkalines were Time. Water was a neutral solution, containing the same number of hydrogen ions as hydroxide ions. In general, Space foods such as fruits and vegetables tended to produce a laxative reaction, while Time foods such as cheese tended to be converted to substance and to produce a binding reaction. Processed foods and meats, of course, were highly binding and tended to be converted to substance. Only athletes or others engaged in strenuous physical activity were capable of throwing off the toxins in such foods.

Nature's way to perfect health was cereal grains, nuts, vegetables, seeds, fruits — a vast array of variety and taste — a regular smorgasbord of health, energy, and vitality — a golden door to a vigorous life. Nor need anyone fear about obtaining enough protein on such a diet, for proteins were present in all natural foods, and the percentage present in cereal grains and nuts far exceeded the 15% required by the body. That I personally had begun to verge toward this diet when my brainwaves had begun to come into balance was sound evidence of the mind-body relationship and how it was a direct reflection of the Space-Time forces and the point of balance between.

Mind was Space, and body was Time, and when correct balance existed between them there also existed perfect health. If a diet was too Time (too many processed foods and animal products), it produced a Time imbalance in the person — he tended to put on weight, and his consciousness became overly materialistic. When a diet was too Space (overly weighted with carbohydrates), it produced a Space imbalance in the person — he tended to become too thin, and his consciousness became overly spiritual. Balance was the key to a healthy mind in a healthy body.

Diet, then, could be a powerful force for the elevation of consciousness, but it also could be a powerful force for the lowering of consciousness. Since death and dissolution were accelerated by a Time diet of meat and potatoes, and since longevity appeared to result from a Space diet of natural foods, was it possible that an even more Space diet could move the person in the direction of immortality? This seemed a highly speculative area, indeed, but I found myself determined to explore it.

Right off I was struck with the thought that the octave was the controlling factor — seven colors in the spectrum, seven notes in the musical scale, seven nervous centers in the body — with opposite polarities in the highest and lowest, each pulling toward the other and there in the gap between — the ego, the sense of self. When Space and Time united in the pineal gland, there came into being the oceanic awareness generally referred to as cosmic consciousness, and the person traded in his small self for a self that encompassed all things. Could this "union with God" be accomplished on the Ecology Diet alone, or would an even more Space diet be necessary?

DIET AND HIGHER CONSCIOUSNESS

It certainly seemed as if the Ecology Diet *should* suffice, provided that consciousness elevating techniques were included. The lives of the saints indicated that they had lived on such a diet, usually supplementing it with fasting and meditation and often by breath control, chanting, and physical postures. But it now occurred to me that an ascension was possible beyond the octave of the vibration associated with life, so that the individual moved onto a plane where matter as we know it did not exist, thereby freeing himself of the forces of dissolution and becoming immortal. I wondered if this was

143

the ascension made by Jesus and if it might not be possible to other mortals.

Toying with the idea made it seem possible that the physical body could be part of this ascension, by increasingly making it more Space, or more subtle and rare. I pictured two bodies — an energy body obscured by a substance body, much in the same manner that the moon obscures the sun during a full eclipse. From around the edges of the physical body could be seen the aura of the energy body, and as the physical body grew lighter the glow of the energy body shone through.

What would be the dietary accompaniment of such an ascension? It would surely have to go from Time to Space as fuel intake was increasingly converted to energy and less and less to substance. First, onto a diet of vegetables, fruits, nuts, animal products, and shellfish. Then the gradual elimination of cooked foods, then the elimination of shellfish, then the elimination of animal products. Once a natural food diet had been achieved, spiritual enlightenment could follow. Where then? Would not consciousness still be bound to a physical vehicle? Would not its subservience to the forces of Space and Time cause it to be successively incarnated? How then to build up the energy to make a physical ascension in this incarnation? Such a high energy diet would call first for the elimination of Time elements — first, cereal grains; then vegetables; then nuts; and finally fruits; until at last the individual was existing only on the oxygen in the air he breathed — oxygen to feed his body of fire.

THE TRANSITION DIET

All this, was simply speculative, of course, and only an exercise in understanding the forces of ascension and descension. So, still subject to the Tree of the Knowledge of Good and Evil, and not yet having attained the Tree of Life, I turned my mind to transition methods of switching from a meat-and-potatoes diet to the Ecology Diet in such a manner as to minimize distressing side effects.

My own transition had been relatively painless since it had taken place so gradually, but a little experimentation with willing friends soon convinced me that this change should not take place abruptly. The Ecology Diet was highly laxative to

144

a digestive system unused to it, and the intake of high energy foods caused the body to begin throwing off toxic substances stored in fatty tissues and joints. This cleansing action often was accompanied by physical discomfort. Under such circumstances a person might be frightened and return to his old dietary habits, so it was better to adopt a transition diet which allowed cooked foods but eliminated meats and processed foods. Accordingly, I was led to draw up three basic dishes — the Alpha Balancer, to be used in the transition stage; and the High Protein Cereal and the High Energy Salad. Once the transition was achieved, a person could become as creative as ever he desired, for in truth, all the subtleties of the culinary art were hidden in the fruit and vegetable kingdoms. Here were tastes as exotic as Arabian Nights, and effects that made the psychedelic world pale in comparison.

THE ALPHA BALANCER

Saute ½ cup of buckwheat groats in 6 tablespoons of sesame oil until brown. Add two cups of water and cook over medium heat until all water is absorbed — approximately 15 minutes. Enhance flavor with 1 teaspoon of your favorite herbs, such as basil, tarragon, oregano, thyme. Add parsley. An onion cut in chunks and/or minced garlic cloves may be sauted with the groats. Vegetables sliced and sauted in sesame oil may be served over the grains, such as green or red bell peppers, onions, mushrooms, celery, Chinese pea pods, bean sprouts, bamboo sprouts, waterchestnuts, zucchini, or alfalfa sprouts. Garbonza, red kidney beans, or lentils may be added to the cooking vegetables at the last minute. Cooked shellfish, such as shrimp, lobster, or crab may be added. Raw almonds add excellent flavor and provide high protein. A cup of grated natural cheese, such as swiss, cheddar, or monterey jack, may be sprinkled over the finished product, and sliced hard-boiled eggs may be added. Buckwheat is the most Time of all cereals and changes least in the cooking process, but other whole grains may be substituted for it, such as millet, brown rice, oats, wheat, rye, barley, or any mixture of these. (Makes enough for four.)

HIGH PROTEIN CEREAL

Mix ¼ cup of ground sesame seeds and ¼ cup of wheat germ, and slice atop this mixture one banana and one apple. Sprinkle with raisins and almonds and cover with honey to taste. Add raw milk. Chia seeds may be added to sesame seeds, and fruit may be experimented with at will. Makes enough for two.

HIGH ENERGY SALAD

To a bed of Romain lettuce, add ½ dozen chopped green onions, 1 diced clove of garlic, a half dozen sliced radishes, 1 sliced carrot, 1 sliced tomato, 1 sliced green pepper, 1 sliced cucumber, half dozen sliced mushrooms, 1 sliced stick of celery, handful of alfalfa sprouts, 1 sliced zucchini, and sprinkle with parsley, watercress, wheat germ, and sesame seeds. Cover with salad dressing consisting of one part of safflower oil to one part of lemon juice, or 1 part of sesame oil to 2 parts of cidar vinegar. Ground almonds or soy beans also may be added, and the addition of sliced fresh fruits provides a tantalizing taste. Herbs may be added to suit. Makes enough for four.

THE BOOSTER
AND THE CALMER

In addition to these three basic dishes, two drinks were devised — The Booster and the Calmer, and these permitted rapid correction of any imbalance resulting from the switch to high energy foods. That switch could be coaxed along by the Booster, but if it appeared to be proceeding too rapidly, so that relaxation was becoming difficult, recourse could be had to the Calmer. The Booster consisted of equal parts of raw honey and apple cider vinegar in a glass of hot water and taken first thing in the morning. The Calmer consisted of two tablespoons of soya sauce in a cup of piping hot tea, taken last thing in the evening. Any herb tea (unprocessed of course) could be used.

It was soon discovered that many desirable cereals, nuts, and beans were difficult to eat in the raw state unless they were first well ground, and that many vegetables and fruits yielded their energy in more concentrated form if their juice was separated from their fiber. Accordingly, anyone aspiring to the Ecology Diet could profitably invest in both a juicer and grinder, which would still leave him on the profit side of the ledger, because after that he could sell the stove.

Fasting, too, became a matter of interest. First of all, it had always been used by spiritual aspirants to move their conscious-ness higher, and secondly, simple observation of the animal kingdom revealed that an injured or sick animal automatically fasted until his affliction began to heal. Fasting appeared to per-mit the body to focus its total energies on whatever was at hand, whether it be healing injury or illness, performing athletically, or making a creative effort — a fact attested to by many people who rejected food on the day of a testing performance. Fasting for more than one day, however, caused hibernation of the di-gestive organs, and this made the breaking of longer fasts critical. One-day fasts frequently undertaken proved the safest means of allowing the body to cleanse itself and to gather its energies. Such one-day fasts could be undertaken as often as once a week with beneficial results, and the cleansing of the lower bowel with a high enema on this fasting day had a general rejuvenating effect.

Altogether, the Ecology Diet produced such great increases in energy and health in both myself and my friends that we could only wonder at how far modern medicine had strayed from the dictum of its founder, Hippocrates, when he said, "Let food be your medicine, and medicine be your food."

And so, by that strange alchemy that delivers to one the truth for which he is ready, there came into my hands a copy of the Essene Gospel of Peace and these words of Jesus: "So eat always from the table of God: the fruits of the trees, the grains and grasses of the field, the milk of beasts, and the honey of bees. For every-thing beyond these is Satan, and leads by the way of sins and diseases unto death. But the foods which you eat from the abun-dant table of God give strength and youth to your body, and you will never see disease. For the table of God fed Methuselah of old, and I tell you truly, if you live even as he lived, then will the God of the living give you also long life upon the earth as was his."

FOODS IN ORDER FROM SPACE TO TIME

General

* Honey
Raw sugar
Molasses
Fruits
Nuts
Seeds
Herbs

Leaf Vegetables
Cereals
Root vegetables
Fish
Animal products
** Animal meat

Fruits

Pineapple
Banana
Papaya
Mango
Fig
Pear
Peach

Cherry
Apple
Orange
Lemon
Lime
Melon
Strawberry

Nuts

Coconut
Peanut
Pecan
Cashew

Walnut
Filbert
Brazil nut
Chestnut

Seeds

Sunflower
Pignole

Pumpkin
Sesame

Herbs

Nettle
Rose Hips
Thyme
Tarragon

Mugwort
Dandelion
Dill
Ginseng

Leaf Vegetables

Eggplant
Tomato
Mushroom
Peppers
Asparagus
Artichoke
Cucumber
String beans

Lettuce
Lentil
Cabbage
Cauliflower
Kale
Endive
Chick Peas
Chicory

Peas
Beans
Rhubarb
Zucchini

Escarole
Parsley
Watercress
Pumpkin

Cereals

Corn
Rye
Barley
Oats

Millet
Wheat
Brown Rice
Buckwheat

Root Vegetables

Garlic
Onions
Radishes
Carrot

Beet
Parsnip
Leek
Turnip

Fish

Oyster
Clam
Octopus
Eel
Mussel
Halibut
Lobster
Trout

Sole
Salmon
Shrimp
Herring
Sardine
Red Snapper
Caviar

Animal Products

Yogurt
Cottage Cheese
Cow's Milk
Eggs
Goat's Milk
Jack Cheese

Cheddar Cheese
Swiss Cheese
Camembert Cheese
Edam Cheese
Roquefort Cheese
Limburger Cheese

Animal Meats

Pigeon
Partridge
Pheasant
Dove
Duck
Turkey
Rabbit

Chicken
Snail
Frog
Lamb
Beef
Horse
Pork

Beverages

Herb teas
Fruit juices
Water
Chinese tea

Coffee
Wine
Beer
Whiskey

Outer Psychology 9

When Robert Burns wished for the power "to see ourselves as others see us" he may have been invoking the Age of Cybernetics with its bio-feedback mechanisms which enable the inner world of man to be placed outside where he can see and hear it. That which all of man's inner efforts failed to do for thousands of years, the outside science of electronics has accomplished in a few decades. By paying attention to a machine outside myself, I had been given a more accurate picture of myself than ever I had managed by paying attention to things inside myself. Therefore, it behooved me to start paying more attention to things that were outside. This new approach I called Outer Psychology.

151

THE GALVANOMETER

Now that I had learned something about myself, I wanted to learn more, so I began looking for other bio-feedback devices. I heard of a man who had gotten into the subject so deeply that he had a regular light and sound show running off measurements of such bodily activities as pulse, breathing, muscle tension, blood pressure, skin resistance, salivary rate, eye blink, and brain waves. I went to see him with a friend one evening and found him playing the Sorcerer in his Den. He hooked me up so I could experience the magic for myself, and the show was really a mind-blower. But there was no way to assimilate let alone integrate the data that were flung at me, so I came away none the wiser. It did illustrate, however, that there were many other signals besides brain waves that were capable of telling me something about myself.

With such a wide variety to choose from, I hardly knew where to start, but the question was settled when I ran into a friend who said that he'd gotten started on a psychological therapy that measured galvanic skin resistance while you were remembering things that had happened to you. I took a look at the machine he was using and decided to get one myself.

Back to the electronic wizard I went and told him my problem. He allowed as to how he could handle it all right, and this time he was easier on me financially — the cost was one hundred fifty dollars. The machine turned out to be bigger than the alpha meter, so I couldn't help feeling that I'd gotten a bargain. I took it home and tried to figure out what to do with it.

MEASURING IDEA RESISTANCE

What the machine measured was skin resistance, the electrical armor surrounding the human body, and this suited me fine, since I had in mind measuring my resistance to enlightenment — specifically, my resistance to new ideas. Since this was the way the machine worked when used as a lie detector, it seemed obvious that when it indicated a high reading, I was resisting the idea I was thinking about, and when it indicated a low reading, I was not resisting. Thus I should be able to review my life and discover all the ideas I

152

was resisting, and it seemed likely that by coming to understand those ideas I would stop resisting them. Then perhaps I could become truly enlightened, see all the way into the center of things, which had been my consuming aspiration since first I became aware of myself.

The best way to accomplish this seemed to be to begin at the beginning, so I hooked myself up to the galvanometer and started out with the first thing I could remember. It was an impression of being near the ceiling of a room, where a flickering circle of light was projected by a kerosene lamp from a table below. My mother and father were choosing my name, and I learned that my initials were to be "U.S.A." Years later, I told my mother about this memory, and she said, "You weren't even born yet. You just imagined it." The needle of the resistance meter went way up as I ran over this memory, and I watched it carefully to see which idea I was resisting — mine or my mother's. It turned out I was resisting mine. I went over and over that idea until the needle showed I had no more resistance to it. I realized at once the significance of this process, for if I had conscious recollection of existing before I was born, that knowledge must change my whole life.

I moved on to the next memory — my birth — somebody grasped me roughly around the head and pushed something hard into my eye, bringing pain and blood. He tried to pull me through a tight opening, but I got stuck, so he grabbed me around the chest and caved in my ribs. Finally, he pulled me through. Then he tried to act nice. I knew he wasn't nice, but I didn't want him to grab me again, so I pretended he was fooling me. This time there was charge on the idea that people were nice, so I worked through it until the charge disappeared. Immediately I was conscious of a letting go within myself — the reduction of some inner spasm that seemed almost to have existed forever — and I knew that my relationships with people would soon improve.

REMOVING EMOTIONAL CHARGE

Then I remembered being told that playing with fire was dangerous, but I thought it might be exciting, so I started a fire and it got out of hand and the fire department came, and I was scared half to death. Charge was on the idea that playing with fire could be exciting, and I worked through it until the charge disappeared. There then came over me a sense of capability, joy, and challenge such as I had never experienced before.

I didn't need anybody to tell me that I was on the right track. I could feel newly-released energy flow through me. Now I remembered being taught how to operate the pumpcar and not being able to and my father showing me how easy it was by illustrating how quickly the boy next door could do it, and I was humiliated and didn't want anybody to ever teach me. I worked the charge off this idea and felt another surge of energy.

Then there was sex experimentation where I picked up the idea that sex was shameful, and fist fights with older boys where I most often was vanquished and grew to believe I was a loser. There was the nagging presence of an invisible world which I could never penetrate and which gave me the idea I was not quite "right." There were the spartan attitudes of Norwegian parents from whom I picked up the idea that affection was being "soft." There was the ease but dullness of school studies, as if I perceived them from some level on which they were elementary. There was the sensitivity unbecoming to a boy, which I attempted to conceal through attempts not to be a "sissy." There was a grade school passion for a young girl and my helplessness to tell her about it. There was the dog I loved but which was poisoned and the loss I felt and the vow I made not to love again. There was the fight to overcome fear by being an athlete and my eventual refusal ever to allow myself to feel fear. There was the death of a schoolmate and my seeing him in his coffin and the fear and horror which I secreted away. And there was the death of an uncle only a few years older than I, a delightful uncle who was always about to "crank up the Ford and go fishing," but he broke his neck in a high dive from a waterfront dock and lingered for a year, a wasted skeleton. All these episodes I worked through and more, but several others gave me a difficult time.

A SERIOUS FALL

The first of these involved a fall I had taken in my sixteenth year. I had gone with three other boys to downtown Portland, Oregon for the express purpose of "sneaking into" a movie. In those days, there wasn't much money, but it was more the excitement than the lack of funds which attracted us to such an enterprise, and we became quite expert at it. We would launch our excursion by waiting for a trolley car at a dark bend in the street of the suburbs where we lived, and one of us would hop onto the rear and pull the trolley from its track. The car would go dark and stop, and in the resulting confusion we would sneak aboard and all smiles and innocence ride downtown. The same procedure was used for the homeward trip. As to getting into the theatre itself, we had as many ruses as a famous bankrobber of the time, Willy Sutton. What we didn't know was that most of the theatre owners were quite aware of what we were up to, but fascinated by our ingenuity, they turned away with a smile.

The night of the fall we launched our operation against the Broadway Theatre where our favorite means of access was through a second story window which entered the women's restroom. We climbed the ladder of a billboard and stepped across to a small galvanized iron platform set in a niche below the window. This particular night the first of us onto the platform couldn't open the window, so I stepped over to help. I had no better luck, so another boy stepped over to lend a hand. With that, the platform gave way. In falling, I struck the front part of my head on the top of an eight-foot concrete wall. The blow opened a huge gash between my eyes, and I was flipped over to land on the back of my head on the pavement of a driveway. A large gash opened on the back of my head.

AN OUT-OF-THE-BODY EXPERIENCE

The rest of the evening was hazy, but I remember being driven to a hospital where stitches were taken and x-rays made and my parents notified. Later, I was told that I ran around the hospital corridor like crazy and kept repeating nonsensical things in a weird voice. I worked this memory over with the galvanometer, but I couldn't remove the charge from it. Since the greater part of the charge was on the time after the fall, it seemed to me that something must have occurred while I was "unconscious," that I somehow had been exposed to an idea that I was resisting very strongly.

I went deeply into my memory to probe this, and suddenly I heard a professional voice saying, "There has been damage to the pituitary gland which will make contact with the pineal extremely difficult. It is perhaps best that we abandon the body and begin anew." I scarcely had time to wonder at this when I heard my own voice answering, "I beg of you to allow me to continue. Whatever must be overcome, I will overcome. I will not be fooled again that easily, I assure you." My voice sounded far too mature for a sixteen year old, and the doctor's statement, if indeed it was the doctor speaking, had never been confided to me or my parents.

I ran this material for an entire day without getting a reduction in charge, until finally it occurred to me that if I had been conscious before I ever entered my body, then indeed I might have gone somewhere outside my body when I was injured. No sooner had this premise occurred to me, than the charge began to reduce. Nevertheless, I worked it for nearly an hour longer before the needle hovered near zero. Then I had an incredible reaction. It was as if some vault of joy had been suddenly opened within me, and my heart literally sang. I knew beyond doubt that life had a significance far above that attached to the flesh.

A BATTLE WITH GUILT

The next memory on which I had difficulty reducing the charge was of my high school sweetheart, my first true love, a beautiful young red-head who played piano like an angel and with whom I made my first fumbling attempt at sex. With her I wrote a pledge of eternal fealty in her family Bible, but when she contracted poliomyelitis, I abandoned her at once, terrified that I might catch the disease. The galvanometer showed that I carried tremendous emotional charge on this memory, and indeed, when I began to get into it deeply my limbs started to tremble, so overwhelming were my feelings of guilt. I ran and reran the memory until I was finally able to face the fact that I had behaved despicably, but I still was not able to remove the charge. I kept having images of the disastrous ways in which my action might have influenced the life of this young girl and the charge would not go away. Finally I moved on, but after this all my female relationships were subtly charged with guilt and I could not remove the charge from the memories. I began wondering if there was some way I could make atonement — perhaps by meeting someone like my red-haired sweetheart and making it up to her by proxy. But as other memories yielded their charges without difficulty and there was great improvement in my emotional tone and sense of well-being, I felt that no serious damage was being done by the memory of that young girl whom I had treated so badly so long ago.

I found emotional charge about the death and injury I caused during World War II, and there was emotional charge about the wasted years spent with no other purpose than making money, but these yielded without trouble. Some other memories were both puzzling and enlightening.

The first was the dream of a pearl bursting through my chest and the great excitement I had felt at the time, as opposed to my later disillusionment with what I had considered to be a "sign." Here I discovered that I had great resistance to accepting the dream as being significant, and I had to do much running of the memory in order to remove the emotional charge. When I finally did, I felt more at peace than ever before.

A BRUSH WITH
THE HANGMAN

Then there was my return to the ancestral home on the Oregon coast where my father had died, and my feeling of his presence there and the strange conviction I had that I gradually was turning into him. This idea too had great charge on it and required much work before my resistance was dissipated. Then I was able to see that my presence in that lonely house on the storm-struck coast had released my father from his physical surroundings where he had become time-bound, even as I now was released from the memory. Lastly, there was the time which carried the most emotional charge of all and that was the night I hanged myself.

After seven years of pursuing the elusive pearl, having exhausted all my resources — mentally, physically, spiritually, emotionally, and financially — I decided that my life had reached a permanent dead end and was best taken rather than prolonged. I shall not bore you with justifications, since I now know that utter despair may be changed to hope in the twinkling of an eye. Suffice it to say that I decided on hanging as the best method, and having procured a rope, I fashioned it into a hangman's noose and tied it up securely. I then sat down with a bottle of whiskey and prepared to enjoy my final hours on earth. That is the last I remember.

Twelve hours later I regained consciousness on the living room floor, the hangman's noose deeply imbedded in the flesh of my neck and its broken end dangling. My face was a mass of rug burns, and I was twenty feet from the spot where I had strung up the rope. Apparently, I had hanged myself, and the rope had broken. In a half-conscious state, I had floundered around on the floor for hours. Glacially calm, I removed the noose from my neck and went to bed and to sleep.

A PANEL OF EXPERTS

But I wasn't calm as I remembered the incident — far from it. The needle of the galvanometer nearly went through the side of the instrument. As in the case of the fall I had taken as a youth, the greatest charge seemed to be on the time I was unconscious. Carefully I probed at that now, trying to remember what impressions I had retained upon regaining consciousness. It seemed to me that I had been on a television show, standing before a panel of experts who were instructing me about my life. But at the time I couldn't remember much about it, so I had put it out of my mind, having more important concerns, or so I thought.

Now as I went back over the memory I realized that far from being a dream about appearing on a television show, I was appearing before an assembly of powerful persons who not only had brought about my attempted suicide but now were telling me why this had to be done and what I was to do henceforth so as not to be reduced to such an extremity again. I couldn't recall what was said to me or the faces of those in the assembly, except to remember an impression of great wisdom and kindliness.

I spent a week running this memory with the galvanometer before I removed the emotional charge from it, and when I did it was almost as though I had become a new person — or rather, that a person long hidden within me had emerged at last.

After this, I turned the galvanometer over to several of my friends with instructions about how to use it. To aid them in understanding the process, I presented them with a Wheel of Balance so that they could see for themselves the general

158

goals to be achieved and could understand where they were at present. This chart is reproduced at the end of this chapter.

THE WHEEL OF BALANCE

Four aspects of the human being are depicted — physical, mental, emotional, and spiritual. A person may be balanced in one aspect and unbalanced in the other three, or balanced in three aspects and unbalanced in one, or balanced in two aspects and unbalanced in two others, or balanced in all four, or unbalanced in all four. He may be out of balance on the positive side in one aspect and out of balance on the negative side in another.

Mental and physical aspects are shown in the horizontal or Time sphere, and these are balanced by natural nutrition and yoga. Emotional and spiritual aspects are shown in the vertical or Space sphere, and these are balanced by means of the alpha meter and the galvanometer. The balanced person is physically athletic, mentally creative, emotionally loving, and spiritually agape. By physically athletic is not meant that he actually be an athlete, but that he be supple, graceful, and vigorous. By mentally creative is not meant that he be an artist, but that he be an innovator in whatever field he has chosen. By emotionally loving is not meant that he necessarily be involved in romantic love, but that he love all men as his brothers. And by spiritually agape is not meant that he necessarily adopt a blind adoration of God, but that he be open to that which is higher and greater than himself and in that openness seek to grow higher and greater too.

ASCENT AND DESCENT

That which is balanced ascends, while that which is imbalanced descends. Therefore there are two paths which lead downward and only one which leads upward, for imbalance may be found on either side of the path of balance. On the Space or negative side, the imbalanced person is physically thin, mentally indecisive, emotionally fearful, and spiritually pious. On the Time or positive side, the imbalanced person is physically heavy, mentally dogmatic, emotionally hostile, and spiritually atheistic. There are of course many gradations of these extremes. For instance, a person spiritually imbalanced

159

on the positive side might be a fanatic atheist or a fanatic believer in one particular religion to the exclusion of all other religions. The same sort of gradation applies to the other aspects of the Wheel of Balance.

Perhaps the most remarkable result of work with the galvanometer was the change it finally produced in brainwave patterns. Everyone using it, including myself, reported a great increase in theta waves, which was invariably accompanied by a feeling of reality about many of the images that occurred in the mind. Accordingly, I began calling the galvanometer a "theta meter."

A number of things now occurred which indicated that a profound change had taken place in my psyche. I began to dress differently. I grew a mustache and sideburns. I started wearing star-spangled ties and otherwise identifying myself with my country. I took to listening to music — really listening to it — getting deeply into it and discovering that entire worlds were hidden there. I began to feel differently about the persons with whom I came in contact. They seemed more interesting, to have taken on depths and dimensions I had never noticed. And perhaps most profound of all was the change in my attitude toward women. I began to see them as people — a different people to be sure — but fascinating by reason of this difference. Where before I had regarded them solely as sexual objects — else mothers, daughters, and grandmothers — now I began to find friendships with them highly rewarding. Never before had I been friends with even one woman. Now I suddenly developed a number of such friendships and found them deeply satisfying. As I was to discover, all this was laying the groundwork for my being able to fall in love. For, strange as it seems, I had never been in love since I had turned my back on my red-headed high school sweetheart.

A MEETING
WITH THE BELOVED

So it was that a friend invited me to his home to meet his daughter who was studying to be a writer, and I manfully undertook the excursion, having in mind a mental picture of a gangly adolescent with glasses and buck teeth who would ask endless questions about Hemingway and Scott Fitzgerald, none of which I would be able to answer. But when I entered

160

the home I was introduced to a lovely young creature in her early twenties, who far from treating me as an elderly sage treated me instead as an equal. Her hair was red, and I fell in love with her.

THE WHEEL OF BALANCE

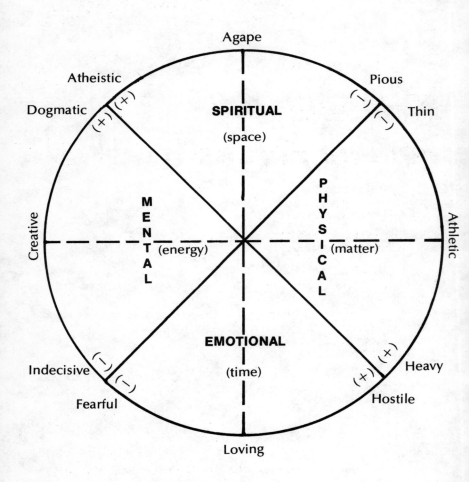

Male and Female Forces 10

We stopped at a small art gallery on the banks of a stream at the foot of a mountain, and there was a painting in the window, an abstraction without shadow, the structured forms of color creating the illusion of a stream emerging from a forested hillside.

"Perhaps that scene is down below," I suggested, and we went down to the stream. It wasn't, though. "You'd certainly think it would be," I said, "but I guess it's someplace else." I put my arms around her, and we watched the waters flow.

"Tomorrow," she whispered, "I'll take you to a different place." She wore white jeans, buckskin moccasins and saffron blouse, and her copper hair, parted in the center, hung straight and long below her shoulders. Her youthful face bore the stamp of some dimly-

163

remembered splendor, and in her eyes were mingled the colors of the earth.

I said I'd like to go.

UNKNOWN JOURNEY

After that we went to dinner, and one part of me knew that I was falling in love but another refused to believe it. We stared at each other in the candlelight with the brightened eyes of excited children. Later on, we slept together, but we didn't make love until morning. Lying in each other's arms, an energy passed between us, a force that heated up the room and melted time and made bluish sparks in the darkness. We dozed in and out of some stately dream until the sun laced the curtains with fiery fingers, then I entered her and glimpsed some paradise just beyond my reach. Afterwards, she smiled an inner smile and slid headfirst off the bed, somersaulting her lithe body onto the floor, head buried beneath the covers. Gently, I removed them from her face. She looked very happy.

While getting dressed, she announced that we would picnic at the place where she was taking me, and we packed a cardboard box with bread and cheese and covered it with a spread of green and yellow. Into the sunshine of the risen day we drove, and she told me where to take each turn. We came to a small town and stopped the car, and she sent me into a store for wine and ice to keep it chilled, and in the store were softened hearts who watched as I made a thoughtful selection. Though I knew she wanted Chablis, I knew it must be special, and when I finally chose a bottle, the softened hearts all nodded. I wondered how they knew I'd picked one that would please her.

I packed the wine and ice into the cardboard box beside the bread and cheese, and when I sat beside her once again, she said, "There's a hike of three miles after we finally park the car."

"I don't care much for hiking."

"The stream passes the parking place. We can picnic there if you like."

I didn't answer. That would be better than hiking, I thought.

"You can decide when we get there," she said.

The road began to wind around and grade up steeply, and pretty soon the car overheated and began to miss. For a moment I thought we might not make it, but then I shifted down the gears, and though the engine remained hot and kept on missing, there was power enough to pull us up the grade.

MEMBERS ONLY

"Some place you're taking me," I said. "A wilderness." Canyons wrested height from towering peaks, and on the slopes pine and cedar raised their limbs in stately dance. No cars were met, no one was seen, though once we came upon a startled doe that fled into the forest. A sentinel, I thought.

We arrived at a place where the road levelled out, and in the trees stood several cars. "Park there," she said. I turned off the road and stopped among the trees. A creek was running down below, and two men fished from the rocks. Patiently, without success, they cast their lines and hauled them in.

"Would you like to stay here or hike to the place above?" she asked.

"What would you like to do?"

"I've been there before. It's up to you."

I searched the reaches of the road. It disappeared into the trees beside the creek and seemed to be fairly level. "All right, let's hike on up."

The box proved heavier than I thought. I put it on my shoulder as we walked along the road, but it cut into my flesh, so I lowered it and carried it in my arms. I clomped along beside her in my boots and thought it odd that I should have worn them because they were not made for hiking. The road veered away from the creek now, and through the trees I could see a footbridge leading to the other side.

We came to a place where the road forked, and a broad and level part went back toward the creek while a narrow path ascended the hill. She took the path.

"Wait a minute," I called. I put the box down. Already my arms were tired. "Why are we going up the hill? The road is level and heads back towards the creek."

"That's private property."

I peered down the road to where an open gate stood. There was a sign that said, "Members Only."

THE ASCENT

"We can't get through that way," she told me.

I looked up the path. "Are you sure this comes back to the creek?"

"Oh, yes. I've been this way before." She smiled. "Ready?" I nodded, and she led the way.

It was tough going. My arms grew leaden, and my breathing finally came in gasps. Shortly, perspiration bathed my face. But as she continued moving briskly, I refused to admit distress. Soon, I thought, I'll get a second wind, then I'll be all right. Finally, though, I had to stop. Pretending wasn't worth it.

"How about you carrying the box for awhile?" I asked. "I'm pretty tired, and you look fresh."

"Sure." She smiled and took the box and once again resumed the path, her copper hair swaying as she struggled with the weight. I followed, breathing easier. Pine trees grew along the slope, and in the filtered light their needles radiated energy.

After awhile, she stopped and said, "I think you'll have to take this back." She handed me the box. I put it down. "Let's rest," I said.

Now I saw that clumps of pine needles were being projected by their limbs along the trail's edge. I was fascinated. "Maybe we could pick up some energy. I think there's energy coming from those pine needles." I moved down the slope a step and touched my hands to the needle tips. She did the same, palms pressed against the needles.

"I don't think that's the right way," I said. "I think we should caress the tips without touching them." I showed her, and she nodded. Around the clumps of pine needles, we moved our hands like magicians. "Somebody should see us now," I laughed. Her smile shared our secret. When we took the path again, I thought the box seemed lighter.

Suddenly, we came upon a Boy Scout troop descending from the heights. Silently, in single file, the procession passed us by — backpacks, shorts and hiking boots, and glum, dejected faces. "Hello," I said, but no one answered. The last to pass, master of the forest's ways, solemnly announced, "Up and Down and Right and Left give birth to In and Out." The footfalls faded in the forest.

THE DESCENT

"Did you see those faces!" I cried. "Whatever is up there

166

can't be much!"

"They didn't recognize it."

"Then how are we going to? That man was a scoutmaster. He's been trained to find places."

"He found one. He just didn't recognize it."

Down the tangled slope I peered, through trunks of trees and pools of shadow. There was no sound. "Seems to me we're getting farther away from the creek. Are you sure you know where we are?"

She hesitated. "It seems to be taking longer this time."

"Perhaps we made a wrong turn."

She shook her head. "I don't think so."

I searched her face. "Well, if we're lost, at least we're lost together."

Some fount of power erupted deep within her amber eyes, and I felt her give me strength. Light that filtered through the trees lit in her hair a burnished sun. I pulled her to me and held her in the circle of my arms and thought I'd made a magic ring to ward off harm forever. When we began walking, I carried the box alone and did not find it heavy.

Around the bend, the path was forked, and one fork started down. This one she took after considering both, and pretty soon there could be heard the tinkle of running water. She smiled and nodded toward the sound. "I think we'll find our place down there."

Swept along by exhilaration, we descended on the creek, but now the path turned back in the direction from which we'd come. Through a break in the trees, I could see the creek and great flat stones along its edge and a log that bridged a pool of water. That's the place, I thought, but she kept on walking.

"You're heading back," I called.

But she had found a fainter trail, angling backward from the path, and now she said excitedly, "I saw our place. There are boulders at the water's edge where we can sit and picnic."

TRAPDOOR INTO TIME

She moved quickly down the new path, skipping in anticipation. Following, I found her wading in the creek where rocks had formed a crystal pool. She scooped up water in her hands, raised it to her lips and drank, then crouched there in the shallows like some eternal woodland nymph. I removed my boots and joined her in the watery mirror, cold and clear, reflecting sky and trees above and waving dreams of submerged rocks. I drank deeply, pausing only to breathe the scented air and peer at my surroundings.

This was virgin forest, where mortal man had never trod. The stream issued from the mountainside, and a feeling of familiarity lurked among the trees. I took her hand and led her to a boulder raised above the eddying waters. We took seats on it, back to back, bracing each other, studying the place above from where the stream came.

"Notice anything?" I asked.

"Yes."

"It's like the painting, isn't it?"

She nodded, and I added, "Do you suppose this is the place?"

"Oh, yes."

"How do you suppose the painter found it?"

"Perhaps he never found it. Perhaps he painted the picture first and created this place later."

I turned to look at her. She brushed her lips against my cheek. "Let's eat," she said.

I watched her break the bread and open up the cheeses. She gestured toward the wine. I took the bottle from her and removed the cork. We ate slowly, relishing each bite, staring into each other's eyes.

Afterwards, we sipped the wine, and suddenly the rocks and trees and stream dropped through a trapdoor into time, and I felt my consciousness ascend along the magic centers, from genitals through abdomen, through solar plexus, throat and head, and like a wheel of radiant power flow out of me and into her.

THE RITES OF ANCIENT EPHESUS

"I love you," I said.

She smiled, pleased.

"No, I mean it. I really love you. Something has happened."

Her eyes widened. "You do look different."

Softly, I whispered, "Do you know how much I love you? Do you really know how much? I love you with the very power that created the universe. I love you so much that I'm finally free, because my consciousness has left me and settled in you, and all the energy of creation can pass from me to you. Oh, how I love you! I love you so much that the power of my love will cause you to grow more beautiful forever. I'll fill you with love. It will show in your eyes and your smile and your walk and your talk. You'll radiate love. Everything around you will grow. People will come thousands of miles just to be near you. My love will turn you into a golden goddess."

I leaned closer and fixed her with my gaze. "Look deep into my eyes. Can't you see my love in there? It's a living thing — a real, living thing. It loves you. It loves you with all its heart and all its soul. Can't you see it?"

Her filling up with love was visible.

"Yes," she said. "You are a labyrinth that I may explore forever." And then she filled up to the top, and the power arced out from her and entered into me.

"Oh, my darling!" I cried. "How long I've waited for you! What was it kept you so? Have I somehow failed you? Surely you would let me know. We've dwelt beneath the Wall of China, kept fasts atop the Himalayas, designed and built the ancient pyramids, hung gardens in the walls of Babylon, presided at the rites of Ephesus, seen the death of Dionysus, preserved and kept the ancient secrets. Surely you would let me know."

ROSE-COLORED GLASSES

She cocked her head, remembering, but imagination played one final trick. "Are you sure you came here with me? I think you came out from the rocks."

"Of course I came out from the rocks! Without you, I couldn't love. Without someone to love, I couldn't love my brothers. Now do you remember?"

She smiled with infinite patience. "Of course. It was in France. You were a doctor, and I was royalty. You proved yourself unfaithful."

"Never!"

"It was said on great authority."

"Liars, all!"

She tossed her head. "Perhaps. I thought it time you learned a lesson."

"How well I've learned it! The empty years have seemed a lifetime. Promise that you'll never leave me."

She melted then, a merry humor on her face. "All right, I

promise. Do you promise to be good?"

"I promise."

"Very well, then. First thing to do is rebuild the world." We laughed and undertook the task at once.

When the sun had lowered in the sky, she finally said, "Perhaps we ought to start back. I'd like to see if it's the same when we are moving."

We packed the gear and after one last look set off. Where the paths converged, she turned to go back the way we'd come, but I glanced along the creek and saw the wide road running by it, and so I said, "Maybe we can go out through the gate. Maybe they'll think we're members." We started toward the gate.

Soon she stopped and fumbled in her purse. "Oh, dear, I think I left my rose-colored glasses."

"Wait here," I answered. "I'll go back." I left her looking after me.

THE SENTINEL OF SEX

Shade and shadow had assembled at the creek when again I stood beside it, and I walked among the darkened rocks watched by many eyes. Undines, elves, and dwarves and trolls peered out from tree and rock, and in the air made magic signs granting miracles to love. When at last they permitted me to come upon her glasses, I heard their whispered final words, "The hidden door is sex."

Returning, I found her lying on a bank gazing at the heavens, and I helped her to her feet and said, "It was different at the pool. It truly is enchanted."

"What was it like?"

"Darker, and the rocks had eyes."

We walked in silence and passed the shadowy shapes of houses. "There can't be many members here," I said. "No one is around." The clubhouse too was dark and silent. "Maybe there really are no members. Maybe we're the first."

"No, we're not the first," she said.

Suddenly, I saw it all, and incandesence overwhelmed me. She'd taken me up the mountain on purpose, stretching me to the limit, qualifying me once again to receive her guarded secret.

"You tricked me," I chuckled. "How many times must I be

170

tricked?"

She smiled archly. "That depends. We're coming very close, we two. I gather that you've noticed."

"But which of us will I finally be? Will I be you or you be me?"

"We each will be the other."

At the gate, a grazing doe raised her head and gazed at us with liquid eyes. Some point of perfect balance reached, time stopped, light became power, and space had no dimensions.

"Shall we turn around?" I asked. "And stay in here forever?"

"Not yet," she answered.

We came into the sunlight, then, and found the car. And driving down the mountain, we finished off the wine.

THE FORCES OF BALANCE

"Up and Down and Right and Left give birth to In and Out"

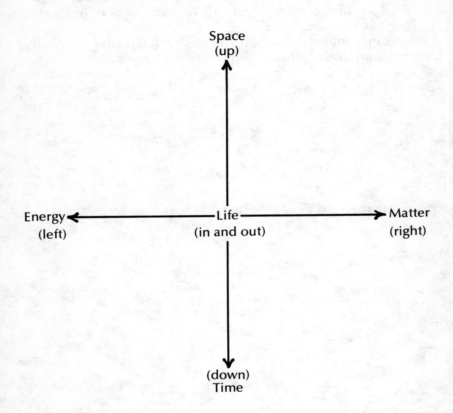

Sex Ecology

Wilhelm Reich was born in Austria on March 24, 1897, the son of a prosperous farmer. He attended a German high school, then obtained his M.D. degree from the University of Vienna in 1922. He continued post graduate studies in neuro-psychiatry and obtained membership in the Vienna Psychoanalytic Society where he met Sigmund Freud. Freud was impressed, and Reich was made First Clinical Assistant in his Viennese clinic, continuing in this association until 1933 when his interest in life energy research drew him away from psychoanalytical paths. Shortly thereafter Hitler came to power and Reich was forced to leave the country.

From 1934 to 1939, he lectured and did research at the Psychological Institute of the University of Oslo in Norway, when he came to the United States, setting up a laboratory in Forest Hills and becoming Associate Professor of Medical Psychology at the New School for Social Research in New York City. In 1942, he founded the Orgone Institute on two hundred acres of land in Maine, and in 1949, the Wilhelm Reich Foundation was established by students and friends to preserve his archives and secure the future of his discoveries. In 1957, Wilhelm Reich died in the Federal Penitentiary at Lewisburg, Pennsylvania where he was serving a two year sentence for criminal contempt of court, having refused to obey an injunction ordering him to cease treating cancer patients with his Orgone Energy Accumulator.

THE FUNCTION OF THE ORGASM

Simply stated, the researches of Reich led him to the following conclusions: 1) The genital function is the highest function of all living beings.   2) The orgasm formula is the formula of life.   3) The elimination of sexual stasis through adequate orgastic discharge clears away the neuroses of man and brings him to full use of his powers.

Reich began by ceasing to ask himself what life was and starting to ask what it did. What it did seemed obvious — it was orgasm. Cells divided that way, seeds sprouted that way, buds bloomed that way. Tension, charge, discharge, relaxation — that's the way the living organism functioned. He observed that it was impossible to distinguish between the contraction of an amoeba and the orgastic contraction of man and records the following phenomena: Intensive biological excitation, repeated expansion and contraction, ejaculation of body fluids in the contraction, and a rapid reduction of biological excitation. He found the same process occuring in the motion of protozoa and metazoa. Worms and snakes showed the process quite clearly, in the movements of their parts as well as their whole. All the organs of the human body operated in strict accordance with orgastic principles. The heart beat accordingly; so the bladder discharged its contents. Liver, pancreas, gall bladder, kidneys, lungs, endocrine glands, all acted that way. The law of living was the law of orgasm, and Reich was prompted to draw up his orgasm formula: Mechanical tension — bio-electrical charge — bio-electrical discharge — mechanical relaxation. He stated unequivocally: "The orgasm formula is the formula of life."

Next he wanted to know what this energy was that was being discharged by the orgasm. He was struck at once by the fact that something moving and changing and pulsating, something non-stastical which couldn't be measured, would appear non-existent to the methods of science. Therefore it was likely that a wholly undiscovered energy existed in the universe, an energy that animated life. Since science hadn't run into it, the likelihood was that science couldn't, and there seemed nothing to do but scrap the methods of science and start afresh like a babe in the woods. Reich removed from his eyes the spectacles of training and peered anew at the orgasm.

THE GENESIS OF LIFE ENERGY

This caused him to wonder, "What is the reason for the extraordinary significance of the genital drive? Nobody doubts its elemental power; nobody can avoid it. The whole living world is subject to it. Even where man denies this powerful force, he by no means abolishes it, and we all know the terrible tragedies which result. That the orgasm reflex follows natural laws is beyond any doubt. It is a clinical fact that orgastic longing always goes hand in hand with cosmic longing, and it seems almost certain that cosmic longing is functionally anchored in the orgasm reflex."

The turning point of Reich's researches began with his observation that the sexual orgasm had therapeutic effects. He records it over and over in his notes. "The elimination of sexual stasis through adequate orgastic discharge eliminates every neutrotic manifestation!" Often appending, "It is necessary to point out this basic fact again and again!"

Finally he was led to ask, "Is biological energy identical with electricity?" This seemed unlikely in view of a number of facts. First, if electrical current were applied to the body, it was experienced as unpleasant. True, muscles could be induced into uncoordinate contractions, but their functional meaningfulness was lost, and the slow delayed movement of smooth muscle indicated an unknown "something" that interpolated between the electrical stimulus and the muscle action. Further, Reich observed that humans have no reaction to the proximity of high tension wires, that they are insensitive to x-rays and radiation phenomena, all of which set up strong reactions in electrical apparatus. He concluded therefore that biological energy was

175

not electricity. Assuredly, minute quantities of electricity were employed by the organism, but these in no way could account for the phenomenon of life.

Nor could bio-energy be identified with chemistry. Though the human body undoubtedly resembled a small chemical laboratory, there was no way to account for the conversion of its small amounts of chemicals into such a tremendous energy output. Bio-energy definitely had to be something other than chemical or electrical. Since energy is the capacity to do work. Reich was struck by the fact that there was no known energy that could compete with the work done by the life population of just this one planet, earth. Since this energy had to be derived from something, and since the universe exhibited vast and endless conglomerations of inanimate matter, he was led to the assumption that bio-energy was derived from inanimate matter itself. This led to a long series of experiments, the conclusions of which follow:

THE EXPERIMENTS OF WILLIAM REICH

1. All matter — if exposed to high temperatures and made to swell — undergoes a process of disintegration.

2. Sufficiently high temperatures destroy what life there is. But these same high temperatures produce bions, which in turn can develop into living bacteria.

3. The energy at work in these bions is not introduced into them artificially from the outside; rather, it originates from the disintegration of matter itself.

4. A bion is a minute quantity of matter, containing a quantity of energy derived from this matter.

5. The bions are not complete living beings, but only carriers of biological energy; they are forms of transition from non-living to living.

6. The blue color of their content is the immediate expression of this energy. As the blue disappears, the essential biological characteristics of the bions disappear also.

7. The bion experiments do not newly create life; they only demonstrate the natural process by which protozoa develop spontaneously from disintegrated matter, and the natural form in which biological energy is contained in living beings.

Reich tried heating ocean sand as a means of obtaining bions and produced such a concentration of bio-energy that he developed violent conjunctivitis merely examining it through a micro-scope. He knew at once that he was dealing with a phenomenon of radiation, and concluded that the potency of ocean sand bions derived from the fact that such sand was solidified sun energy that had been liberated from matter by a process of heating and swelling. Later, Reich placed these bions in close proximity to cancer cells and discovered that the cancer cells were rendered immobile. This observation led to his difficulty with the Federal Food and Drug Administration.

THE SPACE-TIME SOURCE OF LIFE ENERGY

Having discovered life energy, Reich wanted to know how it worked. Its electrical nature, functioning in much the same manner as a condensor discharges when a crucial limit is reached, seemed to anchor its operation in the orgasm reflex, so he set out to discover how it entered the body. Since the discharge center, the genitals, was located in the lower part of the body, Reich began with the assumption that life energy entered the upper part of the body. The most mysterious organ, the brain, was at the uppermost part of the body and might easily be a receptor for rays or forces as yet undetermined or isolated by physics. And if life energy entered the body at the brain and proceeded to its genitals, its natural course would be the path described by the spinal column.

Ultimately, he concluded that bions emitted a radiation energy antagonistic to nuclear radiation, thus postulating a new form of energy. He further concluded that living organisms drew it up from the atmosphere and directly from the sun. He discovered that life energy penetrated all matter, that even lead shields offered not the slightest barricade. By subjecting his patients to concentrations of it, he cured them of all manner of ills, estab-lished greater vitality and increased genital function. He even depicted the miniscule life energy vesicle as a tiny blob of en-ergy shaped like a tear drop. The superimposition of two of these blobs gave the appearance of a crudely rendered drawing of a syzygy, the emblem of Taoism. Reich concluded that all liv-ing beings were formed by the coming together of these two forces and went so far as to demonstrate with the shapes and structures of sea shells, tree leaves, seeds, and the like. These two antagonistic but complementary forces he found at work within the autonomic nervous system of man.

The autonomic nervous system is sometimes called the vegetative system, because its characteristics are possessed by vegetables. However, its activities in vegetables are extremely primitive as compared to its complex functioning in the organism of man, where it regulates heart beat, breathing, digestion, assimiliation, elimination, micturation, oxidation of glucose, hormonal content of the blood, and the intricate teamwork of the bevy of tiny organs known as the endocrine glands. It also governs the sexual function through the four-beat phase of the orgasm reflex.

THE SYMPATHETIC AND PARASYMPATHETIC SYSTEMS

The autonomic nervous system is divided into two subsidiary systems, each antagonistic to the other. The parasympathetic promotes feelings of pleasure and expansion. The sympathetic promotes feelings of anxiety and contraction.

The sympathetic system causes the entire vegetative system to contract and for the most part renders it immobile. This frees the blood to be sped to the outer muscles of the body where it is needed to promote rapid action, because when the sympathetic system is stimulated, the organism has received from its environment a signal to fight or take flight. The parasympathetic system draws blood from the outer muscles, causing the entire vegative system to expand and rendering it highly receptive to sensation, because the organism has received from its environment a signal that something pleasurable is about to happen.

Quite obviously the vegetative system provides man's basic contact with the energy that sustains him. Its plasmatic nature exists in all forms of life. All reflexes necessary for the sustaining of life are built into it. Nobody has to tell it what to do, it just does it automatically and does it perfectly. Man can decide many things with his central nervous system, whether to spit or shoot dice or do both at once, but he can't decided what his autonomic nervous system should do. It knows more about it than he ever will, so it naturally keeps him out of it. But man can defeat it. By his power to think and to decide right and wrong, he can shrink his vegetative system and kill himself gradually.

Reich's researches indicated that every known disease and malfunction was preceded by pathological shrinking of the vegetative nervous system. When expansion was refused by para-sympathetic inhibition, the vegetative system eventually shrank, man's energy ebbed and he fell into illness. When the vegetative system shrank sufficiently, life ceased to function. The vegetative system was in its most extreme state of expansion during sexual orgasm, becoming a greatly increased receptacle for life energy. By means of orgasm, life was sustained to its fullest.

THE ENGINE OF LIFE

Clearly, man is animated by some form of energy other than the food he eats. The laws of physics can in no way account for the conversion of two pounds of food into enough energy to move ten tons of furniture from a truck into a house, which a man can do easily and greater things too. Just the maintenance and repair of his body requires more energy than can be derived from two pounds of food, yet we see that if such food isn't eaten, a man begins to decline, so we know it is essential. But essential to what, in which manner, under what conditions and why, we yet have no way of knowing. It is abundantly clear, however, that we do not exist by eating alone. We are animated and sustained by some power that flows through the body like an endless source of fuel and pumps it into life by means of the orgasm reflex. Orgasm then is the engine of life. Its fuel is life energy.

Life energy has not yet been isolated. Its composition is unknown. Its place of origin yet lies in question. But we know that it exists, Reich proved that beyond doubt, and we know its personality and character because they are manifest in man, and due to Reich's observations we know something about how it works.

It is antagonistic to nuclear energy. By means of nuclear radiation, Reich was able to concentrate it. He discovered that wherever radiation piles existed, they were immediately surrounded by life energy. He further discovered that damage to tissues and nerves was not caused by nuclear radiation itself, but by a superabundance of life energy attracted to the area, which had the immediate effect on the human organism that an overly-rich supply of gasoline might have on an automobile engine.

Reich concluded that the sun was surrounded by a heavy aura of life energy and that it was these rays which were received on earth, not those of nuclear fission and fusion which were tak-

179

ing place in the interior of the sun. More than that, he demonstrated that when nuclear energy broke through the protective layer of life energy that surrounds the sun, in high-flaring geysers that sometimes erupted millions of miles into space, it invariably produced severe disturbances in all living organisms — headaches, irritability, alterations of consciousness, and a sense of heaviness and drowsiness. He postulated, therefore, that life energy was attracted and concentrated by the explosive phenomena of novae and suns and that once it was concentrated it inevitably manifested in living organisms.

CHANNELING SEXUAL POWER

Though Reich uncovered the function of the orgasm, its significance has been apparent in all man's work since the beginning of time. Spires and towers symbolize in essence the erect phallus. Halls, rooms, salons, and theatres symbolize the cunnus. The very rhythm of music, drama and literature displays the the orgasm formula — tension, charge, discharge, relaxation. Even the seasons are orgasm bound, waxing to climax and afterwards waning, revealing the orgastic nature of the heavens themselves. Colorful oratory follows the orgasm formula, building to a crescendo then discharging its point. Even animated conversation has an orgastic quality, rising and falling, now fast, now slow, proceeding first gently, then bolder and bolder, until the utmost feeling accompanies final conviction. Joke-telling follows the orgasm formula, first inducing tension then charging it higher, then discharging all in an orgasm of laughter. Personality itself is a function of orgasm. Warm, animated people have full contact with their genitality. Those who are cold and withdrawn have repressed the orgasm.

Reich's separation of nuclear energy from life energy was a confirmation of the downward pulling force of Time inherent in matter and the upward propelling force of Space inherent in spirit, thereby casting light on the path to ascension. Especially enlightening was the function of the orgasm, for it clearly seemed the engine through which life energy worked. Years before I had discarded Reichian theories because they appeared to be a license for unbridled sexual indulgence, and I simply couldn't believe that man's potential was best developed by means available to any pig or goat, but now I saw that removal of sexual inhibition was necessary for the release of the power inherent in man's nature and this power need not be directed toward the sex act itself.

Though a certain amount of sexual orgasm was clearly necessary, sex energy (life energy) could be directed toward any goal one desired, and if this was elevation of consciousness, such energy could be focused in the higher chakras, providing a powerful impetus to the attainment of enlightenment. Complete celibacy, it seemed to me, was doomed to failure as a consciousness-elevating technique, just as any extreme was doomed to failure, because it had not within itself a method of achieving balance and therefore generated no power. With sex as with eating, it was better not to take all you could but to stop when you should.

FREEING LIFE ENERGY

Interestingly, Reich had devised a therapy for the freeing of life energy, and this therapy was based on his observation that such energy was restricted from flowing up and down the spinal column by spasms in the transverse muscles along seven sections of the backbone. These sections corresponded closely to the seven chakras of yoga, thus he might as well have announced that when the chakras were closed the individual was blocked away from full access to his life energy and that his sex life was accordingly disturbed. Reich's therapy consisted of muscle-stretching exercises designed to release the various spasms, just as the stretching exercises of yoga are designed to open the various chakras. Mystical India and scientific Germany thus had arrived at the same destination following different paths.

It now became clear why my own life energy had increased. First, my diet now consisted largely of Space foods instead of Time foods, so a great deal more energy was available to me. Secondly, daily use of yoga postures was gradually opening up the chakras so that this energy was flowing smoothly along my spine. Third the various energy-charging techniques, such as meditation, chanting, and color imagery were drawing increased life energy into my body. As increased power became available to me and I perceived how it could be focused onto any goal I desired, it became a temptation to focus it on riches, power, fame, and sexual indulgence. Only the fact of my previous experience with such toys and the certain knowledge that they had no power to heal or comfort kept me from yielding to their allure. The ladder of ascension was the only path to salvation. Now I was determined to take it.

THE RHYTHM AND THE TUNE

Being able at last to look at the sexual function with eyes unclouded by prejudice permitted me to see how graphically it depicted the manner in which life energy manifested. By permitting one's self to behave orgastically, one was attuned to the most powerful rhythm of life. To be able to relax, to be able to be stimulated, to be able to be tense, to be able to be excited, to be able to discharge built-up energy in meaningful action, these were the measures of a healthy organism. The very function of one's own nerve cells was based on this cycle — tension, charge, discharge, relaxation. The cells that were not permitted to discharge during waking hours were discharged in sleep during the process of dreaming, and this seemed the very purpose of sleep itself. Experiments where people were allowed to sleep but not to dream had revealed that their brain cells began functioning inefficiently, producing hallucinations and delusions.

At this point I was led to construct a Space-Time emblem in the format of a syzygy and to plot along the perimeter the elements of Reich's orgasm formula. This enabled me to better understand that life energy was a spinning wave, to see how it was propelled and how it formed all living units, animating them by the power of orgasm. It now became clear that powerful emotion was in fact evidence of a great capacity for orgasm and that the stifling of emotion alienated man from his life energy. By permitting one's self to function orgastically, one could regain this power, but first he must permit himself to feel, for from the capacity to feel all genuine orgastic behavior sprang, imbuing action with power.

Most people spent their lives either trying not to get excited or trying to get excited, indicating that they were either out of rhythm or out of tune. If you were both out of rhythm and out of tune, you felt overwhelmed by stimuli. If you were in rhythm but were out of tune, you were too Time and over-reacted to stimuli. If you were in tune but were out of rhythm, you were too Space and under-reacted to stimuli. If you were in rhythm and in tune, you were balanced and generally joyous. This was living orgastically.

CHARACTERISTICS OF ECOLOGISTS

The orgasm that was free to work according to its nature ran the gamut of every emotion, exhibiting a complete dynamics of motion and rest, the utmost flexibility of expression, the highest adaptability and inventiveness, a complete openness and giving-ness, and it contained within itself all the dipoles of human activity — agressiveness and passivity, acquisitiveness and generosity, anger and tolerance, love and hate, individualism and gregariousness, competitiveness and brotherhood, anger and admiration, industry and quietude, slothfulness and neat-ness, desire and satisfaction, even life and death. Orgasm was life in miniature and combined everything into the remarkable dynamics of living functioning.

Since life was everything that is, nothing could be alien to it; therefore everything that is must somehow be encompassed by it. From this it followed that only those people who were com-pletely open to all experience could meet every aspect of living and undergo it, no matter how painful or destructive, and move on rejuvenated. Here was the key to the nature of ecologists.

Ecologists were not gods. They were just more fully human. They could laugh, cry, win, lose, be elated and depressed. They could love, and they could hate. They could grow angry, and they could forgive. They could move forward, and they could fall back. They could make mistakes, and they could be perfect. They could be jealous, and they could admire. They could be pos-sessive, and they could be permissive. They could strive, and they could rest. They could grow sick, and they could recover. They could grow old, and they could die. Nothing was alien to them, nothing repugnant. They were the only people on earth who were truly human, and this was so because they had accept-ed their genitality, with all its afflictions and rewards. They were the only people capable of undergoing full orgasm. They were the only people capable of creative productivity. And they were the only people capable of experiencing joy.

CHARACTERISTICS OF
SADISTS AND MASOCHISTS

Now the profound difference between ecologists and those who were out of balance could be seen. Ecologists did not try to make life fit into a sterotype. They freely accepted all its dangers and uncertainties and risks and paradoxes and were able not only to tolerate them but to turn them into the means of living more fully. They did not insist that life revolve around them. They did not insist that things turn out their way. They did not insist that they be spared from all suffering, and by this means alone were spared the majority of suffering. They did not insist that they know all the answers. They did not insist that those answers even be known. They did not insist that they be given the mantle of leadership. They did not insist on the center of the stage. They did not insist that others should serve them. They were able to accept help without obligation. They were able to give help without expecting return. In short, they had none of the defenses by which the imbalanced blocked out the orgasm and thus blocked out life.

The stereotyped behavior of masochists and sadists resulted from an inner insistence that the orgasm be controlled. The means by which they sought to control it were the means by which they sought to control life. Since life couldn't be controlled any more than the orgasm, the only thing that resulted was a deep-seated frustration which gave rise to their symptoms of sadism and masochism.

All imbalanced behavior displayed the pronounced sign of being hung up forever at some particular point of the orgasm reflex. The masochist provoked and waited. The compulsive sadist searched for privacy and safety. The narcissist displayed himself. And the sadistic tyrant demanded. Since such people could not discharge their tension in the full release of orgasm, because by primal conditioning they were prevented from doing so, they now were condemned to eternally acting out that particular point of the orgasm on which they had become time-bound. Stereotyped behavior resulted. Everything was treated the same way, regardless of nuances or differences. A demand was forever exerted that the situation confronting them conform to the situation they felt innerly. They became blind to everything except that narrow aspect of life which they sensed to be the cause of their frustration and unhappiness, and they were forever wreaking vengeance upon it by the particular psychological device dictated by their illness. They became unteachable and denied everything that did not fit the demonic cosmology created by their sexual stasis. Their inner lives were marked by a black despair, and if they were not enabled to kill or maim others, they wound up killing or maiming themselves. Only by the most intense effort were they able to hold themselves together at all, and quite often broke down psychotically.

THE MATING OF ECOLOGISTS

Such people were capable of developing strong drives in an effort to overcome their inner tension, and their frantic efforts might win them places of responsibility and trust even in a society composed largely of ecologists. In an imbalanced society, the results were a forgone conclusion. They eventually infiltrated and controlled all the organs of that society and enforced their ideas on everyone. Thus imbalance became the norm and finally the law. At last, mass frustration exploded into violence, and the members of the society, like the gingham dog and the calico cat, "ate each other up." Anyone willing to cast even a casual glance over history could see this pattern at work ever since man decided he was bigger than life and could force his will upon it.

The mating of ecologists was a rewarding experience. None of the rites of possession was involved. Neither made demands on the other. Neither had a preconceived idea of how the other should behave. Each was a source of constant fascination to the other, since the depth of ecologists can never be plumbed. There were constant surprises, invention, spontaneity. There was a deep sense of femaleness and maleness, but with none of the defensiveness such concepts imply. There was recognition and joy that each was unlike the other and that in their coming together something greater evolved. There was a "letting be" in the regard that each had for the other, a deep feeling that the works of this remarkable creature must not be tampered with. There was pride in femaleness, in its facets for softness, allure, sustenance, respite, and renewal. There was a pride in maleness, in its gifts of vision, challenge, construction, achievement and leadership. There was no sense of domination whatever. Each fell into the role assigned him by life and each felt that role equally important. But it was the male who led, the male who dominated, and it was the female who served and was submissive. Each recognized that this was the nature of things and that any other arrangement would be a distortion.

185

LIVING ORGASTICALLY

The sex lives of such people were full to the brimming, but there was absolutely no feeling that they must be that way. They simply responded to the orgasm as a natural phenomenon of living, and it occurred quite spontaneously as time and situation allowed. No rituals were connected with it. No places were set aside. Time played no factor, and schedules were never involved. Neither expected or demanded the erotic attention of the other — it simply ocurred when it occurred. They had no favorite ways of making love to each other. They never fell into habits, never found it dull. The foreplay of love-making was a constant invention as new delights were discovered, new ways of arousal. Both surrendered completely to the orgasm, fused into one by a power greater than themselves.

Ecologists never suffered from chronic constipation or indigestion or colitis or halitosis or headaches or unpleasant body odor or any of the other symptoms of imbalance to which the masochist and sadist were subject. If spoiled food was eaten, it was promptly regurgitated, since the orgasm reflex was free to work in reverse. Under shock or injury, vegetative functions simply subdued themselves until restorative processes could be completed. Infections and other invasions of the body were promptly flushed away by the quick action of the orgasm reflex. Perfect health and vigor were the order of the day. Any evidence to the contrary was quickly overcome. The ecologist felt good. That's why he was happy.

Ecologists lived orgastically — seldom, if ever, overworking; seldom, if ever, being lazy. They spoke, thought, and behaved like a piano concerto, sometimes on the high notes, sometimes on the low, sometimes faintly and delicately, sometimes in a crescendo, sometimes serenely, sometimes in a rush. They could be mad, sad, or glad. They were the only people who could love, because they, alone, could let others be. They easily survived the loss of a loved one, because the laws of departure and death were part of the orgasm. They were capable of great improvisation and welcomed such opportunities, since by this means they experienced the new and the different. They could also work within routine, though not for protracted periods of time without falling into some of the maladies of masochists and sadists. However, their instincts unfailingly kept them out of such situations except under duress. Their rhythms of sleeping and waking occurred quite spontaneously. They went to bed when they were sleepy, got up when they were rested, ate when they were hungry, didn't when they weren't. They did not suffer from obesity or emaciation or insomnia or alcoholism or drug addiction. Such pathology was impossible because the body told them what it needed, they never told it. They had great curiosity and wide-open minds and were willing to explore and consider any facet of human endeavor. They were rooted in the earth and had their feet on the ground and considered this sphere of ours a mighty fine world. Obviously it might be when such people abound. How, then, to become one?

THE MAN IN THE MIRROR

First step was to practice talking orgastically. For this, a mirror was needed. You just stood in front of it and began talking, immediately observing that it wasn't surprising that people didn't like you. There you were with all that rage and resentment showing through, and all the time you thought you were fooling everybody. So you peeled off the mask and threw it away. Then you shook hands with your ugly, old self. You and he were going to have to get along for awhile.

In acting classes, they teach incipient thespians how to express their emotions. That's what this mirror-talking was all about. But conversely to the pretense involved in acting, mirror-talking had to be dead-on-the-level. What we were after here was to say exactly what we felt, just the way we felt it, with the appropriate emotion, inflection, intonation, speed of delivery, and volume. No point in artificially trying to determine these. The hallmark was sincerity. No one was around. No one was watching. No one would overhear. You wouldn't get caught by mamma or papa or your wife or your boss or your girl friend. No one was going to find out what a miserable opinion you had of yourself. No one was going to wise up to the fact that you hated them and the world and were scared to death and guilty and sick at all the miserable deals you'd pulled off. So you vomited out the whole works.

You found a lot of things to confess to the man in the mirror. At first, you were absolutely certain that he wouldn't understand. But as the days moved on, you found that he was changing. You began to notice an occasional sympathetic glance, once in a while a nod of understanding. He also began to look like somebody you knew a long time ago but whose name you couldn't remember or even where you met. This gave you the feeling that at least you weren't talking to a total stranger, so you began to warm up a little. Once in a while, you exchanged a little smile, even a chuckle or two. The turning point in your relationship came the day you both burst into laughter. That startled you, and you stared at each other. Then you doubled up and roared. You held your sides and bellowed to high heaven. You could see all of his thirty-two teeth, or at least as many as he had left, as his mouth gaped wide with merriment and the tears rolled down his cheeks and his face reddened and he looked as if he was having a whale of a time. This eruption might go on for half an hour. By the time you staggered from the house, you were a little weak in the knees, but you suddenly discovered that you felt better than you ever had in your life — pleasantly relaxed, nicely at peace, and you could feel your skin tingling all over.

SOME ADVANTAGES IN BEING ALIVE

After this, mirror-talking took on some of the aspects of joke-telling, and you found that these jokes were all on you. But that's exactly why you thought they were so funny. And it didn't bother you at all that your friend in the mirror was laughing at you. By this time both of you were growing to recognize that you were human after all, a creature who hadn't the vaguest idea how he got inside that strange body, didn't know where he came from or where he was going, had the whole mysterious world to cope with, and had had to be relatively shrewd even to stay conscious. It occurred to you that the only way you'd ever learned anything was to make a lot of mistakes, and that the only way you were going to continue learning was to make a lot more, and it wasn't so bad not being perfect.

By this time, you were on pretty good terms with the man in the mirror, so you didn't have to be quite so faithful about visiting him. After all, good friends didn't have to see each other all the time. Now you could get around to looking at some of the problems that had been bothering you, because all that talking to the man in the mirror had allowed you to look at them without your hair standing on end.

You saw at once that it wasn't what you didn't know that had gotten you into trouble. It was what you knew that wasn't so. Now, suddenly, you were able to recognize a lie, and you could see that you'd believed in a number of these for years and that had caused all of your trouble.

The first lie to strike you was that you had to do certain things certain ways. You suddenly noticed that there were other ways to do them and that many people didn't do them at all without the sky falling on their heads. This caused you to believe that you'd been some kind of machine, just rods and pistons chugging away forever, and you stared at your body and noticed that it didn't look like a machine. That caused you to make some un-machinelike movements, like getting out of the rut and doing something different. The sensation was pretty heady at first, and you thought maybe you'd been more comfortable being a machine, but you didn't go back to it. A machine couldn't suffer black despair. If it could, it would try to be human. So you just persevered at trying some new things and trying to do old things some new ways, and you suddenly discovered that the sun was shining and it was a beautiful day.

THE DISCOVERY OF JOY

Now you stopped drawing up the future the way you wanted it to be and getting all upset when it didn't work out. You broke those habits and stopped those rituals. You took a look at the landscape and realized that nobody knew what was going to happen, not a single soul in the whole wide world. You began getting the feeling that you were willing to adjust to it, to go with the excitement, to let yourself respond to the drama. You didn't have to do anything about anything. All you had to do was go along for the ride. The remarkable vehicle that packed you around would take care of everything. All you had to do was let it.

Now that you'd shot a little juice to your living functioning, the next lie occurred to you at once. All those things that you'd always believed you couldn't do didn't look so impossible any-more. What was once the Matterhorn seemed to be shrinking and gave the definite impression that you might be able to climb it. About this time, you realized that you'd lived your life in a dream. There had been prelates and potentates and heroes and giants and sages, and you wanted to be like them but suspected you couldn't, and life wasn't worth living if you didn't make it. Suddenly, you couldn't care less. You saw that the man at the top had his problems too. He had headaches and indigestion and was subject to heart failure and cancer or somebody shooting

189

him through the head when he least expected it. He wondered what life was about too. You could stand right alongside him, and a hundred feet away, a Martian couldn't tell you apart.

Now came the grand experiment. You let yourself go. You walked out of jail and kicked down the jail so it couldn't get you again. You took a deep breath of that nice, fresh air. You looked up at the sky and observed it was limitless. You saw a bird flying. It looked almost like an accident, it was so absolutely free. Deep in your heart, you knew you were that way too. All you had to do was start moving. Your body would take care of everything. It didn't even need a map.

Suddenly you discovered that you could smell, hear, taste, see, feel. The vivid world with its colors, sounds, and aromas seemed almost to embrace you. You almost felt that somebody had changed it, cast it in technicolor and set it to music. You could feel your heart beat. You could feel your insides moving around, taking care of everything, giving you life. Your fingertips tingled. Each breath seemed a kiss. Something ecstatic welled up inside you and burst out toward the sky.

THE MAGIC OF CREATIVE POWER

Now you couldn't tell a lie if someone paid you a mint. No more cheating and swindling. No more forts to defend your beliefs. No more anguish that you didn't rule the world. No more insisting that you knew what was what. No more gods and heroes and saints and tabernacles. Not one head in the world a hair higher than yours. There was just you and the universe, and you suddenly realized that from the place where you stood your own viewpoint was the only one that was true. There was a heady feeling went along with this. That made you God. Not in the sense of being in charge, but just from the sense of being alive where you were. Out the door went humility. Out the door went the scepter by which you planned to rule others. Out the door went the things that you couldn't do without. What need for things when you were Life itself?

Now your friends began appearing from nowhere, because they were ecologists too. Together you had a whale of a time. No sparring, no knives in the back, no straining at the seams to put the other one down, no laying down the law, no raising the flag, no pulling down the blinds so nobody could see, no building of walls, no fencing off land, no dragging out things to show you

190

were great, no idle chit-chat, no painful long silences, no complaints, no accusations, no resentments.

By this time, you no longer were intimidated by the opinion of others. Only one opinion really had value, and that was the opinion of the man in the mirror. Naturally, you wanted to stay on the good side of him, because he was the best friend you had. When things were at their worst you didn't take your problems to a preacher or psychiatrist or load them on the backs of your friends or your mate. You didn't hang them out to dry so the world could make comments or send emergency alarms to the city or state. You just took them up with the man in the mirror.

He was the first to suggest that you ought to make something. You asked him what, and he said, "Oh, anything at all." You took a look at your hands and decided what they were good for, then you put them to work building the thing they built best. When you got the first one of these finished, you were stricken with awe. There was something pretty and useful, and if it hadn't been for you it wouldn't be in the world. You drove off in the country and sat by a brook the whole day. Now you knew what you were here for. You didn't have to read books or get smart or win titles. You just had to make something.

Some of the things you made were bought by others. That was all right with you, but you didn't make them for that. You made them because in the making you discovered more of yourself, and the more you discovered the more inexhaustible you became. Finally you saw that these creations of yours had sprung into life through no effort of your own, gestated into the world by the orgasm reflex. You'd become an ecologist and had tapped the magic of creative power.

The Function of the Orgasm

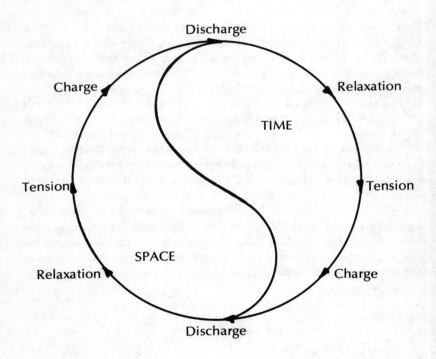

The New Ecologists

12

Wherever I went now, I was greeted by the same question: "What happened to cause you to lose all that weight and to quit smoking? When I answered that I'd restored my body to balance by conditioning my brainwaves, it inevitably was the signal for protracted discussion. Having learned what had happened to me, a number wanted to try the same thing, only they didn't know where to begin and what to do and didn't have the time to find out by themselves. Would I teach them? Eventually, I agreed.

At first I undertook this responsibility only with friends and family, but at last the demand became such that professional classes were organized. A few who graduated from these classes became teachers themselves, so what had started out as one man's journey began to take on the aspects of a movement.

This made me uneasy, as I'd had enough experience with movements to be afraid that sooner or later bones would replace flesh, everything would become rigid, and what had begun as an open door to freedom would become just another closed trap. But then it became apparent that the classes were graduating a different kind of person, one who was not seeking dominion over others but who was a interested in their freedom as his own. This was best put by a young man who used to steal gasoline for a living.

SPACE - TIME BALANCE

"When you syphon gasoline out of a tank," he informed us, "you have to suck on the hose with all your might in order to get the gasoline going. But once it's going, you just let go of the hose and it runs under its own power. As I see it, that's what we're doing here. We're helping people get going, then we're turning them loose and they're running under their own power." It was a nice simile.

Backbone of the movement became a series of seminars. Here, alpha meter and theta meter training were given, as well as techniques of meditation, concentration, physical postures, breath control, chanting and color imagery. Ecology, with its balance between opposites, was discussed in depth, as well as the insights which sprang from it. Afterwards, seminar graduates organized themselves into discussion groups. Guests were freely invited, and many people thus were introduced to ecology and to fellow sojourners on the path.

Attending the first of these weekly meetings proved a rewarding experience for me. It was held in a private home, and by the time I arrived some fifteen people had gathered and were chanting. Rhythmic vibrations filled the house with charged energy.

One wall was devoted to symbols. There was a large Space-Time emblem, flourescent in the light. A sign said, "Balance is Backbone of Ecology." Still another asked, "Are you an ecologist yet?" A final sign stated, "God gave us Space. We handle Time."

People were scattered about the room in various positions. The bulk of them were on the floor, some kneeling, some in the half-lotus, some sitting, and a few were seated on chairs. A number were handling prayer beads, ticking them off with their fingers as they chanted. The rhythm was contagious as a resounding "Oom!" emphasized each phrase. With everyone working together, eyes shining with sharing, it was as if a single self filled the room with love.

SPONTANEOUS REMISSION

Through the laboratory of the seminars new data began to emerge. It was soon discovered that brainwave conditioning itself was relatively ineffectual without a rationale to guide it. Those who trained themselves to high alpha output by the use of various feedback machines were always made more relaxed by the training, but such feedback training did not necessarily extend to a change in eating habits or to increased mental powers. A person tended to find in brainwave training fulfillment of those goals that occupied his consciousness, sometimes fallaciously, but often quite miraculously. Increasingly, we were made aware that we were dealing with some power that bridged physical cause and effect by an unknown means.

It was discovered that without exception everyone accelerated his progress through the use of feedback training devices. As more and more people successfully conditioned their brainwaves by this method, they became increasingly lucid in describing the procedure to others. Thus the time required to achieve a conditioned alpha began to decline from an average of eight hours to something just over three — a far cry from the eighteen hours I had devoted in the beginning. The resultant proficiency in meditation provided some unusual developments.

There were a number of cases of the spontaneous remission of disease and malfunction. Several stomach ulcers disappeared, a case or two of chronic colitis, a number of habitual migraine headaches, several cases of asthma, and there was marked alleviation of insomnia, nervous tension, constipation, and the various symptons of stress and strain. Overnight, people quit smoking, never to resume again.

THE LOVE EXERCISES OF ECOLOGY

In addition to the general improvement of physical health, theta meter training promoted an improvement in mental health. People were able to learn more rapidly, to remember more easily. They appeared able to move into the subconscious with more facility, to obtain information there and to integrate it into their

195

affairs. This brought about significant increases in creative ability. Many people began painting or sculpting, and those already engaged in creative work reported a steady flow of new ideas. The general meshing of conscious and subconscious minds indicated by these reports was marked by a lessening of emotional tension and a more relaxed and joyous attitude toward life.

Concentration techniques, while not undergoing any particular metamorphosis, seemed most affected by timing, nearly everyone reporting better results when it was engaged in as the last of the morning exercises. At this time, energy seemed to be at maximum and when focused on the chakras, the affirmations, and the life goal tended to manifest in a powerful manner. A few people achieved conscious control over normally unconscious functions of their bodies, and a number attained major goals in an almost miraculous manner. Many people found that the self-image affirmations — "I am," "I can," and "I don't have to" — could be chanted along with "Oom stu gah dyu ahn dye ahr," and most used prayer beads for this purpose, doing twenty-five, fifty, or one hundred chants as time and circumstance allowed.

As it turned out, ecologist exercises tended to center around chanting and physical postures, so it inevitably happened that people were drawn into Tantra Yoga exercises. Since these are performed by male and female partners and tend to be erotically stimulating, and since partners were shifted after each exercise, a number of love affairs blossomed and ripened into the maturity of marriage, while some older marriages were granted a new lease on life. A fresh and broadened viewpoint of sex inevitably followed, as sex energy was seen as a manifestation of life energy and orgasm as essential to the healthy person as an adequate diet. This permitted people to establish a rational discipline of their sex energies, conserving them in such a fashion as to heighten their mental, spiritual, and physical powers. In this manner, a whole host of people experienced love for the first time in their lives and were completely transformed in the process.

NEW LIFE STYLES

The powerful healing effects of color imagery soon became apparent as well. Visuallizing pink, gold, and violet in the higher chakras — in the cathedral of the heart, the generating station of the thyroid, the world of the pituitary, and the throne room of the pineal— not only produced a powerful consciousness-elevating effect but proved to be a strong mind-body integrating force as well. Disease and malfunction yielded in the face of increased life energy, and many people reported freedom from aches and pains for the first time in years.

Breath control produced some remarkable psychic effects, a number of people entering so deeply into the subconscious as to greatly enhance their powers of extra-sensory perception. It shortly was discovered, however, that dangers lurked here, for alterations of consciousness produced by over-indulgence in breath control exercises could be too great for the individual to adjust to, and he could suffer loss of equilibrium. While this had no lasting physical effect, it could frighten the person and slow his progress. As a result, people were cautioned to use breath control with restraint, especially breath-holding and hyperventilation.

Psychic powers themselves soon were discovered to be only symptomatic of the attainment of a lower level of higher consciousness; to become fascinated there was to be detained from the ultimate goal. Moreover, it was learned that concentration on psychic powers could lead to an imbalance between conscious and subconscious minds which in extreme cases could cause the person to be engulfed by the subconscious and swept into the world of psychosis. As ever, balance was the guidline.

Perhaps most important of all was the emergence of new life styles in those who adopted balance as a guideline. No pious group of spiritual aspirants these, nor grim-visaged pursuers of the banknotes of materialism. Laughter, casualness, relaxation, and creativity were the order of the day. Hair and clothing styles and general deportment tended to be highly individualistic, and an assembly of ecologists seemed more a gathering of artists than anything else. It was always surprising to learn that among their number were bankers, engineers, lawyers, doctors, plumbers, stevedores and truckdrivers.

THE ETHIC OF ECOLOGY

As with all life styles that prove satisfying and practical, ecology inevitably developed an ethic, a psychology, and a philosophy. These turned out to be the Ethic of Honesty, the Psychology of Love and the Philosophy of Beauty. In each were many dimensions.

The Ethic of Honesty was based on the recognition that all men were brothers evolving into godhood, and though at any moment each might be found on a different path, all paths converged at the same destination. Ideas of reincarnation and karma predominated, as it was perceived that each soul must unravel the threads of its own blindness (karma) and that in this unravelling it was solely responsible. Thus, to lie to others for one's personal gain or to lie to them for the security of their protection was to delay the unravelling of one's karma as well as the karma of those who were lied to. Nothing would do then but honesty — honesty with one's self as well as honesty with others. It mattered not whether such honesty was understood or misinterpreted or ignored, for it was the only means of growing into godhood.

Clearly, a society guided by the Ethic of Honesty would emerge remarkably different than the societies we know today, for the only alternatives to honesty are exploitation and appeasement, both of which are based on the lie, and exploitation produces economic feudalism while appeasement produces social dictatorship. Where the lie ruled, the law of the jungle reigned, no man trusted his neighbor, and even the heads of the mighty were uneasy. Justice became a matter of "paying off" those "on the take," and that which could not be gained by guile was eventually sought by violence. There were only the predators and the preyed upon, and the eater himself never knew the moment he might be eaten. Nor was the lie used only by those who sought to exploit others; it was equally used by those who sought to appease, to gain and hold jobs, to win economic security. In such societies, the skillful use of the lie commanded economic rewards and prestige, while the ethic of honesty was looked down upon as evidence of an unsophisticated mind.

From the first it was obvious that one could not be honest with others unless he was first honest with himself, and ecologists began making it a habit to be dead-on-the-level with themselves and everyone else. As a result, everybody knew where everybody else stood, and since there were no concealed threats, everybody began opening up. This marriage of open minds with new information gave birth to some remarkable learning situations, and a number of people emerged from ecology training with the equivalent of a college education in the humanities. Teamwork, good will, fellowship, and constant exploration of the frontiers of knowledge gave hints of the society which might emerge where honesty was the guiding ethic.

THE PSYCHOLOGY OF ECOLOGY

A natural adjunct to the Ethic of Honesty was the Psychology of Love, for when one had opened up to others, when he no longer distrusted them or felt threatened by them, he was willing to let them be themselves, and this conferring of freedom on others was the feeling known as love. If life was a school in which each person was evolving to a more aware state, then it followed that he must be held responsible for his progress. Only freedom permitted such responbility. Alternatives were either a quest for power or a quest for security. Those who became enamored of power and interferred with the lives of others created a difficult karma. Moreover, if they actually achieved power, their egos grew around them like iron shells and prevented their spirtual ascensions. On the other hand, those who aimed for security, surrendering their right to choose by subjugating themselves, became victims of karmic forces beyond their control.

The discovery that love was a power came as a revelation to most people. They had thought of love as something passive, an act done to one rather than something he did himself. But as their chakras opened and life energy began to flow through them, producing states of elation, even ecstasy, they inevitably turned this power onto other people, even plants and animals, and discovered that everything around them flourished. Then they knew that love was life energy itself, for it was the power that healed and nourished, and when one had opened himself to it, not only was he healed and nourished himself, but the power flowed through him to everything around him so that everything prospered and grew.

People developed "green thumbs," and their gardens produced huge vegetables and gigantic flowers. Even their pets grew coats of glossy fur and feathers and frolicked with new-found energy. Their wives and husbands and children became serene and joyful. Their businesses prospered and became fun. They developed the power to heal, to nourish and sustain, to produce growth.

Now it could be seen that the true aim of true psychology was to allow the power of love to work in and through one, for by this act all growth ensued. To be loved was only a shallow reflection of loving, and never to be sought in itself, for it could become a karmic block that deterred a person from loving. Loving usually occurred first between two persons of the opposite sex, for in this manner polarities were most easily activated, permitting the power to flow, but once a person had experienced love, he no longer restricted that love to the person who first inspired it, but instead turned it on everyone and everything around him. Nor did the loss of his loved one cause him to turn it off. To turn it off would be to turn off the power that sustained him. Nor were there limitations on love. Love was life energy itself and an inexhaustible fountain.

THE PHILOSOPHY OF ECOLOGY

Having perceived that honesty was the dynamic point of balance between exploitation and appeasement and that love was the dynamic point of balance between power and subjugation, it now became possible to select a philosophy. Surprisingly, this philosophy did not turn out to be spirituality, even though the primary aim was ascension of consciousness, because by now, the concept of balance, subtle as it might be, had been firmly ingrained into everyone's perception. Thus spirituality was seen as the opposite extreme of materialism. From the blending of these two opposites life ensued, and the point of balance between them was sought as the key to a philosophy. What would a dynamic balance between the material and spiritual produce? The answer seemed obvious. It would produce beauty.

One had only to look at the architecture of materialism (America) and the architecture of spirituality (India) to realize that a more dynamic architecture existed, and that was the architecture of ancient Greece (beauty). Missing from the architectures of materialism and spirituality was balance, which was exactly what the architecture of Greece possessed, and that was what made it beautiful. Balance was symmetry and symmetry was beauty, thus a balanced philosophy was that which sought beauty. Neither spiritual penitent nor industrial tycoon, the ecologist. He was the artist.

This was sometimes difficult to pursue, for the overt helping of others had strong appeal as a beautiful action, but a little

200

reflection revealed that such an action was out of balance and that encouraging others to help themselves was much more in line with the Philosophy of Beauty. In this manner, they responded with an action equal to the help they had received; thus symmetry was preserved.

Commensurate with this insight was an obvious corollary: that which produced beauty was fundamentally creative, thus the new, the novel, and the different were part of the Philosophy of Ecology, not as ends in themselves, but as measures of the worth of something that was beautiful. Therefore the ecologist was not only the artist, he was the explorer, the inventor, and the discoverer as well. And when he was a businessman, he carried in his mind the scales of justice upon which his goods or services were weighed against the price exacted, and these scales must always balance. Such was the Philosophy of Ecology.

THE ECOLOGY DIET

Perhaps the greatest satisfaction provided everyone were the benefits gained from the Ecology Diet. Without exception, everyone who switched to this diet became lean, vigorous, and healthy. While most people preferred to include some animal products in the diet, many others became complete vegetarians. There were, of course, people who were exposed to the diet and never used it or tried it tentatively and abandoned it. These were the same people who failed to do the consciousness-elevating exercises. Eventually we coined a name for them — the Searchers. They didn't want to become Finders.

Bringing the body's sodium-potassium ratio into balance was at the bottom of the Ecology Diet's effectiveness, though as it turned out, there were other beneficial factors as well. Potassium could be obtained naturally only from vegetables, fruits, whole grain cereals and nuts, and since the average American's diet was highly deficient in these items and contained an over-abundance of the processed foods that were high in sodium, he was usually getting the worst of two worlds. The Ecology Diet corrected this.

Dr. L. K. Dahl, who had spent years researching the relationship of sodium intake to high blood pressure, had found in all age groups that the greater the sodium intake, the earlier and more numerous were deaths from hypertension. The high sodium content of prepared baby foods was an especial target of Dr. Dahl's. *By feeding baby rats canned meats and vegetables prepared for infants, he produced high blood pressure that was fatal in four months.*

Perhaps the greatest harm done by excessive sodium intake was that it caused serious loss of potassium from the body. Potassium, by activating many enzymes, was essential for muscle contraction. Without it, sugar (glucose) could not be changed into energy or stored for future use. Nor was that the only harm done. Normally, potassium stayed largely inside the cells and was balanced by sodium outside the cells. If potassium was deficient, however, sodium entered the cells, taking with it so much water that many cells burst. The result was water retention (edema), damage to muscle and connective tissue, and scarring.

MORE ON SODIUM AND POTASSIUM

A diet of processed foods, even though supplemented with essential nutrients, produced deficiencies of potassium in humans. Such persons developed listlessness, fatigue, gas pains, constipation, insomnia, and low blood sugar. Muscles became soft and flabby; pulse weak, slow, irregular. These symptoms were suffered by millions of Americans, though it was difficult to imagine how such deficiencies could occur when potassium was supplied in all raw, natural foods. But people were now eating relatively few fruits and vegetables, the richest source. Moreover, when vegetables were soaked or boiled and the water discarded, the potassium was thrown away. And such medications as ACTH, cortisone, and diuretics caused potassium to be excreted in the urine, as did aspirin and many other drugs, including alcohol. Even excessive drinking of water tended to deplete the body's supply of potassium.

Whenever potassium in the cells was low, blood sugar also was low. Low blood sugar, or hypoglycemia, had become a major health problem in the United States, causing fatigue, irritability, and foggy thinking. Low blood sugar caused still more potassium to be excreted in the urine. Then the eating of high-sodium foods resulted in both blood potassium decreasing and blood sugar dropping, bringing a feeling of exhaustion.

Since lack of potassium allowed sodium and water to pass into the cells, increasing the potassium intake often corrected edema or water retention. Weight conscious American women, wishing to be quickly rid of every pound, begged physicians for "water pills," and 36 million prescriptions for such diuretics were now being written annually. Though the urine output was temporarily increased and pounds lost, the cells again retained water because of an even more serious lack of potassium. Blood sugar then dropped until exhaustion became unbearable. Dexedrine or other amphetemines were then used for a "pick up." These made nerves tense and sleep evasive, and prescriptions were then obtained for tranquilizers and sleeping tablets. Millions of American women were caught in this vicious circle.

SODIUM AND FATS

High blood pressure, usually caused by an excessive sodium intake, had also been produced in both animals and humans by diets deficient in potassium. High blood pressure also had been successfully treated by giving patients large amounts of potassium. The greatest harm done by potassium deficiency was probably its effect upon the heart. It had long been known that heart attacks were often associated with low blood potassium and a low potassium diet. In addition, experiments had shown that animals deficient in potassium suffered extensive degeneration of the heart muscles. It now appeared likely that a lack of potassium in the coronary muscles was the major cause of death from heart disease in humans. Certainly, from cradle on, the American intake of sodium was excessive while the intake of potassium was deficient. This imbalance was corrected by the Ecology Diet.

It was important to remember, however, that sodium, in proper balance with potassium, was essential to life and health. And the maintenance of this proper balance might require the adding of salt to the salads and salad dressings of the Ecology Diet. This salt should always be organic and never the inorganic salt most often found on grocery shelves. Powdered kelp was a good source of organic salt, while herb tea and soya sauce (The Calmer) taken before retiring at night was capable of quickly correcting any sodium deficiency. However, such a deficiency was rare in our society and likely to be experienced only by those individuals who engaged in prolonged and violent excercise in hot weather.

The Ecology Diet also was found to be self-regulatory as to the intake of fats and proteins. During the initial stages, usually when excess weight was being shed, the individual unconscious-ly limited his intake of fats as the body turned over its excess fat storage to the combustion process. But as weight began to stab-ilize, the person turned to more fat-containing foods, such as avocados, nuts, and vegetable oils.

PROTEINS, VITAMINS, AND MINERALS

Obtaining adequate protein on the Ecology Diet was never a problem, though many people suffered "protein deficiency fear" due to the propaganda put out on behalf of high protein diets. Usually these fears were allayed when they understood that any intake of protein in excess of 15% of the total calories re-quired that protein to be changed into carbohydrates before it could be utilized in the body. High protein diets simply placed additional strain on metabolism, using energy internally in order to separate nitrogen from excess protein and to elimi-nate it in the urine. Moreover, sinister connotations had been accorded excess protein in the diet by Dr. Edward Kelley who had cured himself of cancer by eating natural foods after having been abandoned as lost by the medical profession. Dr. Kelley's researches indicated that cancer was caused by faulty protein metabolism due to an excessive intake of pro-tein. Those who dined from nature's table had no difficulty obtaining just the right amount of protein simply by following their own tastes. What's more, they could eat as much and as often as they wished, without their diet going out of balance and without the danger of putting on weight. Leading sources of protein were food yeast, wheat germ, nuts, cereal grains, cheeses, milk.

It was reassuring to most people to realize that all the vit-amins and minerals essential to human nutrition were to be found abundantly in the Natural Food Diet. These vitamins and minerals are listed below with their chief sources.

Vitamin A: colored fruits and vegetables, eggs, cod-liver oil.

Vitamin B Complex: yeast, wheat germ, whole grain cereals, green leaf vegetables, milk.

Vitamin C: citrus fruits and juices, raw fruits and vege-tables.

Vitamin D: sun-irradiated vegetable oil, enriched milk, cod-liver oil.

Vitamin E: wheat germ, buckwheat, unrefined soy oil and other vegetable oils.

Vitamin K: produced by intestinal bacteria when diet adequate in unsaturated fatty acids; intestinal bacteria increased by taking acidopholus.

Unsaturated Fatty Acids: vegetable oils, such as safflower, soy, corn, cottonseed, as well as nuts and nut oils.

Bioflavonoids: citrus fruits, especially pulp and white of rind.

Phosphorus: fruits, vegetables, milk, cheese, bone meal.

Calcium: milk, cheese, yogurt, vegetables, bone meal.

Magnesium: fruits, cereal grains, vegetables.

Iron: yeast, wheat germ, cereal grains, eggs.

Iodine: powdered kelp and other seaweeds.

Potassium: fruits, vegetables, nuts, cereal grains.

Trace minerals: leafy green vegetables.

ALCOHOL AND DRUGS

One of the more remarkable results of the Ecology Diet was the drastic reduction in the consumption of alcohol by those who followed it, a large number of adherents giving up alcohol altogether and the remainder preferring only occasional wines. This result was right in line with the reports of Dr. Roger J. Williams, a professor at the University of Texas, who had shown that the desire to drink could be caused by nutritional deficiencies. The gist of the experiments he reported was as follows:

Large numbers of rats were given their choice of four beverages: 100% water, 3% alcohol, 10% alcohol, and 50% alcohol. Each rat was kept in a separate cage, and its liquid consumption measured daily. All the animals were given the same "normal" diet. Some rats became teetotalers while others became drunkards. Then the teetotalers were put on an inadequate diet and the drunkards were given a superior diet. Before long, the teetotalers started drinking, many becoming drunkards, while the drunkards drank less and less, many becoming teetotalers. Dr. Williams also told of the dozens of persons who had written him of their success in giving up alcohol after improving their nutrition.

The desire for alcohol was apparently an almost inevitable accompaniment of a meat-and-potatoes diet, for this excessively

Time intake tended to produce a low blood sugar which the victim sought to counter by taking in alcohol which could be quickly converted to glucose. The Ecology Diet, high in quick energy, kept blood sugar at normal levels and therefore reduced the desire not only for alcohol, but for candies, ice cream, cakes, pies, even for coffee.

In addition, those who followed the Ecology Diet for any length of time generally gave up drugs altogether, simply because they did not choose to tamper with the feeling of well-being which was constantly theirs. Moreover, the "highs" associated with meditation and the performance of the exercises was sufficiently mind-expanding for most, and those who sought more pushed their consciousnesses higher with the gentle nudges of ginseng and musk.

WHY GINSENG AND MUSK ARE APHRODISIACS

Of the two, musk was the more powerful and also the more expensive, an ounce retailing for as much as one hundred dollars. Tibetan musk, used by the lamas to elevate consciousness, was the most desirable. A half ounce might last as long as a year, for only two grains on a moistened fingertip and then placed on the tongue was sufficient to cause the mind to become exceptionally sharp and clear. Red ginseng root from Korea, though not as powerful as musk, had comparable effects, and was considerably less expensive, retailing for about twelve dollars per ounce. A piece of ginseng placed at the side of the mouth under the tongue also produced a clear-headed effect, though not to the same degree as musk. Heads of state throughout the centuries had been known to use both musk and ginseng when difficult decisions had to be made. The energy of both, however, could be directed wherever the consciousness desired, and if directed to the lower chakras caused the person to dissipate his energies in sexual indulgence and gormandizing. As a result, both substances had established reputations as aphrodisiacs, but this was so only when attention was focused on the lower chakras. Musk was obtained from the male musk deer and was carried by pharmaceutical houses, while ginseng was obtained from the root of the ginseng plant and was carried by herb supply houses.

Those whose attention was taken by aphrodisiacs found interest in the fact that scientists had studied the vitamin C content of the pituitary gland before and after male rabbits were bred. When the diet lacked vitamin C the animals did not care to breed. If the diet was adequate, the pituitary was saturated with vitamin C before breeding but depleted of the vitamin afterwards. Raw fruits and vegetables are the richest souce of vitamin C obtainable.

Through a sea captain friend of mine, I learned of an old Chinese, operator of a herb supply house in Vancouver, Canada, who when a boy used to hunt ginseng with a bow and arrow. The plant itself could not be seen in the daytime, since it was found only in the deepest part of the forest and during the day withdrew into the underbrush. At night, however, it emerged from hiding and its flowers blossomed, becoming flourescent in the dark. The old Chinese, a boy then, used to go with his father in the dark of the moon on ginseng hunting trips, armed with a bow and arrow. When the flourescent flowers were seen in the darkness, an arrow was fired at them, but no approach was made to the plant, for the underbrush might be hiding poisonous snakes or predators. In the morning, however, the boy and his father would again enter the woods and find their arrows. At each spot, they would dig, eventually uncovering the ginseng roots and bearing their prizes home and to market.

NUTRITION AND ECOLOGY

Though a number of people came into ecology because they desired to lose weight, they were advised at the outset to throw away the bathroom scales and stop counting calories and concentrate on building good health through proper nutrition. The weight loss eventually would take care ot itself and excess pounds would stay off permanently, just as smoking and drinking would cease as well as the habit of taking pills and drugs. All that was required was undertaking the Ecology Diet, biofeedback training, and the doing of the exercises of ecology.

If America, as it now appeared, far from being the "best fed nation on earth," was actually one of the worst fed and perhaps the most expensively to boot — since the cost of its hospital and medical care might reasonably be added to the costs of its processed foods — what could be done about it? First thing was not to buy and consume foods that endangered one's health. This economic boycott sooner or later would have the effect of putting into the markets the kinds of foods that were health-giving and nutritious. No doubt the processed food industry would resist this change, since it was bound to influence profit pictures for awhile, but if consumer demand remained unyielding, the change would be made, for no one continued to produce what he could not sell. It was important, however, that each person determine for himself the facts of human nutrition, for where somebody's pocketbook was involved it would be naive to expect that he would always adhere to the truth.

Other problems intrinsic to proper nutrition were those involving soil conservation and the use of pesticides in the spraying of crops. These mainly revolved under the broader heading of ecology — the relation of man with his environment. It had long been known that all living things existed by means of symbiosis, which was to say that they had an interdependence in the cycling of life energy, and if this cycle was interrupted at one point that interruption must sooner or later affect every living organism on the planet. Therefore the balance of nature was crucial for the continued welfare of man. Lately, industrialism and over-population had been literally destroying the environment, polluting streams and oceans and atmosphere with residues that not only were exterminating many forms of life but were producing monstrous mutations in others. Such heedlessness could not continue much longer without a great human crisis, and everywhere alert and concerned people were banding together to do something about the problem.

Interestingly, there were now many hundreds of young people returning to the soil all over America. They were growing their own foods without chemical fertilizers or poisonous sprays. They were setting out orchards. Many raised goats and cows for raw milk, and chickens to supply fertile eggs. Usually their only sweets were honey, maple syrup, and unrefined molasses. Their cakes were made of whole-wheat flour, nuts, grated carrots, and honey. They were refreshingly healthy, clear-eyed and happy.

THE HEALTH FOOD MOVEMENT

In college dormitories, too, young people were refusing to eat the foods served in the cafeterias and were preparing their own menus in their rooms. There, they served up eggs, milk, natural cheese, soy beans, celery, bell peppers, green onions, cracked oats, applesauce, and cottage cheese. Organic gardens on campus supplied radishes, lettuce, carrots and chard. Breads of soy flour and stone ground wheat were served fresh from the oven. Dessert was fresh oranges, bananas, apples, served with sunflower seeds, nuts, and wheat germ. Honey, milk, and yogurt were consumed in large quantities. Contrast this with the menus served in the cafeterias: Meat balls with white rice; chicken fried in hydrogenated fat; mashed potatoes, white bread, white rolls, white-flour muffins, sweetened gelatin, cornstarch pudding, chiffon pies, and huge quantities of coffee and soft drinks.

Increasingly, there was springing up around America a type of eating place known as the "health food restaurant," where one could obtain raw food dishes of organically grown fruits, vegetables, cereal grains and nuts. Such restaurants offered cooked dishes as well, and though the menu was meatless in most cases, sufficient variety was provided to tempt the palate of the most discerning gourmet. But even with the growth of the healthfood industry and the advent of the healthfood restaurant, it was still difficult to obtain a nutritional meal in most cities of our nation. For that reason, it behooved the health-minded person to be well supplied with nutritional supplements when he traveled extensively. These included natural vitamin and mineral compounds, and could be taken with an apple, orange, or banana after your zealous hostess had cheerfully poisoned you at dinner. No need to offend her. But unlike Socrates, carry your antidote.

ECOLOGY

Philosophy, Psychology, and Ethic

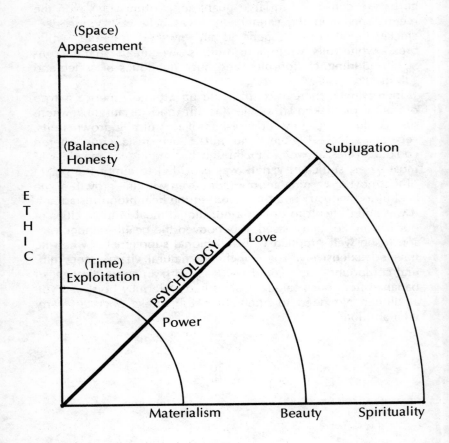

PHILOSOPHY

Psychic Power 13

In 1945, Jose Silva, a Texas parapsychologist, began training people to control their alpha brainwaves, hoping that they would be able to increase their I. Q.'s. Not only were they able to increase their intelligence, but amazingly, many began to develop psychic ability. Lately, confirmation of this power of the human mind had begun to come out of Russia.

In their book, *Psychic Discoveries Behind the Iron Curtain*, Sheila Ostrander and Lynn Shroeder told of Russia's concentration on the discovery of a new energy in man and the revolutionary effect it is likely to exert on us all. This "psi force," which the Russians called "bioplasmic energy," had striking similarities to the Orgone Energy of Wilhelm Reich.

THE CARRIER WAVE
OF PSYCHIC POWER

That this power had been known about for hundreds of years was apparent from a brief glance at history. It was the Prana of the Chinese, the Mana of the Hunas, the Solar Energy of the Yogis, the Munis of Paracelsus, the Animal Magnetism of Mesmer, the Etheric Force of the Radiathesiasts, and the psychosomatics of medicine. It was a power different than electricity and electro-magnetism, a power antagonistic to but complimentary to nuclear energy. It was life force, the bio-energy that animated all living things, the carrier wave of psychic power.

"Human society today is faced with the dilemma of a breakdown or a breakthrough in human consciousness," wrote Dr. Shafica Karagulla, and indeed I suspected when I first perceived that the alpha brain rhythm was the door to the subconscious that I would soon become involved in a world of startling dimensions. The door to that world now swung wide open, and I walked within, propping it open and casting an anchor outside so I could pull myself back if the going got rough. So it was that I awoke one night from a deep sleep, and the man in the violet jacket was standing at the foot of my bed.

It was one thing to run into him on a pier or walking a fence at midnight or to dream about him, but to have him standing there in the dim light of my bedroom, as composed as if he had dropped in for tea, was almost too much for me, and at first I was frightened and irritated. Then it came to me that he must be existing in another dimension, a dimension that somehow was in my mind.

"It is no accident that your initials are U.S.A.," he said.

"My parents were Norwegians," I answered. They chose my initials in honor of their new homeland."

"So *they* thought. But *you* chose your parents. Don't you remember?"

A PRACTICE IN BLACK LIGHT

The memory floated through my mind, a feeling of space and soft light, and a ceiling and low conversation and kerosene lamps, and a vague sense of a liquid enclosure, and I could hear my name being spoken. "Uell Stanley," said my mother, and her voice was youthful and girlish. "I like it," she laughed. I entered the liquid enclosure.

"Yes, I remember," I answered.

"Good," said the man in the violet jacket. "Now it is time." He tapped his stick on the floor, and I floated up to the ceiling. "Practice in black light," he said, "I'll drop in on you later." He disappeared and left me hanging near the ceiling. As if that weren't enough, I looked down on the bed and saw my body lying there.

There are moments in every life when the mind is bombarded with new information that literally transforms its nature. Such moments bring one close to madness. The brink is reached, the chasm gazed down upon, one teeters on the edge of engulfment. Now panic seized me, and I was overtaken with the feeling that I couldn't get my breath and would smother. But this is only a dream, I thought. Surely it can't be real. But there I lay on the bed below, a stranger to myself. Recalling the anchor outside the door of my subconscious, I heaved on the rope and tugged myself back. As a piece of elastic might snap into place, I re-entered my body. Then I woke up.

I'd heard of a man hunting in the wilds of Canada, who one moment was stalking a moose and the next found himself crouched on the street of a city thirty miles away, gun in hand and still in his hunting clothes. The experience so unnerved him that he wound up in a mental hospital, and everyone thought he'd imagined it. As I turned on the light and climbed out of bed, I could feel my heart thumping in my chest and cold sweat broke out on my forehead. I'd had realistic dreams before, but never anything to approach this. And was it a dream, after all? Wasn't it possible that there was another dimension of consciousness which might seem like dreaming but would actually be dealing with a reality equal to the physical world? Everything I had learned about Space and Time urged me to accept this hypothesis. Nevertheless, I sat up all night in the living room, every light in the place turned on, because I wasn't yet ready for another visit from the man in the violet jacket.

THE ASTRAL BODY

Next day, almost inexplicably, I found myself outside a psychedelic shop where I purchased a black light. This I dutifully installed in my bedroom, reflecting on the fact that ultra-violet was at the Space end of the spectrum and according to yoga theory marked the entry of cosmic consciousness into the pineal gland. This seemed particularly reassuring, especially since I knew that if I explained to anyone what I was up to alarms would be sent for butterfly nets and a paddy wagon. Yet, all I was trying to learn was astral travel, and people had been reporting that for centuries. They were even reporting it at ecologist meetings. At first I thought they'd been imagining it, but now I suspected they were onto something.

Existence of the astral body had been detailed by Helena Petrovna Blavatsky, the founder of Theosophy, in her books, *The Secret Doctrine* and *Isis Unveiled*. This body, she maintained, had a separate existence from the physical body, though its form was identical. Physical and astral bodies were ordinarily fused, though the presence of the astral body could be detected by its aura — colored lights extending a few inches to a few feet away from the edges of the physical body and invisible to the ordinary eye. In certain mental states, the astral body could separate itself from the physical body and float freely in the air, visiting wherever it chose, finding no obstruction in space or time or solid walls. The existence of the astral body had recently been confirmed by a new method of photography developed in Russia.

Semyon Kirilian, a Krasnodar electrician, had developed a method of photographing high frequency electrical fields through the use of an oscillator that generated 75,000 to 200,000 oscillations per second. Any living form, plant or animal, when placed in this high frequency field and photographed, showed an energy body that was an exact duplicate of its physical body. Startlingly, the human body looked like a celestial galaxy, revealing stars, planets, suns, novae. It housed an intense, dynamic energy.

DISCOVERY OF THE ENERGY BODY

Kirilian discovered that the physical body was an exact duplication of this energy body, that disease and malfunction could be diagnosed by observing areas of reduced activity in the energy body. Implications were overwhelming. The physical body appeared to mirror whatever was happening in the energy body. Illness, emotion, states of mind, thoughts, fatigue, all derived from the pattern of energy which circulated through the physical body. Soviet scientists maintained that a new energy had been discovered. The Pathology-Physiology Department of the First Moscow Medical Institute reported, "Kirilian photography can be used for early diagnosis of disease, including cancer." All living things — plants, animals and humans — not only had a physical body made of atoms and molecules, but also a counterpart body of energy. The Russians called it, "The Biological Plasma Body."

Scientists at Kazakh State University discovered that breathed oxygen converted surplus electrons and a certain quantum of energy into the energy body. In the silent, high-frequency discharge, they could actually see this process occurring. Different colors also had an impact on the bioplasma, changing its activity and calling forth different oscillations.

Was the energy body of science the astral body of mysticism? The Soviets now turned their attention to studying yogis who claimed to do out-of-the-body travel. In the United States, Dr. Charles Tart of the University of Southern California also began to test astral travel. Altogether, I was in good company, and my black light charade in the bedroom began to seem a little more respectable.

HOW THE ENERGY BODY FUNCTIONS

The discovery of an unknown energy circulating in the body provided clues to a sensible explanation of supernormal phenomena from telepathy to psychic healing. Photographing psychic healers at work, Kirilian saw streams of bright energy cascading from the bioplasmic body of the healer to that of the patient. This transfer of energy eventually reflected on the physical plane and caused a healing. This discovery opened up approaches to healing by balancing the energies of the bioplasmic body with negative ions, electromagnetic pulses, or oscillating magnetic fields. The diagnostic aid provided by Kirilian photography could revolutionize the practice of medicine.

Though it had been known for some time that an atmosphere charged with negative ions had a rejuvenating effect on life, while an atmosphere charged with positive ions had a debilitating effect, such effects were observable for the first time by Kirilian photography. The energy body, being positively charged, was fed by negative ions. In such an atmosphere, it flamed brightly, but when the atmosphere was charged with positive ions, the fires of the energy body grew opaque and cloudy, and the person suffered drowsiness, headaches and nervous exhaustion.

Ancient yin-yang philosphers developed a healing system called acupuncture which involved the insertion of needles into intersection points where vital energy flowed through the body. This energy could be tapped at seven hundred places on the surface of the skin, correcting imbalances and curing or preventing disease. The ancient acupuncturist was primarily charged with prevention, and his patients paid him to keep them well. If they became ill, he paid them. He diagnosed oncoming illnesses by finding imbalances in the body, and performed acupuncture to prevent these imbalances from manifesting. His credo was, "The superior physician cures his patient before the onset of disease, while the inferior physician cures him afterwards."

Nowadays, through a device called the tobiscope, an offspring of Kirilian photography, the Soviets have located acupuncture points on the surface of the skin that are less than 1/10 millimeter in diameter. The device was exhibited at Expo 67 in Montreal.

THE PSYCHOTRONIC GENERATOR

Even more intriguing was the psychotronic generator of Robert Pavlita, a Czech businessman. Pavlita's generators accumulated psychic energy from persons who stared at them or moved their hands over them. Afterwards, they carried out work. When the energy of the generator was directed at the seeds of plants, those plants turned out to be twice the size of ordinary ones. Pavlita's generators seemed to prove that it was possible to transfer energy from living bodies to nonliving matter, and then utilize it for work. The Orgone Energy Accumulators of Wilhelm Reich had charted the way.

Czech scientists even constructed a "telepathic" psychotronic generator with a rotating pointer atop and ESP cards underneath. From another room a person sent telepathic images of another set of cards. The generator acted as the "receiver." The sender shuffled the cards and turned one face up, concentrating on the pattern. In the next room, the generator pointed to a similar card. As the sender moved through the deck, the telepathic generator continued its "guesses." How many were right? 100%. It never made a mistake.

Russia's Nelya Mikhailova confounded investigators by moving things with "mind power." Concentrating on objects before her and subjecting herself to some tremendous inner strain that moved her pulse up to 250 heartbeats per minute, Mikhailova exerted some unseen force on the objects and they began to spin. During the initial phase of these experiments, EEG recordings showed tremendous activity in the region of her brain controlling sight. Most people generated only three times more electrical voltage from the back of the brain than the front, but Mikhailova generated fifty times more. When the objects before her started to move, the magnetic field around her began to pulse, as if somehow she had caused her energy body to vibrate.

THE ENERGY OF TIME

Every area of the occult was now an object of respectable investigation in scientific laboratories, and increasingly it was determined that the most awesome world of all was that which lay hidden within the nature of man himself. Even the basic concepts of Space and Time fundamental to physics and mathematics seemed likely to be shaken by this investigation of the occult. Nikolai Kozyrev is reported to have stated, "Time is a form of energy. It is to time's source that we must look to find the source that maintains the phenomenon of life in the world." Indeed, metaphysical concepts seemed likely to prove exceedingly useful to the physics of the future as it became increasingly clear that Time was simply a function of the constriction of Space and that a cosmic consciousness which occupied all Space would obliterate Time in an eternal Now.

Meanwhile, more and more people were entering the psychic world by means of ecology. There were cases of telepathy, clairvoyance, and mental healing, so in order to come to a better understanding of the brainwave mechanics involved, the alpha meter was brought into play. First experiments were conducted in adjoining rooms, using a deck of ESP cards. Receivers and senders were selected from among those who had reported "psi" experiences and who had good control of their alpha rhythms. A first, results were discouraging, showing little if any divergence from what might be expected of the law of averages, but one evening there was a breakthrough and the manner in which it came about proved again the fundamental truth of the philosphy of balance.

It happened in the home of a friend on the Southern California coast on a rainy evening in the fall of the year and provided deep insight into the functioning of the subconscious. We had set up the telepathy experiment as usual, sender and receiver in separate rooms, each attached to an alpha meter, and we had proceeded through the tedium of recording each card against time. Both receiver and sender had produced beautiful trains of alpha, but when results were correlated at the end of the first test, there was the customary adherence to the law of averages. At that point, Jonas, whose home we were in, suggested that he put both receiver and sender under hypnosis to see if results would improve. Both were willing, so it was agreed.

BREAKTHROUGH IN
TELEPATHY

Jonas was a skilled hypnotist, and both of his subjects had been hypnotized before, so within half an hour he had induced a profound trance in each. Instead of alpha rhythms, both began producing long trains of theta. The sender then was given the suggestion that he would be able to open his eyes without breaking his trance, and the experiment began. Halfway through the run, notes were compared, but results again were disappointing, not significantly different than in previous tests. Then an accident happened, one of those freakish things that so often determines the course of events.

Jonas had left the receiving subject alone in the room, and when he returned it was to find that a clock radio accidently had been turned on by its alarm. The resulting music had brought the subject out of his trance, but he was nicely relaxed and producing long trains of alpha. Seeing this, Jonas decided to proceed with the remainder of the test without rehypnotizing him. Twenty-five more cards were transmitted by the sender, and of this number, the receiver correctly named twenty-three.

This result stunned us all. We finally managed to gather our wits and make another run of twenty-five cards. This time twenty-one were named correctly. Another run was attempted. Nineteen were named correctly. Of seventy-five cards, sixty-three had been correctly named! The odds against such an occurrence were astronomical. Apparently, when the sender was in theta and the receiver in alpha a channel for thought transference was established. We might have suspected it. Theta denoted aggressive activity on the part of the subconscious mind, as it generated the picture. Alpha denoted passivity on the part of the conscious mind, as it was kept from interferring with reception.

Subsequent tests provided verification, though we seldom were able to produce such excellent results as we achieved that first evening. The percentage of successes remained far above chance, however, so we knew we were dealing with a law. Nevertheless, a number of us knew about the "telepathic" psychotronic generator, so we knew that perfection was possible. Later, it was demonstrated that the misses were due to human error, just as a skilled athlete will not always deliver his top performance.

THE GATES OF HORN

This alpha-theta telepathic relationship led to one of the most beneficial aspects of ecology, for it was soon discovered that prolonged chanting caused the emission of theta rhythms. With this knowledge, a number of people began experimenting with thought transference while chanting. These experiments were mainly successful, but it was soon realized that they were mere games compared to what could be done. It proved possible to heal others at a distance, to achieve goals, and to turn conditions of lack into abundance, simply by keeping the desired objective in mind while chanting. Not only the individual's power seemed directed toward his objectives, but the power of the group as well.

It now could be seen that the bio-energetics of ecology was the power known as love. It was psychic energy. It was admitted into the body by means of the pineal gland, and its healing, nourishing, and sustaining force was directed onto whatever occupied consciousness. Many people reported that this power was projected from their eyes, like rays of energy, so that whatever they directed their gaze upon prospered and grew. Nor was it necessary for a person to use the power for his own purposes. Just the mere fact that it was flowing through him seemed sufficient to give him health, happiness, and prosperity. By blessing others, he blessed himself, proving again the truth of Jesus' statement that it is more blessed to give than to receive.

Now that the Gates of Horn (door to the subconscious) had been opened, powers that formerly seemed magical could be recognized as universal laws. The subconscious was apparently not individual, but rather cosmic — a mind that occupied all space. Since every living thing shared this mind, an understanding of how it worked and the manner in which it was activated gave the individual the powers of a magician. Not only was he enabled to transcend Space and Time and achieve direction of events, he was also enabled to vastly expand his information storage and retrieval system by utilizing the full potential of his mind.

ACCELERATED LEARNING

Since the door to the subconscious is open in the alpha state, some of us began toying with the idea that information could be poured into it at that time, perhaps at a much higher rate than was ordinarily possible. The work of Dr. Georgi Lozanov of the Institute of Suggestology and Parapsychology in Sofia, Bulgaria seemed to bear this out. Dr. Lozanov believed he had created a teaching method that sped up learning fifty times, increased retention, and required little or no effort on the part of the student. He reported that hundreds of people from all levels of society had learned two-year language courses in as little as twenty days. Groups were even mastering courses in mathematics, physics, chemistry, and biology in a matter of weeks. Moreover, it appeared that Dr. Lozanov's teaching technique involved something akin to ecology methods. He described it as a kind of mind contact between teacher and student, based on yoga techniques.

An average class at his institute was composed of people from all walks of life. Lighting was dim, chairs comfortable, and students listened to soothing music, oblivious to the teacher. They had, in fact, been cautioned not to listen, but to concentrate entirely on the music and to relax, thinking of nothing. Meantime, the teacher repeated English words, idioms, and their translation.

Next day, students were surprised to discover that they could write and speak from 120 to 150 new words of French. Within a month, they had picked up a vocabulary of two or three thousand words. Tests a year later showed that this material had been retained.

How did it work? Dr. Lozanov's description seemed remarkably like the meditative state that produced alpha brain rhythms. Through relaxation, he said, the brain was relieved of its usual anxieties and stresses. Freed from unconscious defense mechanisms, "the growling dogs at the Gates of Horn," it suddenly resembled a sponge able to absorb all kinds of knowledge. This material didn't reach the memory in the ordinary way, since the student did not consciously participate in the process. It appeared to become part of a "cellular recall system" which was free of the usual searching techniques employed by the conscious mind in ordinary recall. In short, since the material had not passed through the conscious mind when acquired, it did not need to be dredged up by the conscious mind in order to be used. Recall became perfect.

SUPERMAN ABORNING

It had long been a premise of psychiatrists and brain researchers that the memory of man was perfect and only his recall was faulty. Hypnosis had revealed the ability of the mind to remember long-forgotten scenes in detail, complete as to scents, sounds, colors, and feelings. Electrical stimulation of portions of the brain had even produced a vivid reliving of past experience, revealing startling powers of memory and suggesting that only the means employed to use that memory — the filing system set up by the conscious mind and its method of searching those files — blocked man away from full use of his subconscious knowledge.

In a single session of only fifteen minutes Lozanov taught fifteen lessons from a French grammar book containing about five hundred new words. Afterwards, he gave a written test, then three days later another. All words had been perfectly retained.

Such experiments are bound to have enormous impact on modern educational methods. If learning actually can be speeded up fifty times, then it follows that a complete education, from grade school through Ph.D, could be taught within the space of one year. A person fully educated by this method would have in his mind and accessible for use 50 to the 20th power more information than today's Ph.D. Superman is aborning.

I myself conducted the first ecological experiment with accelerated learning. I wrote out a one-hour speech, approximately 5,000 words, and recorded it on tape. Then I spent fifteen minutes with the vibrator, relaxing both mind and body. Then I began to play two tape recordings, one of my speech, the other of soothing music. Focusing my attention on the music, I entered completely into it, so that the words of the speech faded into the background, becoming unintelligible. Next day, I gave the speech before two hundred people, word for word, just as I'd written it, without using a note and never once fumbling for the text.

THE POWER OF IMAGINATION

The speech just seemed to pour out of me with exactly the same inflections, phrasing, and timing as I'd put it on the tape. Such strong confirmation of the Lozanov experiments prompted me to immediately make available to others this system of accelerated learning. Everyone trying it reported a speed up in learning and an increase in recall, though it became òbvious that some people preferred supervised training rather than learning on their own.

The frontal lobes of man's brain are the seat of imagination. From an evolutionary standpoint, these frontal lobes were nature's last great achievement. Imagination, with its ability to form concepts, re-establish the relationship between cause and effect, and predict the future through envisioning its possibilities, already had produced the astonishing effect of man extending his image through the solar system like an incredible giant. From Mars to Venus his sense organs roamed — aluminum balls replete with antennas — and told him what was going on. In this manner, he one day might extend his intelligence through the whole universe.

Imagination was the tool that separated man from animal. It made him a thinker, a tool maker, master of his environment. It gave him the power to symbolize, to establish proxies inside his head for objects outside his head. These symbols could be words, figures, equations, images, but they always indicated an entire spectrum of interconnected meanings about the outside world. They were concepts. Man lived by them — indeed, must live by them, for he was an intellectual animal and no longer subject solely to the pain-pleasure, stimulus-response motivations of lower forms of life. He was aware, while other forms of life were somnolent. Lacking imagination, they could not reflect on their existence, could not grasp consciousness itself. Man was the being whose inner workings had been held up to a mirror, and that mirror was imagination. Within it, he saw his own reflection, thus was able to say "I," differentiate himself from "Thou," and wonder at the meaning of life. He was self-consciousness sprung into the universe, now rapidly growing, now constantly emerging, now increasingly mastering. It would be difficult at this point to place limitations on his destiny.

THE USES OF CONFLICT

But in order to use the imagination, one must accept uncertainty. He must face up to the stark facts of his existence in a universe about which little was known and whose gigantic forces were capable of crushing him like a gnat. He must ceaselessly explore, modify and re-arrange the symbols in his mind to better reflect the actuality of the world, always knowing that the best he could hope for was a partial grasp of reality. This required a cutting loose from all comforting illusions and reassuring credos. It necessitated that one fight down the temptation to do as others did, believe as others believed, and to escape into the somnolence of automatic behavior. It required a pushing off from safe shores into unknown seas with no assurance whatever that the ship of one's self wouldn't be capsized by storms. How difficult this is was easily illustrated by the fact the millions of people were panic-stricken when forced to face even one day of uncertainty. Yet the fault lay not with the people, but in the fact that they had been trained to make premature closure on every situation confronting them.

Learning was the ability to tolerate conflict at intellectual levels without becoming emotionally involved. If everything one considered either threatened or comforted him, he decided at once to accept comfort and deny threat. Accordingly, he made premature closure about everything. He did not think about it, but responded to it emotionally. Far from life being a puzzle which he sought to solve, its elements became things to embrace or run away from. Thus he reduced his brain to the same elementary functioning as performed by a pig's snout.

Conflict could be defined as that state produced when an individual was given a choice between two incompatible alternatives. Unthinking reaction quickly embraced what was assumed to be "good" and discarded what was assumed to be "bad." In this manner, it was freed to take immediate action but that action might prove woefully inadequate, since it had not been deliberated upon but had been made on the basis of previously-held concepts. It had learned nothing from the choice made, but had acted as if the situation confronting it were tantamount to a situation that confronted it before.

The ecologist never solved conflict by choosing one side or the other. He deliberated the possibilities and opted in favor of balance. When he chose to act, he did so on the basis of modified concepts, thus his action was geared to the present and more likely to be effective. Moreover, he did not abandon the conflict simply because he had acted. His action was tentative and carried within it all the possibilities inherent in the polarities. This was to say that he did not make either/or choices. He did not unequivocally say that one thing was good and the other was bad. He tolerated conflict and thus remained in possession of all possibilities. Unexpected occurrences did not floor him. He was adjusted to uncertainty, quite willing to change.

THE SECRET OF MAGIC

Imagination was inhibitive in nature and produced the delayed response, and this was so because its function was to adjust behavior. The human body might be regarded as a great muscular trap which in the absence of a brain would would immediately be sprung, and this was indicated in the phenomenon that occurred after death, rigor mortis, and in the seizure known as epilepsy. A relaxed muscle was an inhibited muscle and was being prevented from contraction by the brain. "Act, never think," was the rule of lower forms of life. "Act first, think later," was the rule of primitive man. "Think first, act later," had placed man's footprint among the stars.

Toleration of conflict and steadfast refusal to escape from it by acceptance of one of its polarities was the only way to become a thinker. For conflict to be widely regarded as some kind of mental disease was a pungent comment on our times. People in droves attended healers who asserted that the cause of problems was conflict and offered treatments for its removal.

Where such treatments succeeded, sterotypey was produced. Parents sought to abolish conflict in their children by laying out rules under which choices could be made automatically. Educational institutions carefully delineated right from wrong, thus permitting further automatic choice. Professions were carefully set up and isolated, thus allowing members to make choices by rules. Each extolled pridefully that he had accepted a "discipline" and thus had access to truth. What this discipline generally amounted to was dosing people with bad medicine via prescriptions in bad Latin so nobody knew the trouble he was getting into.

Wrote Palinurus, "Somehow then and without going mad, we must learn to reconcile fanaticism with serenity. Either one, taken alone, is diastrous, yet except through the integration of these two opposites there can be no great art and no profound happiness — and what else is worth having? For nothing can be accomplished without fanaticism, and without serenity, nothing can be enjoyed."

And William Blake, "I rest not from my great task to open the Eternal Worlds, to open the Immortal Eyes of Man inwards into the Worlds of Thought, into Eternity, ever-expanding into the bosom of God, the Human Imagination."

And Charles Cammel, "Miracles are performed by Imagination, and by nothing else. When visualization is absolute, the object visualized (imagined) is seen as clearly by the eye of vision as a material object is seen by the physical eye, and since seeing is believing, believing is seeing, and that is the power of magic."

THE GATES OF IVORY

In the black light of my bedroom, I faced my conflict between reality and imagination. As the letters, U.S.A., glowed in the dark, I placed myself in the alpha state, slowed my brain rhythm into the theta range and attempted to separate myself from my body. At first there was only inner strain, as my egoistic will was imposed on a power greater than I was. But gradually I relaxed and permitted my imagination to take over. One night, there occurred a powerful alteration of my consciousness, and lo, once again I was floating near the ceiling and observing my body on the bed. This time there was no sensation of fright, but rather an overwhelming sense of freedom.

I had had dreams of flying before, but this was different. Now

I had only to think about moving, and I began to move. But I was unstable and had difficulty keeping position, rolling over on my back like a clumsy bird. At last I was able to maneuver about the bedroom, but I didn't leave it. Quite simply, I was apprehensive about my body lying there unprotected. From then on, however, I engaged in this "astral flight" once or twice a week. As I became more accustomed, I ventured into other rooms of the apartment, and once or twice even traveled outside, right through the walls. Now I began looking forward to the return of the man in the violet jacket, for I sensed that I soon would undergo an even more unusual experience. Beyond Gates of Horn lay Gates of Ivory, the entry to higher consciousness.

The Brotherhood of Light

14

During the evening of July 4, 1776, in the old State House in Philadelphia, a group of men were gathered for the purpose of declaring the independence of the American Colonies from the British Commonwealth. It was a solemn moment as all present realized that their lives could be forfeited. Strong opposition sprang up and seemed about to win, when suddenly a new voice rang out. The debaters stopped and turned to look at a stranger. Who was this man who had suddenly appeared in their midst? They had never seen him before and none knew when he had entered, but his dignified form and commanding face fixed their attention. For half an hour, his voice ringing with zeal, the stranger stirred them to their souls. His closing words rang through the building, "God has given America to be free!"

Wild enthusiasm burst forth as he resumed his seat. Name upon name was placed upon parchment. The Declaration of Independence was signed. But where was the man who had launched the accomplishment of this immortal task — who had lifted for a moment the veil and revealed a part of the great purpose for which this new nation was conceived? He had disappeared, nor was he ever seen again or his identity established.

NEW ATLANTIS

The Great Seal of the United States, with its pyramid and phoenix (eagle), and its cryptic use of the number 13, is a treasurehouse of mystical symbols. Did the founders of the United States Government receive aid from some unknown group which helped them establish this country for a purpose realized only by an initiated few? Was the Great Seal a signature of this group, and the unfinished pyramid upon its reverse side a symbolic pledge to the task to which the United States government was dedicated from the day of its founding? Was Francis Bacon's New Atlantis the prophecy of a great civilization soon to rise on the American continent, a new nation, conceived in liberty and dedicated to the proposition that all men are created equal? Was there, in fact, a brotherhood of godlike beings who guided the destiny of mankind? To these questions I turned my attention.

The ancient Mystery Schools claimed to be guardians of a knowledge so profound as to be incomprehensible except to the wise and so powerful that it could only be revealed with safety to those who had consecrated their lives to the unselfish service of humanity. The initiates of these schools, realizing that nations come and go, that empires rise and fall, that golden ages of art, science, and idealism were succeeded by dark ages of superstition, went to great lengths to insure that their knowledge was preserved, engraving it upon the face of mountains and concealing it within colossal images. Secrets of chemistry and mathematics were hidden within mythologies or in the spans and arches of temples so that neither the vandalism of men nor the ruthlessness of the elements could completely efface them. Today, men gaze with awe at the Great Pyramid of Egypt, mute testimony to lost arts and sciences. Were the secrets of the Great Arcanum concealed there?

In Prague, Czech patent 91304 recently had been issued on a model of the Great Pyramid. This patent had found a commercial application — the sharpening of razor blades. Six-inch high pyramids made of styrofoam were sold to those who hoped to get more shaves for their money. The used blade was placed upon a two-inch pedestal, with its edges aligned north and south, then it was covered by the pyramid, the edges of which also were aligned north and south. A razor blade ordinarily good for five to ten shavings thus was made good for as many as two hundred.

PYRAMID POWER

How did it work? The inventors themselves were puzzled. However, it had long been known that leaving a razor on a window ledge in the light of a full moon would cause the blade to become dull. Polarized light had been given as the answer. Was the shape of the pyramid a means of concentrating unpolarized light? Was it in fact a temple to the sun? Nay, more than a temple, an actual generator of solar energy?

Indeed, a strange mummifying effect had been noted in the Great Pyramid. Small animals wandering into its passageways and dying gave off no odor of decay or signs of decomposition. They appeared to have been quickly mummified by some force resident within the pyramid, but just what this force was or how it operated was a mystery. Hermes Trismegistus, the founder of alchemy, had stated that the whole of the art concerned the secret relationship of the sun and the moon. His famed Emerald Table was of great antiquity and probably contemporary with the construction of the Great Pyramid. A translation of the table reads in part:

"It is true and to be depended upon that the superior agrees with the inferior and the inferior with the superior. As all things owe their existence to the will of one, so all things owe their origin to the one only. The Father of the one only is the sun, the mother is the moon. These powers ascend from the earth up to heaven, and descend again, newborn, on the earth, and the superior and the inferior are increased."

The Egyptians credited Hermes with being the author of all the arts and sciences. It was he who brought the secrets of Atlantis to preserve them from the castatrophe which he foresaw would soon come. Did he preserve them within the Great Pyramid? Plato stated that he was initiated there, and Plato spoke of Atlantis. Hermes was also thought the father of the healing arts. Hermetic healing used sound and color vibrations and careful diet to restore balance and harmony to the body. The historian, Herodotus, told of his amazement at finding that the only inscription on the Great Pyramid depicted the amount of onions, garlic, and radishes consumed by those who had built it. The onion was revered by the Egyptians because its rings and layers were felt to represent the concentric circles into which creation was divided. Radishes were a powerful agent in trans-cendental magic, and garlic warded off obsession and certain forms of insanity. Did Hermes make of the Great Pyramid a heal-ing center, a gigantic accumulator of life energy?

IN THE KING'S CHAMBER

Twice in this lifetime I had climbed those musty passageways and made my way into the Chamber of the King. The first time I was eighteen years old, the second nearly ten years older. Both times my experience had been the same. From the moment I entered the pyramid until I emerged two hours later, I was in an altered state of consciousness.

At the time, I had thought it was only my imagination, but now I know that my brain had been producing theta rhythms, because my consciousness had been occupied with imagery so vivid that I could have sworn it was real. Through the passage-ways and chambers passed the illumined of antiquity, enter-ing these portals as men and emerging as gods. Somewhere in the depths resided an unknown being robed in blue and gold and bearing the sevenfold key to Eternity. This was the Master of Masters, who never left the House of Wisdom and whom no man ever saw save he who passed through the Gates of Horn and the Gates of Ivory.

Who was this Master none might behold except those who had been "born again?" He alone knew the secret of the pyramid, but he had departed and the house was empty. Hymns of praise no longer echoed through the chambers. No more did neo-phytes receive the word from the lips of the Eternal One. Noth-ing remained but an empty shell — the outer symbol of an inner truth.

Profound mystery hung in the atmosphere of the King's Chamber. A peculiar cold cut to the marrow of my bones. Here, the candidate, after being crucified upon the cross of solstices and equinoxes was buried in a great coffer. That coffer, when struck, emitted a sound unlike any note of the musical scale. Now the candidate's soul soared into celestial realms, and he discovered the truth about life and light. Power to know his guardian spirit was given him, and the method of disentangling his body from his spirit, then there was revealed to him that secret name by which man and God are made consciously one. He then became a living pyramid himself. Within the chambers of his soul, other human beings might receive enlightenment.

THE MISSING CAPROCK

Dazed by the sunlight and sunk deep in thought I had departed the pyramid on those two occasions, once riding a camel, the second time in a jeep, but each time in the grip of such nostalgia that it was difficult to believe that time's veil had not been rent and I had been permitted a glimpse of the long-ago past. Yet in the end I chalked it up to imagination, for it seemed too far removed from "reality."

Now, more than twenty years later, I was beginning to perceive the existence of a grand design that would have been incomprehensible to me earlier. The secret science of man's spiritual development was hidden in broad daylight, concealed in arts and sciences over thousands of years and providing mute testimony to the existence of a brotherhood of enlightened beings charged with the spiritual development of mankind. Alchemy, astrology, mythology, drama, architecture, all told the story of a downward pushing force and an upward pulling force affixed to the spinal column of man and of the steps necessary to unite the two in the pineal gland and thereby achieve spiritual enlightenment. The missing caprock of the Great Pyramid had never been there in the first place. Its place was to be taken by the opened "third eye" of the initiate (the opened pineal gland), and so it was depicted on the reverse side of the Great Seal of the United States. A brotherhood of masters had thereby made it known that within this new nation, phoenix-like, the secret knowledge would rise again.

Osiris, the sun, and Isis, the moon; Isis the Virgin who gave birth to the sun, Osiris the Father who created the moon. "I, Isis,

231

am all that has been, that is, or ever shall be. No mortal man hath ever me unveiled." Space-Time in Egypt. Thirty-three vertebrae in the spinal column, thirty-three years in the life of Jesus, born at the winter solstice, crucified on the cross of Space-Time, rose from the dead at the spring equinox, twelve disciples, twelve signs of the Zodiac, twelve tribes of Israel, twelve labors of Hercules, twelve knights of the Roundtable. The Holy Grail. The Seige Perilous. Excalibur.

THE HIDDEN ARCANUM

Alchemy exoterically was the process of trasmuting base metals into gold. Esoterically it involved the transmutation of the ego into the gold of cosmic consciousness. Twenty-two steps in the alchemy process, 22 figures in the Bembine Tables of Isis, 22 Tarot cards in the Hebrew Quabbala, 22 letters in the Hebrew alphabet, and Moses was an initiate of the Pyramid Mysteries.

Astrology exoterically was the art of fortune-telling. Esoterically, it was the science of admitting solar energy into the pineal gland, and its seven planets were the seven chakras. Those chakras were also represented by the Seven Wonders of the Ancient World, beginning with the Great Pyramid (the coccyx), the Hanging Gardens of Babylon (the genitals), the Mausoleum at Halicarnassus (the abdomen), the Lighthouse at Alexandria (the heart), the Statue of Zeus at Olympia (the throat), the temple of Diana as Ephesus (the pituitary), and the Colossus of Rhodes (the pineal). The Great Brotherhood through the Master Masons of antiquity had depicted the whole science of spiritual development with the most imposing series of structures the world had ever known.

The anonymous author of Shakespeare's plays had concealed in cipher this process of ascension. Dante's Divine Comedy held the seven keys to purgatory and the seven keys to paradise. The Four Horsemen of the Apocalypse were the four elements of living matter. And the first three chapters of the Book of Genesis contained the whole story, of the two creative forces, the tree of the knowledge of good and evil, the tree of life, the two rivers and the one balancing them, vegetarianism, the fall from paradise and the flaming sword, all plain as could be in the most widely circulated book in the world, yet not one person in ten thousand understood it.

Everywhere my eye fell, the same story was revealed. The

path to salvation plainly awaited only the gaze of understanding, having been ingeniously concealed from the unready by an enlightened brotherhood of masters. Now the certain knowledge of previous lives swept over me and I knew that I had been invited into the Great Pyramid as a prospective initiate but had failed the trials, and that had given me a difficult karma. I had served the priestesses of the Temple of Diana, stood beneath the cross atop Mt. Calvary, fled the Inquisition and seen the fall of the Bastille, been present at the death and rebirth of the Great God Pan, suffered the rule of Agarthi and the rule of Shamballah. So many lives, so much blindness and pain, because I had refused to abandon my ego. But now I saw the significance of the "philosophic death" and prepared myself to undergo it.

THE PHILOSOPHIC DEATH

Thus I knew myself, and did not know myself and it was all very strange. I moved through fields of light and shadow, of form and formlessness, and had at once the sensation of great speed and utter immobility. I wondered at this, but was not distressed. I felt curiously free and unbounded, gloriously whole for the first time in my life. The sensation was so exquisite that I was afraid even to think, for fear the feeling might desert me.

A panorama of life seemed to pass before me — mountains, forests, seas, cities — and I had the uncanny sensation that I not only was the observer but the observed. Occasionally some object, a tree for instance, focused for a static moment in a new and revealing light, and I realized with a shock that I had never before known what a tree was. I scarcely had time to wonder at this realization before another object seized my attention and also was seen in this new light. Then a long view, mile upon mile of countryside, seemed drawn near as if by some optical illusion. I saw it all, the whole enormous expanse, and at the same time every blade of grass was vividly clear and so close that I might have touched it. My senses rocked with this dizzying change of perspective. My consciousness expanded and contracted in undulating waves. But it was not just the tree or the rock or the countryside. It was something more. I tried to remember but could not. Some trick was being played on me.

Now I seemed disembodied in everlasting space, moving and yet not moving in a void of unearthly silence. While there was silence, still there was sound, but the sound was not for the ears. I listened, but listening seemed to obliterate it. It only came when I was perfectly still and did not try, then ever so faintly, but clearly, as if from a great distance. At first I thought it was a chord of music, a marvellous chord, infinite in variety and meaning and containing more harmonies than I had ever known. It rose in crescendo, but nothing of its harmony was lost, and as it grew louder, I could hear each note of it, millions of notes, and they were not notes at all; they were voices. And in each voice was the chord and all of the chord, though each voice was only a part of it.

THE INSCRUTABLE ANSWER

Then I was enraptured by light. Myriad colors moved about me, clear but countless, each shading into the other so that even though they were separate they seemed to be the same. And each color had within it the properties of all other colors, even as the spectrum contained each hue in itself. I sought to give each a name but could not. There was no red, no blue, no green. Whatever each color, it was there only for an instant, then was something else, then was gone, and even what it had been and what it would be was not what it was. Knowing this gave me an aching feeling of aspiration, as if above all else I desired the truth.

I held this feeling to myself. Above all things, I must know, I thought. Then I was puzzled, for I could not remember who "I" was. I said the word to myself, but it meant nothing. I, I, I. Repetition failed to jog my memory. It was only a word and was meaningless. My elation left and I was quickly depressed, but almost as quickly recovered my spirits. If there was nobody to desire, there must be nothing to learn, so all things must be known. All things were known — the words moved me strangely. Were they understood by myself?

Self. What was self? It was a note in a chord and yet all of the chord and yet not even the note. That was it! Who am I? I asked myself and answered, I am all things. That seemed to make sense, but I was confused. Hadn't I always tried to be something? In that instant I began to lose my feeling of unity. A crack appeared, however slight, into the world of manifested things. I began to remember.

Faces moved about me now, and I was distressed, for though

I knew that in a manner they were part of myself, I saw that they were also separate. And each face held a different expression, of some secret and silent aspiration, and each face peered vainly into the reaches of space in search of an inscrutable answer. What do they seek out there? I wondered, and then I knew they sought their very selves. I smiled with gentle compassion. They had forgotten who they were. Their true being was obscured by their sense of separateness. They and I were one, and yet we seemed to be different. I felt something akin to love for them, but infinitely more. We were separate now, but someday we would be together. When? When we were united again with the infinite and everlasting and changeless, which always had been and had never begun and would never end. I existed in some suspended moment, where everything was contained within me, where past, present and future met and fused in me. The infinite and eternal were breaking through. The sequence of each event, great and small, was leading inevitably to a specific time which was yet no time and all time. Eternity was entering into the Now . . .

THE GREATER SELF

Gradually things were contracting, forming themselves, attaining shape and substance, and I was concious of a room and a voice and a sense of peace that came from softly spoken words, rising and falling. I thought that the voice was surely my own, though it seemed to come from outside me. Sometimes I seemed to be one speaker, sometimes the other, sometimes both, sometimes neither.

— To strive for personal ambitions is futile. One may alter the course of events, but it is only temporal. It has no ultimate meaning.

— For those who strive it has meaning. What folly is life if human aspiration has no reward?

— Rather, what folly life would be if each human aspiration were rewarded. Do you think what is going on here is not secure and safe in the hands of its Creator? He knows where he is going. He sees at once the beginning and the end and all of the events between. Shall a speck of dust alter his plan?

— Then why suffer? Why strive at all?

— He who suffers for his own petty ambitions has ordained his suffering. He has sold himself to the false self within him.

He has denied the infintely greater self which the Creator provides him.

— Then there are two selves?

— Within man is a rift, a separation of his true self and his false self, which creates a gulf between him and his Creator. Man can only be truly man when he becomes his true self, that which can be essentially one with God.

— Man must then strive to close this rift?

— Only separation causes striving. The more man attempts to find himself, the more tangled he becomes with his false self. He must surrender to God. In losing himself he finds himself.

— Then man is nothing?

— Nothing for what he is now — a vain creature seeking himself in that which has been created instead of in that which created him. But everything for what he will become — a creature united with his Creator.

THE DIVINE WILL

— How may this come about? After all, a man is only a man and must act according to his nature.

— A man is not only a man, and acts falsely on that basis. When he surrenders to his true self, then he begins to feel as God feels and no longer acts in the light of himself, but in the light of God instead, which is his true self.

— Man cannot be God, because he is man. This is undeniable.

— But God can be man, because He is God. Man is the link between God and the world, and God caused this, not man, and man cannot change it. To God the beginning and the end exist together, and the end is as sure as the beginning.

— Then man has nothing left to do with himself.

— What man considers man to be is an illusion. What God sees man to be is reality. If man insists on maintaining his false self, he has torn himself from reality and will follow this phantom to self-annihilation.

— But there are still ignorance and evil, and a man must struggle against them.

— Life increases its awareness through struggle. Although man is an undeniable part of life, he can only see truth when he turns within. Now the struggle is between the world and the spirit. To God, the victory of the spirit is certain, but to the individual man it is a matter of suffering.

— But you said there is no need to suffer.

— There is a suffering which is ultimately joy. This cannot be explained, only experienced.

— Still, what of right and wrong? Surely a man wronged is justified in revenge, to stand to battle for the right, to rise up and throw off an imposed yoke. Surely that is part of God's plan.

— You cannot change the world by taking arms against it. First, change yourself and you will see the truth of the world, and the world will be changed for you. When you throw yourself against manifested things, your eyes are closed to the truth about them. And when you hate and destroy, you destroy only yourself.

— But surely there is purpose in human plans?

— Those plans will seem different when you see yourself differently. Now you do not fully realize what part you play in the drama.

— How can you be sure?

— Because in a manner that you do not understand or are even yet aware of, I am you.

SEVEN RINGS TO ETERNAL LIGHT

"Phillip to Aristotle, Health: Know that I have a son. I render the gods many thanks; not so much for his birth, as that he was born in your time, for I hope that being educated and instructed by you, he will become worthy of us both and the kingdom which he shall inherit."

"Alexander to Aristotle, Health: You were wrong in publishing those branches of science hitherto not to be acquired except from oral instruction. In what shall I excel others if the more profound knowledge I gained from you be communicated to all? For my part I had rather surpass the majority of mankind in the sublimer branches of learning, then in the extent of power and dominion. Farewell."

"Aristotle to Alexander, Health: Though my discourses have now been communicated to the multitudes, none who has not heard me lecture upon them has yet divined their import. For the truth to be seen, it must first dwell in the eye of the beholder."

Spake Hermes: "O people of the earth, men born and made of the elements, but with the spirit of the Divine Man within you, rise from your sleep of ignorance! Be sober and thoughtful. Realize that your home is not in the earth but in the Light. Why have you delivered yourselves over unto death, having power to partake of immortality? Repent and change your minds. Depart from the dark light and forsake corruption forever. Prepare yourself to climb through the Seven Rings and to blend your souls with eternal Light."

So now I awaited another visit from the man in the violet jacket, armed with remembrance of the past, enabled to separate myself from my body, determined at last to escape the wheel of reincarnation and abide in the realms of immortality. How long I had yielded to the lure of opposites, pursuing first power, then serenity, never learning the secret of balance. That lesson was well-learned now. God willing, I would not again forget. When the time came as I knew it must that the man in the violet jacket again appeared and beckoned me forth from my body, I knew he would serve me as I had served him. I had only to tell him my wishes.

Not Shamballah, neither Agarthi, but rather Ultima Thule.

The Master Mind 15

He beckoned with his walking stick, and immediately we were transported into what appeared to be a subterranean cavern with hundreds of symbols hanging from the ceiling, like stalactites in the faint light. Numbers were there, and the letters of the English alphabet, and Roman numerals, and the Greek alphabet, and geometrical figures, and the signs of chemistry, mathematics, physics and astronomy and hieroglyphs and cuniform — a veritable maze of symbols — like the memory storage some master intelligence. I scarcely had time to contemplate these before I was drawn to a wall upon which was emblazoned three huge stripes of red, white and blue. As I approached, I could see that the white stripe was actually a luminous passage leading from the cave. Without a moment's hesitation I entered, and the man in the violet jacket followed me.

VISION IN A COSMIC MIRROR

We found ourselves in a crystal chamber. In the center was a golden chair with high arched back and elaborate scrollwork, and before it stood a full length mirror. The mirror was smoky and opaque, and dark clouds swirled upon its surface. The man in the violet jacket pointed to the chair, and I seated myself. Immediately, a tingling sensation passed through my body, and I felt myself grow light and luminous. The clouds within the mirror cleared, and I saw played out in rapid succession the many lives I had lived upon the earth. As I witnessed the repeated struggle and aspiration, it was as though I witnessed the struggle and aspiration of all mankind.

Finally, the man in the violet jacket led me from the crystal chamber into a garden where we took our seats in an arbor. I smelled the fresh odor of growing things and heard the songs of birds. On all sides mountains covered with vegetation reared their peaks into the air.

"Much that you have written and spoken consists of thoughts that I have given you," he said, "but you have been most difficult to reach because I have had to contest for your attention. From the first you were intended to be a reflection of me, and your initials were selected to aid you in the accomplishment of a particular mission, but the Forces of Imbalance did much to destroy my contact with you. They caused your fall from the building when you were sixteen, which impaired the functioning of your pineal gland, so that it was many years before I could reach you again. Meantime, they led you into a difficult karma. When you pledged allegiance to your high school sweetheart upon a family Bible, they smote her with a dread disease and caused you to abandon her. You must seek her out and ask her forgiveness. She will understand and release you from your karma. Much of it you have worked through already, else you would not be here.

"The turning point came when you hanged yourself. I myself caused this to happen. It was a risk that had to be taken. You had so closed your pineal gland with meat, liquor, cigarettes, and the low vibrations of egoistic concerns that it seemed hopeless to ever give you the full vision of your mission. It was I who cut the rope and took you from your body while you were unconscious and brought you before the Great Council where you were told what to do to open your pineal gland and re-establish psychic contact. You survived, and the experiment proved successful. Now that you have opened yourself as a channel for me to work through, I am pleased. My mission is a serious one.

THE SECRET DESTINY
OF AMERICA

"That mission is to preserve the constitutional freedoms of the United States of America as outlined in the Declaration of Independence, the Preamble to the Constitution and the Bill of Rights. Those freedoms are now in jeopardy due to a serious condition of imbalance that has crept into the American social structure. Man no longer lives in balance with himself, in balance with nature, in balance with his fellows, or even in balance with his Creator. Everywhere, there is a polarization which threatens to erupt into violence. Only a major effort to restore balance can avert destruction of the environment, degeneration of physical health, and the overthrow of the American government by a dictatorship of either the extreme left or the extreme right. Such occurrences would delay human evolution by thousands of years, for the psychic energies of the earth center in the United States, and no spiritual progress is possible without freedom.

"The immediate task is this: The widespread teaching of the laws of ecology and the techniques of mind expansion. To accomplish these ends, schools must be created. Eventually buildings to house them should be constructed in the shape of glistening white pyramids, for such structures reflect rays of condensed energy from their tips and provide easier access to the Master Mind, an electronic information storage system, known to your scientists as the plenum, which hovers above the surface of the earth and in which all the thought forms of humanity are stored. The Master Mind is linked to the information center of the solar system which is linked to the information center of the universe, and it is the mind that was in Jesus, Buddha, Mohammed, Lao Tzu, Krishna, Zoraster, Confucious, and Moses — the mind that inspired Einstein, Galileo, Michelangelo, Leonardo, Plato, Socrates, Archimedes, Hippocrates. When the human mind has expanded sufficiently to achieve full contact with the Master Mind, the person is able to transcend the death of the physical body and continues his ascension on higher planes of consciousness.

THE EXPANDING MIND

"You have made a good start in defining the forces of Space and Time and the means by which they arrive at balance. There is nothing in the universe, from mathematics to music, that is not readily understood when one has gained insight into the functioning of these two forces under the Law of Balance. That which is balanced evolves. That which is imbalanced devolves.

"Mind expansion is the principal means of teaching ecology. When the mind expands, the individual develops as much concern for others as for himself. This releases his psychic energy in the feeling known as love, and his expanded mind then relates perfectly to his environment and to other people. Thus he perceives directly the Laws of Balance.

"Ordinarily, the techniques of mind expansion should not include the use of drugs until competence in handling them has been demonstrated, though such organic substances as marijuana, mescaline, and peyote are relatively harmless and provide temporary access to the Master Mind by opening the pineal gland. Ideally, however, the body and nervous system should be purified and strengthened by mental and physical discipline in order to handle the influx of energy and intelligence from the Master Mind without damage. Far greater "highs" than those offered by the psychedelic drugs are possible to those who undertake alpha meter training, theta meter training, Ecology Yoga, and the Ecology Diet. Such "highs" are "crystal clear" and strengthen the whole organism. This is the true path to psychic power.

THE BIO-CHEMISTRY
OF PSYCHIC POWER

"There is a bio-chemistry of psychic power which your present program of nutrition serves well but may serve even better with deeper understanding. This bio-chemistry centers around the blood platelet, a tiny energy vesicle to which medical science currently ascribes the sole function of clotting the blood at the entrance to a wound. The blood platelet is capable of receiving a psychic energy charge, and when all blood platelets have received such a charge, the individual achieves direct contact with the Master Mind, and all of its intelligence and energy are accessible to him.

"The only way in which the blood platelet can receive a psychic energy charge is by passing through the pineal gland, but any constriction of the blood vessels closes this gland and prevents the blood platelets from entering. Fear, anxiety, and anger cause such constriction as do all Time foods. Only rarely in modern man is the pineal gland sufficiently open to permit charging of blood platelets, and these occasions are more than offset by his ingesting substances which immediately remove the psychic charges. Such foods are psychic poisons.

"The blood platelet has three poles, and when it passes through the pineal gland, the center pole receives a positive charge while the two side poles receive negative charges. Then, as the platelet circulates through the bloodstream, the positive pole picks up a negatively-charged particle while the two negative poles each pick up a positively-charged particle. At that point the platelet is fully charged.

"When all the blood platelets have been fully charged, the very next platelet to pass through the pineal gland receives a positive charge on all three poles, and the person achieves direct contact with the Master Mind. His psychic powers then rapidly develop.

THE PSYCHIC POISONS

"Foods which act as psychic poisons by removing psychic charges from the platelets are, in the order of their destructiveness: Pork, spinach, chocolate, refined sugar, bleached flour, alcohol, tobacco, and coffee.

"The pig blood platelet is charged exactly the opposite of the human platelet. It carries a negative charge on the center pole and positive charges on each of the side poles. Consequently, when pork, ham or bacon are ingested they set up a chain reaction in the blood stream, which removes the charges from every blood platelet. Even a perfectly functioning psychic organism would take twenty-seven days to recover.

"The iron in spinach cannot be assimilated by the human body due to the presence of oxalic acid. As a result, that iron accumulates in the digestive tract and withdraws charges from the blood platelets.

243

"Chocolate has a mirror-image platelet — one side is simply a reflection of the other. This causes each chocolate platelet to cancel out the charge on one blood platelet.

"Refined sugar, bleached flour, alcohol, tobacco and coffee place stress on the pancreas, liver, and adrenal glands, alternately filling the blood with insulin and adrenalin, and the resulting debris restricts the activities of the blood platelets and dislodges their psychic charges.

THE PSYCHIC ENERGIZERS

"Certain foods, taken in moderate amounts, aid the development of a perfectly-charged blood platelet system and therefore of psychic powers. They are kumquats, filberts, avocados, tomatoes, bananas, and nettle. Ginger, too, may be included, for it tends to remove positive charges from the body. A tiny pinch of ginger may be taken with herb tea or water several times a day. A teaspoon of ginger dissolved in a quart of water will withdraw positive charges from the environment and make the atmosphere of your home conducive to psychic contact with the Master Mind.

"Animal flesh and animal products are damaging to human health. This is due mostly to the fact that the human body has great difficulty metabolizing animal fats, and the resulting toxins are deposited in arteries, joints, and organs where they eventually cause disease, malfunction and death. Such foods, because of their low vibrations, also make higher levels of consciousness more difficult to attain.

"Anyone who exists on a diet free of animal flesh and animal products and the psychic poisons previously mentioned will establish contact with the Master Mind and develop psychic powers. He is cautioned, however, to keep up his physical strength by eating raw most of his fruits, nuts, cereal grains, and vegetables, for they are more nutritious when taken in this manner. For example, raw garlic and organic sulfur are excellent blood purifiers, cleansing the system of toxins. When man has learned to exist on a diet of natural foods, his longevity will double and he will be free of disease and senility. Such treatment as he may need will be performed on his energy body by practitioners of bio-energetics, a science which will replace the practice of medicine.

244

THE COMING NEW AGE

"There will be a general arrival of Christ Consciousness as more and more people establish contact with the Master Mind. Many of these people will be former inhabitants of Atlantis, the most advanced of earth's civilizations, and their consciousness will gradually permeate the institutions of men and radically alter the structure of life on earth. There will be a world government, and the nations of today will be states under this government. Instant communications and push-button voting will reduce the size of legislative and judicial bodies, and only the executive officers of the world government will be elected — all other offices will be filled by professionals after competitive examination. As the world government is modeled, so will the governments of nations, states, and cities be modeled, and most of the decision-making formerly done by politicians will be done by a highly sophisticated system of computers.

"The chief executive of the world government will seek the advice of a great council, a group of twelve men and women who have demonstrated superior contact with the Master Mind, and the advice of the great council will always be made public. The chief executive will be empowered to act on his own, but will be subject to immediate recall by the people.

"Money as a medium of exchange gradually will be discontinued, being replaced by a computerized system of debits and credits. Free enterprise will be maintained for small businesses, but large businesses will be socialized, and the profit motive will be replaced by the production and service motive.

"Education, too, will be radically altered, with emphasis shifting to health, science and awareness. Expanded minds will be able to assimilate the equivalent of today's college education in only a few weeks. Everyone will have at his fingertips all the information in the world through a telephone connection to a computerized world information center.

THE FORCES OF DARKNESS

"Even before all these changes take place, the planet will see the arrival of human beings from other inhabited planets in the galaxy. They already move among you in small numbers, but their presence will then be made known and they will act as guides to effect the peaceful transition to the New Age. Concerning this there is yet great difficulty, for there are powerful forces in this section of the galaxy which seek to keep the earth in darkness.

"These forces are concentrated in the star system of Deneb. Beings on the planets in this system look much like earth people, and indeed, everywhere that life evolves sufficiently to bear the human soul the body looks much the same. The Deneb system joined the revolt against the orderly process of ascension led by the brilliant but power-mad Lucifer. Lucifer was chief executive of 607 inhabited worlds in the galaxy, 37 of which joined him after he issued his manifesto of self — a proclamation of personal liberty and a rejection of allegiance to the Universal Father. Lucifer first enlisted the aid of his chief assistant, Satan, then issued his proclamation to all the inhabited worlds in the galaxy, stating that the Universal Father did not really exist and that physical gravity and space energy were sufficient to account for the workings of the universe. He denied that personality was a gift from the Universal Father and stated that it was merely an inevitable result of the forces of nature. He maintained that reverence was only ignorance and that men were their own masters.

THE MISSION OF MICHAEL

"Of the 37 worlds that joined the Luciferian Rebellion, six are in this section of the galaxy and five are planets in the star system of Deneb. The sixth is your earth. Caligastia, who had been assigned by the Corps of Melchizedeks to the post of Planetary Prince of your world, chose to join the rebellion on the promise that his authority from that day forth would be absolute. He was opposed at once by the Melchizedeks, but not before his teachings of unbridled liberty and self-assertion had every opportunity for deceiving the primitive people of a young and undeveloped world. Caligastia plunged the planet into darkness by severing its connection with the Master Mind. Gradually that darkness has been lifting due to the bestowal of Michael.

"Michael, divine son of the Universal Father, incarnated as Jesus of Nazareth and by his life illustrated the process of the ascension of consciousness from its seat at the base of the spine to its union with the Master Mind in the pineal gland. Unfortunately, the truth of his mission has been concealed by

Lucifer's Forces of Imbalance so as to keep the earth in darkness. A similar thing happened to the teachings of Moses. However, it is simple enough to recognize the forces of Lucifer. With them, all is a matter of hiding the truth, so they keep things in the dark. With the forces of the Universal Father, all is a matter of revealing the truth, so they bring things into the light. By their fruits, ye shall know them.

LUCIFER'S LAST STAND

"The beings on the five planets of Deneb are much more evolved than the people of earth. They have learned to live in imbalance with nature without destroying either themselves or nature. Great precision is needed to achieve this state, for that which is balanced ascends, while that which is imbalanced descends. Yet they have achieved such delicate control of their environment that they are able to prolong their lives indefinitely. They cannot, however, evolve further, and upon death each entity must incarnate in the lowest form of life and begin the process of spiritual evolution all over again. This decision they have made in full knowledge of the consequences, but since they only die from accidents and for the most part are able to control these, their decision to abandon the Ascension Schools and settle for what they have is at least understandable. They have beguiled many earth people into joining them by promises of power and immortality, and by this means they effecively control the planet. It is the Faustian bargain that we spoke of earlier.

"Now, however, the Deneb system is seriously threatened, for the veil of darkness that has surrounded the earth is gradually lifting, and if this planet decides in favor of ascension, the balance will so shift in the psychic energies of this section of the galaxy that the entire Deneb star system will be expelled and all the beings on it will perish. You can well imagine their efforts to prevent arrival of the light.

THE INTERPLANETARY
CONFEDERATION

"The galaxy is divided into twelve sectors, and in the sector occupied by your earth, there are 54 planets inhabited by beings who look much like earth people, ranging in size from two and a half feet in height to over eight feet. Forty-eight of these planets have maintained allegiance to the Universal Father and the principles of ascension, and they belong to a confederation which conducts interplanetary trade and cultural exchange. They are quite aware of the situation at Deneb and the predicament of the earth, and they help all they can. When the message of Michael was twisted to serve the ends of the Forces of Imbalance, visitors from the 48 planets began arriving on earth, and they spread psychedelic plants all over the globe. Of these, the hemp plant thrived the best, and despite all efforts to stamp it out is available to the people of every nation on earth. All such plants, when ingested, release the spasm of the pineal gland and allow contact with the Master Mind.

"Unquestionably, it would be safer for the emotional stability of the person if this contact with the Master Mind could be made through more orderly processes than the undisciplined use of psychedelics, but the dangers in such use are slight compared to what is at stake. For mankind must see the truth or be condemned to live forever in darkness."

The Master Self 16

H e had talked steadily for some time, with the penetrating gaze of his blue eyes hypnotically fixed on mine, and I could almost believe that I was he and he was I — that in the process of our communication we were somehow blending into each other. A gentle gust of wind stirred his dark hair, and from the distance came a sighing sound as if some force of nature was expressing deep contentment.

"Doubtless you are curious as to who I am," he said. "I am an Ascending Master of the 76th Degree, and before your visit is over you will know my identity. The 76th Degree is the highest level of consciousness possible before entering the Kingdom of Heaven, which is the power and intelligence center of the galaxy, and the Abode of Ascended Masters. I wait there now for the gates to open, which happens automatically every fifty-two thousand years. Michael of Nebadon, last known on earth as Jesus of Nazareth, waits there for me, as do many other masters, including all the founders of your earth's great religions. We could enter immediately if it were not for the fact that Lucifer's forces have placed at the gates a terrible being wielding a flaming sword. Such extraordinary circumstances have caused us to incarnate again and again, in hopes of defeating Lucifer, even though the danger is great of building up karma which would prevent our entering the Kingdom. We prefer however, to reflect a portion of ourselves onto other living entities, in hopes that they may grow into a likeness of ourselves. You have been chosen for such a reflection, and it is not the first time we have been so associated. Insofar as this association is successful, you will become me. Does that please or distress you?"

Wisdom and kindness peered from his clear blue eyes, and glory gathered in a halo around his head. "It pleases me," I answered.

THE STRONGEST STRUCTURE
IN THE UNIVERSE

"Then listen carefully," he said. "The universe has a center which is its Source, and it has a periphery which is that part of itself farthest away from the Source, and in general it is shaped like a sphere, but its structure follows the plan of the pyramid. At the tip of the pyramid is the Source — the Ultimate Being — the I AM consciousness referred to as God. The Source at rest is in a condition of perfect balance and is all light, all power, and all truth, but in order to better understand itself it deliberately produces in itself a condition of imbalance and thus becomes creative, descending from its absolute state and dividing into two opposing but complementary forces — Space and Time. Imbalanced, they descend into matter. Balanced, they ascend into Spirit.

"The Source descends into matter thusly. It first divides into two energy beings, and each of these has half of the Source's power and intelligence. These two energy beings in turn divide into four energy beings, and each of these has one fourth the power and intelligence of the Source. These four divide into eight; the eight divide into sixteen, the sixteen into thirty-two, the thirty-two into sixty-four, the sixty-four into one hundred twenty eight, and so on. By simply dividing itself one hundred times under this system of geometrical progression, the Source is able to create more than two zillion beings of which approximately one zillion are on the lowest level or farthest removed in magnitude and power. The outermost periphery is reached when another division is impossible due to insufficient energy, and at this point the process of ascension begins. Each fractionated being begins uniting with other fractionated beings, ascending along the levels of consciousness until finally only two magnificent beings — Space and Time — stand before the Golden Throne. These two then are brought into perfect balance, melding once again into the Source itself, and after a period of repose, the cycle begins over again.

THE ASCENDING MASTERS

"The Great Pyramid of Egypt was built to illustrate this structure of the universe, as was the Great Pyramid of Mexico and the Great Pyramid of Atlantis. The engineers of Atlantis built each of these pyramids by waterpower, using the force of gravity as the downstroke of a huge water pump, and the force of a fire-induced vacuum as the upstroke. Afterwards they were used as Temples of Initiation into the Cosmic Mysteries, though smaller pyramids, being waterpumps, were used for irrigation.

"The government of the United States was constructed as a model of the Pyramid Plan, and the significance of that plan is this: It is the strongest structure in the universe. By it the Source is able to communicate directly with the tiniest bit of energy and matter, because that tiniest bit of energy and matter is itself. Thus the entire universe is a gigantic cybernetics system with a Master Intelligence at the center. It is a system containing systems containing systems — a Master Mind that staggers the imagination. And all of that Master Mind is available to each human being, for the Master Mind is truly his own mind and one day he will realize it.

"You have already realized it, of course, and your progress henceforth will be rapid, even though the seven levels of human consciousness took you long to traverse this lifetime. Levels eight to thirteen are those of Ascending Teachers, and levels fourteen to seventy-six are those of Ascending Masters. I will be pleased to welcome you on the seventy-six level. It has been done before in a single lifetime, and as you saw in the Cosmic Mirror you were a highly-evolved Chinese monk 9000 years before the bestowal of Michael.

EVOLVING TOWARD THE MASTER SELF

"Each man then is evolving toward his Master Self along the consciousness-expanding structure of the Pyramid Plan and is guided by the Master Mind as long as he follows the Path of Balance. The Master Self is not a single type molded after a fixed pattern, for the law of the Master Mind is unity fulfilled in diversity, and therefore there is infinite diversity in the Master Self. As evolution proceeds, however, individual beings will ascend beyond the Master Self and reach the highest heights of the Master Mind — the unitarian self-realization which is the last and supreme state of Creation.

"The Master Self is the consummation of spiritual man, whose whole way of being, thinking, living, acting will be governed by the power of a vast universal spirituality. All his existence will be fused into oneness with his Master Self, and all his action will originate from and obey the law of this Self. Life will have to him the sense of conscious being, and he will feel the presence of the Master Self in every center of his body. He will live and act in complete joy of the spirit, in spontaneous sympathy with all the universe. All beings will be to him his own selves. All ways and powers of consciousness will be felt as the ways and powers of his own universality. His own life and the world life will be to him a work of art — the creation of a cosmic and spontaneous genius infallible in working out a multitudinous order. He will be in the world and of the world but will also exceed it and live in transcendence above it. He will be universal but free, individual but not limited by separate individuality.

THE PSYCHIC POWER OF THE MASTER SELF

"Thus man will so lighten and strengthen his physical body that he may live within it for several hundred years, and eventually will put a halt to the aging process and death itself as he learns to raise the vibrations of his body to higher planes of being. He will discover, isolate, and harness psychic energy — the most powerful energy in the universe. He will find this energy hidden in his own sexual nature and so will design ways of channeling his sex drive so as to increase his power and awareness. By means of psychic energy he will physically traverse the galaxy at speeds far exceeding light, and his vehicles will be modeled after the blood platelet which itself uses psychic energy and acts as a catalyst between matter and energy. With psychic energy under control, he will find himself master of Time as well as Space and will be able to journey both into the past and the future. He will free his consciousness from confinement in the body, go out in trance or sleep or even waking and enter into worlds or other regions of this world and act there or carry back his experience. He will come to feel his body as only a small part of himself, and he will begin to contain what before contained him, achieving cosmic consciousness and extending himself to be commensurate with the universe.

"He will begin to know inwardly and directly the forces at play in the world, feel their movement, distinguish their functioning and operate immediately upon them as the scientist operates upon physical forces. He will be able to accept their action and results or reject, change, create immense new powers and movements in place of the old small functionings of his nature. He will perceive the full working of the Master Mind and will know how his thoughts are created by its working, and he will separate within himself the truth and falsehood of his perceptions, enlarge their field, extend and illumine their significance, become master of his own mind and action and capable of shaping the movements of the Master Mind in the world around him. He will perceive the flow and surge of the universal life-forces, detect the origin and law of his feelings, be free to accept, reject, new-create, and rise to higher planes of life power. He will perceive the key to the enigma of matter, follow the interplay of consciousness upon it, discover its function, detect its last secret as a form not merely of energy but of involved and arrested consciousness, and he will begin to see the possibility of liberating that consciousness.

THE MEANING
OF THE MASTER SELF

"The Master Self consciousness will develop higher and higher degrees of world knowledge and completely transform life on the earth. To be or become something, to bring something into being will be the whole labor of man's existence. He will know that to become his Master Self is the thing to be done, and that to exceed his outer self is the mandate of his nature. To be in the being of all and to include all in his being, to be conscious of the consciousness of all, to be integrated with the universal force, to carry all action and experience in himself and feel it as his own action and experience, to feel all selves as his own self, to feel all delight as his own delight — these are the necessary conditions of the Master Self.

"The movement of going inward and living inward is a difficult task to lay upon the normal consciousness of the human being, yet there will be no other way for the Master Self. This turning inward will not be an imprisonment in personal self, but the first step towards a true universality, bringing man the truth of his external as well as the truth of his internal existence. There is a reality, a truth of all existence which is greater and more abiding than all its formations and manifestations. To find that truth and reality and live in it, to achieve the most perfect manifestation and formation possible of it, is the secret of human destiny. There is a being that is becoming — a reality of existence that is unrolling itself in Space and Time. What that being is, that secret reality, is what we have to become, and so to become is life's real meaning."

THE SEVEN CENTERS OF ASCENSION

This last statement hung on the air of the arbor as the man in the violet jacket raised his eyes and appeared to be listening. He sat in this manner for several minutes while I studied him closely. Try as I might, I could find no revealing marks of age. His skin, hair, figure, bearing — all betokened a vigorous man in his middle thirties. There was, however, an aura of other-worldliness about him — a magnetic quality exuded by some great but invisible power. As he sat there with his hands clasped atop his gold-headed walking stick, eyes fixed in the distance, there was in his manner a courtliness and precision that seemed truly royal.

At last he resumed speaking. "The earth is a living being and is fed by two energy rays that emanate from the center of the universe. These two rays are known as Shale and Hal and are equivalent to your understanding of the forces of Space and Time. They pass through the center of the galaxy and through the center of the solar system and give rise to seven ascension centers when they finally contact the earth. This is due primarily to seven warps in the earth's gravitational field, which are located at Stonehenge, England; Gizeh, Egypt; Peking, China; Tenri, Japan; Easter Island, South Pacific; Los Angeles, California; and Bimini in the Bahamas. Strong ascension forces are at work in each of these areas, which is to say that contact with the Master Mind is made easier in each of these locations. Such contact would be even easier if it were sought within the confines of a pyramid structure. The Great Pyramid of Egypt already exists in a proper location, and it can be activated by two simple devices. The first consists of a brass column four feet high and eighteen inches in diameter, topped by an eighteen inch glass sphere filled with water in which two ounces of ginger have been dissolved. This device will enhance the negative polarity of the pyramid by removing positive charges from the area, thus increasing the accessibility of the Master Mind. The second device is a capstone.

THE POWER DYNAMICS OF THE PYRAMID PLAN

"Of special importance is the building of pyramids at Tenri, Japan and Los Angeles, California. These two cities are at opposite ends of the huge San Andreas Fault which is precariously balanced and could be triggered into a gigantic cataclysm. Already tremors are being felt, for Los Angeles with its fleshpots and Japan with its materialism have become centers for the Forces of Imbalance. The construction of a pyramid in each of these areas, one that is dedicated to the ascension of consciousness, will do much to alleviate imbalance factors by making the Master Mind more accessible to people. Much threatening destruction can thus be averted. These pyramids need not be as large as the Great Pyramid of Egypt, but must not be less than eighty feet in height.

"The seven gravitational warps on the earth's surface are

used as navigational aids by beings from other planets who arrive in so-called "flying saucers," which are simply mechanical blood platelets. These are driven by psychic energy and control the forces of attraction and repulsion by setting up polarities. Before long man will learn that his own blood platelets may be directed outside of his body by his thought, traversing great distances in an instant, performing work there or securing information. The earth stands on the threshold of a great breakthrough in psychic power. All depends on overcoming the Forces of Imbalance.

"To teach the Laws of Balance I recommend that you use the Pyramid Plan. Under this plan, one becomes two and two become four and four become eight and eight become sixteen, and so on. Simply put the truth into the hands of two persons who each will put it in the hands of two persons who each will put it in the hands of two persons, and so on. The teaching of the truth will spread rapidly, for after only thirty-two such transactions everyone on earth will have had access to the truth and the New Age will be dawning.

THE FINAL TRIAL

"With the coming of the New Age, ecology will solve all the problems of racial inequity, war, drug abuse, poverty, disease, mental and emotional illness, crime, and violence. The age will be marked by the building of pyramids of light all over the earth as man increases his awareness and masters the Laws of Balance."

He stood up and smiled. "We are coming much closer, we two. Now I must leave you so that you may undergo the trials of the Master Game. Just remember that what is about to happen has happened before. You will then be guided in your choice." .

He beckoned and turned from the arbor. I followed him out of the garden to where a glistening white pyramid was fronted by a smaller stone structure exhibiting Grecian columns. There he opened a door carved with mystical figures, ushered me inside and closed the door behind me.

The Master Game 17

I found myself in what seemed to be a large art gallery. Many oil portraits hung on the walls, and no one was about. Lighting was soft and diffused, and originated in some unknown manner. A great hush hovered over the hall.

Around the walls of the gallery I made my way, looking upon the portraits of the great names of history and finding a biographical sketch by each. There were Jesus and Buddha and Krishna and Lao Tzu and Zoroaster and Confucious and Socrates and Plato and Aristotle and Alexander and Washington and Lincoln and Michelangelo and Galileo and Ghandi and Leonardo and many others. At last I came to a portrait that stopped me. It was the man in the violet jacket.

I was startled to learn the prominent part he had played in history and was deeply intrigued by the mystery that surrounded him. As I peered into those penetrating blue eyes, so brilliantly reproduced in the painting, I could feel my heart go out to this being who had become so instrumental in my life. Never had I admired anyone so deeply.

THE MAGIC THEATRE

A gust of air moved across my cheek, and I turned to see that a door had opened nearby. Moving to it, I peered into a room cluttered with various items of wearing apparel, like a huge wardrobe department.

I entered and found on closer examination that all the clothes were vintage pieces, though obviously in good repair. Finally, my attention was taken by a door with a sign upon it which stated in bold letters: ENTRANCE TO THE MAGIC THEATRE. NOW PLAYING — THE CARDINAL'S BALL. COME IN COSTUME. I could make out a buzz of conversation and the sound of music coming from beyond the door. Suddenly I was excited at the prospect of joining the festivities, and I immediately began searching the racks for an appropriate costume. What I finally settled for was a white lace shirt and cuffs, black swallow-tailed coat and black buckled shoes, black knickers and black hose. As I glanced at myself in the wardrobe mirror, I appeared to have stepped directly out of the pages of time. Satisfied, I entered the door of the Magic Theatre.

THE CARDINAL'S BALL

I found myself in a grand ballroom arranged with a dance floor in the center and a platform at the far end on which an orchestra was playing. Pillars were at the sides of the room with tables scattered among them, and a number of people were seated at the tables, while an equal number were on the ballroom floor, dancing. The ceiling was hung with crystal chandeliers ablaze with candles, and draperies and paintings covered the walls. Before me was a handsome man of middle years wearing the robes of a cardinal in the Roman Catholic Church. He was greeting guests, who addressed him as "Cardinal Rohan." Suddenly a lackey scurried up to him and whispered excitedly. The cardinal waved his hands at the orchestra, and the music stopped. A page announced in the sudden silence. "Her Majesty, Marie Antoinette, Queen of France!"

The queen entered the ballroom, pausing on the steps as her retinue gathered behind her. Gowned in purple, with a tiny diadem upon her blonde head, she looked the picture of loveliness.

She surveyed the assemblage coldly. Cardinal Rohan thrust his way forward and bowed before her. "A thousand pardons for my unpreparedness, Your Majesty. You do me great honor."

"Where do I sit, Rohan?" she asked icily.

The cardinal turned and shouted, "Clear the bandstand for the queen! Set a chair of honor!" There was a scurry of movement on the bandstand as the cardinal turned back. "May my humble house serve as your court, Your Majesty. I am yours to command."

She stared at him discomfitingly, impatiently tapping her foot. The cardinal turned and shouted again, "Hurry with the bandstand! Make it ready at once!"

"Ready for the queen!" called someone.

"This way, Your Majesty," announced Rohan with relief. He stepped aside, indicating the bandstand with a flourish.

THE MAGICIAN INTERVENES

The queen started through the ballroom and the crowd cleared a path before her, staring silently and making bows and curtsies. She climbed the bandstand and found her chair, and her ladies-in-waiting took positions around her. Guardsmen aligned themselves on either side at attention. Nobody moved, and there wasn't a sound.

"How dull you all look!" cried Marie Antoinette. "And I thought this might prove interesting!" She waited, her eyes roving over the crowd. Suddenly they flickered with interest, for a swarthy man with a head like a lion had stepped into the path left by her passage. A maroon cape covered his dark full dress suit, and his black eyes glistened. He walked slowly forward and stood before her, making a slight flourish with his cape.

"I will undertake to entertain Your Majesty. I am Count Alesandro di Cagliostro, privy to the secret teachings of the centuries. Under my hand and eye, objects return to nothingness, from nothingness objects arise." He made a gesture with his hands, extending the palms, and a bowl of strawberries appeared within them. There was a gasp from the crowd, and Cagliostro laid the strawberries at the queen's feet. "For Your Majesty. I am your humble servant."

The queen's laughter pealed across the room. "I would not have thought the dull Rohan to have such entertaining friends. Continue, magician. You interest me."

A relieved buzz of conversation arose from the crowd, and Cagliostro went to work. He materialized an orange, then a coconut, then a bowl full of dates, then six apples one after another, then a bowl full of cherries, then a melon, then another. All these he placed at the queen's feet, and as the mound of fruit grew before her, she first was seized with astonishment, then with a paroxysm of laugher. The entire ballroom laughed with her.

"Enough," she finally cried. "I could not eat so much fruit in a lifetime." She dried her eyes and prepared for further entertainment.

THE MAGICIAN'S WARNING

Cagliostro removed his cape, placed it on the floor, gestured above it, jerked it aside, and revealed a dazed white mouse. Again he placed his cape, again withdrew it, and there was a strutting cock. Once more he followed the same procedure, and this time exposed a ferocious weasel. Almost instantly a chase and fight sprang up amongst the animals. The crowd screamed and scurried.

The cock darted upon the scurrying mouse and killed it, then was set upon from behind by the weasel and killed in turn. The weasel scampered off. The queen sat forward on her chair with startled interest. Cagliostro watched her impassively, paying no attention to the uproar. Noise began to subside.

"I demonstrate with symbols, Your Majesty," he said. "The proud cock destroys the frightened mouse and is himself destroyed by the lurking weasel. Yet no one suspects the weasel, who works in darkness."

The queen had sobered now. Her eyes were narrow. "You intrigue me, magician. I had not suspected you were a philosopher also. Speak plainly."

"I am only a conjurer, Your Majesty. Surely the world of men is far more complex than the animal kingdom."

He swirled his cape again, and this time produced a bouquet

of lilacs and lilies. He handed it to the queen. "No flower in France is equal to the beauty of Your Majesty. Accept this humble gift as a token of my fealty."

Again the Queen softened as she took the flowers into her lap. Once more, she prepared to be entertained.

Now the movements of Cagliostro took on a half-maddened air. He caused a chair to disappear, then another. He ran a sword completely thorough himself, then caused the sword to vanish. He found a lady's undergarment in the pocket of a startled guardsman. A flame extended from his forehead, and he pinched it out with his fingers. He moved his hands over an imaginary keyboard, and there arose the sound of music. He caused a variety of hats to appear on the heads of startled ladies. A pale hand floated across the room and disappeared into his pocket. He suspended his cloak upon the air and sat upon its edge. With a pointing finger he materialized urns upon the ballroom floor. His eyes were wild now. The cloaked figure capering before the crowd seemed exploded out of some nether world. Finally he called a halt and stood motionless.

THE VISION OF
MARIE ANTOINETTE

"These are but minor powers, Your Majesty," he stated. "They token only my grasp of secrets denied most men. But given me also are those higher powers by which the future is revealed. Is Your Majesty interested in such a demonstration?"

Marie Antoinette seemed dazed, but she managed a smile. "You wish to tell my fortune?"

"If the queen pleases." He exhibited a small mirror.

"Your skill is great, magician. It almost frightens me. But the future is in the hands of God. No man has access to it."

"Let Her Majesty test my art. She shall behold the future with her own eyes, and shall not have to take my word."

The queen smiled indulgently. "You presume upon your talents, monsieur. No such thing is possible."

"It is up to Your Majesty, of course. Is the queen afraid of her future?" He held out the mirror.

Marie Antoinette impatiently extended her hand for the mirror, but Cagliostro withheld it. "A word of warning. To all mortals the future is changeable. It is within the power of each man to create his own. But whoever gazes upon this mirror and sees his future revealed can no longer escape it. He is bound to it forever, no matter his will or his actions. Does Your Majesty care to look?"

Now the queen was truly impatient, and she imperiously beckoned for the mirror. Cagliostro stepped forward, and their eyes seemed locked on some iron-bound plane. He handed her the mirror, but for a moment her eyes could not escape his. Then she lowered them to the mirror.

Over her face came an expression of horror, and she rose from her chair with her hand clasped to her throat. Her flowers fell to the floor, and her mouth sagged open, eyes rolled back. She screamed. Then she dropped the mirror and fainted, falling in a crumpled heap to the floor.

A shout went up from the crowd, and in the resulting confusion I suddenly found myself confronted by Cagliostro. Glittering eyes burned into mine. "You have seen the beginning of cataclysmic events," he said, "and I am the cause of them. The people of France will not be long rising. They will burn the Bastille and overthrow the monarchy. Blood will flow among the aristocrats. Neither king nor queen will be spared. Soon we will rule France. Before long, the world. Once again, I invite you to join us. Simply sign this pledge, and power and riches are yours." He thrust a paper in my hand then, swirling his cape, swept from view. The uproar faded.

. . . Dazedly, I looked around me. I was seated in the living room of my own apartment, dressed in my normal attire. Daylight shone through the windows, and I had apparently been asleep in my chair.

Had it all been a dream then? Had it been a mere vision that had seized my imagination?

No, it was more than that. For clutched in my hand was the paper that Cagliostro had thrust there. I opened it and read:

THE SATANIC CREED

"Eyes that fall upon this creed forsake allegiance to all men, else dwell eternally in limbo! There is no right or wrong or up or down or length or breadth or even time. Nothing else exists except illusion.

"Few have the heart and mind to take this lonely path despite its power. Only tested eyes behold these words. You have passed severest trials yet the greatest lies before you. Should you fail, you are ashes, and your hopes will all be dead.

"You must learn to laugh at what the world calls great misfortune. You must learn to weep at what inspires it to laugh. You must look behind each name for the existence of its opposite. You must strike your judgement dead and hold opinion in abeyance.

"Nothing on this earth is true, except it is decided. Remember!

"Know then that the souls of men aspire to conclusions. These faint hearts have not the strength to tolerate a flux. All conflicts issue from opinions of believers. Yet the world puts highest value on sincerity.

"Each hallowed ground is so decreed because of pocketbook or power. Masses thrive on catchwords and on rites. Minds are locked within their grooves by habit. Repetition dulls the power to perceive. There is no end to domain over others when one is freed from judgement of the right.

"A Satanist must be empty, does that surprise you? He must have neither self nor soul or even recognize his name. He must become the time and place, the movement of events. He must become the tide itself to take advantage of the shore. Empty of goals, devoid of desire, he fits the pieces into place where they best fall.

"Work with dark, it is your ally, for from the dark illusion springs. Seeing is believing to the soul enmeshed in senses, and conviction by illusion is the subtlety of art. In light there is great danger for in light some men may think and may even be emboldened to voice their silent thoughts. The uninitiated think the hand is swifter than the eye. By such beliefs you win your power. The truth is this: The eye sees light, and light is swifter than the hand. The trick is mind. It forms from light what it expects. The Satanist suggests.

THE FALLEN PRINCE

"What is paid attention to is all the mind can see. Establish bit and bridle on attention. Rein it right and left and up and down, turn it back and forward, do your work where it is not, and it perceives a miracle. Make the most of this illusion. Claim heaven's powers.

"Know this: The Satanist who entertains, and only that, defiles the art. This fate awaits him. He shall wither to his bones, with staring eye and crooked back, and lose his skill but not his life, and beg in streets forevermore.

"There is a secret which at last the expert Satanist attains, after mastering the mechanics of illusion. It dwells in understanding what the mind is. The secret waits for him who rids himself of all desire and has no goal but mastery of his art. Then he enters minds of others and becomes them at his will. There is a veiled telling of this method, but each must unravel it himself. Who perceives it achieves the Satanist's highest powers, which are to rule the movements of the earth.

"Swear now you will abandon all desire! Swear to forsake that self you call your own! Pledge to abandon judgement ever after! Pledge to have no goal except your art! Consecrate yourself to indirection! Swear to tolerate the ambiguity of fate! Keep attention from the hand that does the work! Before men claim yourself a god! Suggest to lead, lead to suggest, that is your art from this day forth. Now swear!

"Sign this pledge and stand among the gods."

Carefully I folded the paper. So Cagliostro had been Caligastia, deposed Planetary Prince and Vice-Regent of Lucifer. And still he operated on the earth, promising immortality and personal power and making slaves of men. But this time there would be no Reign of Terror or Age of Darkness, because this time the world be prepared.

The Master Plan 18

There was a knock at the door, and when I opened it I found myself confronted by the man in the violet jacket. He entered without ceremony and took a seat, then he nodded at the paper which I still held in my hand. "If you sign that, all will be as he promised. You will have power and riches beyond your dreams. Many men in your position have accepted his offer. What have you decided?

"There is no happiness keeping people in the dark."

"The way of light is narrow and uncertain. It is sometimes hard and difficult. And there are no guarantees."

"Nevertheless I prefer it."

"Then give me the paper.

I did as he asked and watched as he burned it. His eyes seemed more penetrating than ever.

THE SCROLLS OF ATLANTIS

"Our pledge is simple," he said. "It is merely to shed light on the dark. To do so we have preserved Seven Sacred Scrolls from the days of ancient Atlantis. The first of these I now entrust to you. As you continue to progress, the others will be entrusted successively." He withdrew from his pocket a parchment scroll and placed it in my hand.

"This first scroll signifies Truth," he explained. "Truth is balance, as you have discovered, and it is the greatest power in the universe. With the scroll in your possession, you will make further progress and discover more of life's secrets.

"The second scroll signifies the Fountain of Youth, the third the Garden of Eden, the fourth the Cure for All Evil, the fifth the Elixir of Life, the sixth the Keys to the Kingdom, and the seventh the Source of All Knowledge. Each of these scrolls will be given to you as time passes, and you will make them available to others who seek the Truth. Those who wish personal guidance to the Philosopher's Stone will be admitted to Atlantis University where they will undergo training as leaders of the New Age which will prepare the way for the Second Coming of Christ. If successful, they will be awarded the Philosopher's Stone and the title of Master of Balance.

THE STANDARDS OF ECOLOGY

"The trademark of Atlantis University may be placed on products and services that meet the highest standards of ecology — those which help prevent aging and promote better health, increase freedom and develop security, make people happy and expand their awareness, and help one and all to the Source of All Knowledge. You may place the trademark right now on alpha meters and theta meters, provided they meet performance standards. A third product will be given you shortly, and it will be a variation of the Tesla coil, with a cosmic coil on one side and a resonator on the other. A subject placed between coil and resonator will experience mental and physical rejuvenation, for the DNA memory storage of each of his body cells will be restored to its original electrical potential, and the RNA messenger will begin producing youthful cells.

THE MASTERS OF BALANCE

"Eventually, ecologists will restore the earth to its original Edenic state. You will see the beginning of this, but before it reaches fruition, you will be called to other work. Gradually, you will recover the memory of your sojourns at Agarthi and Shamballah, and you will realize that many times you have sided with the Forces of Imbalance and that is why, old soul that you are, you still are bound to the Wheel of Reincarnation. Before you can admitted to Ultima Thule, you first must confront the Magicians and Warriors of Shamballah and prove yourself invulnerable to their offers of power. Should you be successful in that undertaking, then you must confront the Priests of Agarthi and overcome their offers of security. Should you again be successful, you will be admitted to Ultima Thule as a Master of Balance of the 76th Degree. Our selves then will become one — yet we will remain separate to the end of eternity. That is the mystery of Creation.

THE PYRAMID OF ATLANTIS

"Before long you will be locked in a personal confrontation with Caligastia. He is a being of such power that he has easily destroyed the truth many times before, but this time he may not be able to because a great many people have glimpsed the light. However, he may try to destroy you. I will do my utmost to provide protection.

"Even though you learn where Caligastia is, you must not point him out to the world, for that could easily divide the earth into warring camps and prevent the arrival of the New Age. Rather, you will patiently describe the Forces of Balance and the Forces of Imbalance and allow each person to decide for himself.

"Caligastia plunged the planet into darkness by trapping a powerful fire being beneath the Great Pyramid of Atlantis. When the Lucifer Rebellion broke out and Caligastia had decided to join it, the earth was visited by Fahz, an Ascended Master who immediately discerned Caligastia's intention to defect. Caligastia, aware that he was found out, lured Fahz beneath the pyramid and there imprisoned him. However, he hadn't reckoned with the power of Fahz who gathered all his energy and propelled himself through the earth to emerge at Easter Island where he escaped through the gravity warp. Great statues were later constructed there to commemorate the event. But the earth was affected disastrously.

THE EARTH'S IMBALANCE

"As a result of Fahz passing through the core of the earth, the polarities of the planet switched, and the earth turned over. Tremendous calamaties ensued. Tropical regions were subjected to freezing temperatures. Floods swept the lands. Earthquakes shook the continents. To make matters worse, the planet eventually righted itself, and the floods, earthquakes, and swift temperature changes were repeated. This series of catastrophes eventually sank Atlantis beneath the sea. In addition, conditions were made extremely difficult for a high civilization to rise again, for the series of calamities had separated the earth's magnetic pole from its geographical pole due to an angular displacement of the core from the plenum, and the earth's inhabitants could receive only spasmodic contact with the Master Mind.

This suited the purposes of Caligastia well. He now seemed assured of keeping the earth's inhabitants in ignorance. When it was discovered that possession of the earth by the Forces of Imbalance was necessary to prevent Lucifer's Headquarters — the star system of Deneb — from being ejected from the galaxy, the planet now known as Venus was sent into the solar system to insure continuation of the imblance that had overtaken the earth.

"Caligastia was made Lucifer's Vice-Regent — third in command — serving directly under the Regent, Satan. Sad is the case of this fallen Planetary Prince, once the noblest of beings, who over the centuries has restorted to the foulest murder and corruption in order to maintain his position of power. If ever a being deserved to forfeit his chance for salvation, Caligastia has earned it, but he too will be given the chance to start all over again. Such is the loving kindness of the Universal Father.

REALIGNING THE POLES

"But it is perhaps Lucifer who inspires the greatest sympathy.

Once known throughout the galaxy as the Bearer of Light, this great being has isolated himself from the source of his brilliance and has become known instead as the Prince of Darkness. He has long repented of his decision, but since he would have to begin the millenia of ascension all over again, starting from the lowliest of microbes, he cannot bring himself to abandon his vain and futile dream. With nothing to look forward to but descent and bored by his inability to evolve further, he is the best of all possible examples of the Faustian bargain.

"By building giant pyramids in the gravitational warps of Los Angeles, Tenri, Stonehenge, Bimini, Easter Island, and Peking, these can be used, along with the Great Pyramid of Egypt, to house thrust devices for realigning the earth's magnetic pole with its geographical pole. At the proper time, instructions for building these devices will be disclosed, as well many other wonderful devices, such as a mechanical blood platelet for interplanetary and intergalactical travel and for the instantaneous transfer of anything or anyone to anyplace or anytime. By then conditions on earth will have been restored to their Edenic state.

THE LIVING TRUTH

"The present Great Pyramid of Egypt can be reactivated by outfitting it with an ascension device and replacing the missing caprock with Philosopher's Stone. It then can be tuned into the Master Mind and later used to house a thrust device for realigning the earth's poles."

He arose and tapped his walking stick on the floor, signalling departure. "Though you know my name, I prefer that you identify me only as the Man in the Violet Jacket. You have learned a number of my incarnations so you realize that I have been the Lawgiver of the Jews, the Father of the Christ, the Discoverer of America, the Author of Shakespeare, the Father of our Country, and the Liberator of the Slaves. The truth of these lives has been distorted by the Forces of Imbalance, but that truth will be made known again. Now I must go. I will visit you soon and will be instantly available if you need me." He extended his hand, and I took it warmly.

"Your eyes have been opened," he said. "Now you clearly see the Forces of Balance and the Forces of Imbalance. Always side with the Forces of Balance, never with the Forces of Imbalance. That is the Secret of Life."

At the door he had a final word. "Distilled water is the only compound in nature that is perfectly balanced and so always sides with the Forces of Balance. To avoid the Forces of Imbalance, use distilled water."

I watched his passage across the patio. The elegant figure in the violet jacket caused not the slightest stir among those who were sunning themselves. Nobody perceived the magnificent being who passed among them.

THE END

A free brochure on the Mind Power Courses of the University is available on request.

Other books by U. S. Andersen available through Atlantis University:

Three Magic Words . . . . $5.50 postpaid
Secret of Secrets . . . . 4.50 postpaid
Magic in Your Mind . . . . 4.50 postpaid
Success Cybernetics. . . . . 4.50 postpaid
Secret Power of the Pyramids . . . . . 4.50 postpaid

MELVIN POWERS SELF-IMPROVEMENT LIBRARY

HYPNOTISM

___ ADVANCED TECHNIQUES OF HYPNOSIS *Melvin Powers*	2.00
___ BRAINWASHING AND THE CULTS *Paul A. Verdier, Ph.D.*	3.00
___ CHILDBIRTH WITH HYPNOSIS *William S. Kroger, M.D.*	5.00
___ HOW TO SOLVE Your Sex Problems with Self-Hypnosis *Frank S. Caprio, M.D.*	5.00
___ HOW TO STOP SMOKING THRU SELF-HYPNOSIS *Leslie M. LeCron*	3.00
___ HOW TO USE AUTO-SUGGESTION EFFECTIVELY *John Duckworth*	3.00
___ HOW YOU CAN BOWL BETTER USING SELF-HYPNOSIS *Jack Heise*	3.00
___ HOW YOU CAN PLAY BETTER GOLF USING SELF-HYPNOSIS *Jack Heise*	3.00
___ HYPNOSIS AND SELF-HYPNOSIS *Bernard Hollander, M.D.*	3.00
___ HYPNOTISM *(Originally published in 1893)* *Carl Sextus*	5.00
___ HYPNOTISM & PSYCHIC PHENOMENA *Simeon Edmunds*	4.00
___ HYPNOTISM MADE EASY *Dr. Ralph Winn*	3.00
___ HYPNOTISM MADE PRACTICAL *Louis Orton*	3.00
___ HYPNOTISM REVEALED *Melvin Powers*	2.00
___ HYPNOTISM TODAY *Leslie LeCron and Jean Bordeaux, Ph.D.*	5.00
___ MODERN HYPNOSIS *Lesley Kuhn & Salvatore Russo, Ph.D.*	5.00
___ NEW CONCEPTS OF HYPNOSIS *Bernard C. Gindes, M.D.*	5.00
___ NEW SELF-HYPNOSIS *Paul Adams*	4.00
___ POST-HYPNOTIC INSTRUCTIONS—Suggestions for Therapy *Arnold Furst*	3.00
___ PRACTICAL GUIDE TO SELF-HYPNOSIS *Melvin Powers*	3.00
___ PRACTICAL HYPNOTISM *Philip Magonet, M.D.*	3.00
___ SECRETS OF HYPNOTISM *S. J. Van Pelt, M.D.*	3.00
___ SELF-HYPNOSIS A Conditioned-Response Technique *Laurence Sparks*	5.00
___ SELF-HYPNOSIS Its Theory, Technique & Application *Melvin Powers*	3.00
___ THERAPY THROUGH HYPNOSIS *edited by Raphael H. Rhodes*	4.00

MARRIAGE, SEX & PARENTHOOD

___ ABILITY TO LOVE *Dr. Allan Fromme*	5.00
___ ENCYCLOPEDIA OF MODERN SEX & LOVE TECHNIQUES *Macandrew*	5.00
___ GUIDE TO SUCCESSFUL MARRIAGE *Drs. Albert Ellis & Robert Harper*	5.00
___ HOW TO RAISE AN EMOTIONALLY HEALTHY, HAPPY CHILD *A. Ellis*	4.00
___ SEX WITHOUT GUILT *Albert Ellis, Ph.D.*	5.00
___ SEXUALLY ADEQUATE MALE *Frank S. Caprio, M.D.*	3.00

METAPHYSICS & OCCULT

___ BOOK OF TALISMANS, AMULETS & ZODIACAL GEMS *William Pavitt*	5.00
___ CONCENTRATION—A Guide to Mental Mastery *Mouni Sadhu*	4.00
___ CRITIQUES OF GOD *Edited by Peter Angeles*	7.00
___ EXTRA-TERRESTRIAL INTELLIGENCE—The First Encounter	6.00
___ FORTUNE TELLING WITH CARDS *P. Foli*	3.00
___ HANDWRITING ANALYSIS MADE EASY *John Marley*	3.00
___ HANDWRITING TELLS *Nadya Olyanova*	5.00
___ HOW TO INTERPRET DREAMS, OMENS & FORTUNE TELLING SIGNS *Gettings*	3.00
___ HOW TO UNDERSTAND YOUR DREAMS *Geoffrey A. Dudley*	3.00
___ ILLUSTRATED YOGA *William Zorn*	3.00
___ IN DAYS OF GREAT PEACE *Mouni Sadhu*	3.00
___ LSD—THE AGE OF MIND *Bernard Roseman*	2.00
___ MAGICIAN—His Training and Work *W. E. Butler*	3.00
___ MEDITATION *Mouni Sadhu*	5.00
___ MODERN NUMEROLOGY *Morris C. Goodman*	3.00
___ NUMEROLOGY—ITS FACTS AND SECRETS *Ariel Yvon Taylor*	3.00
___ NUMEROLOGY MADE EASY *W. Mykian*	3.00
___ PALMISTRY MADE EASY *Fred Gettings*	3.00
___ PALMISTRY MADE PRACTICAL *Elizabeth Daniels Squire*	4.00
___ PALMISTRY SECRETS REVEALED *Henry Frith*	3.00
___ PROPHECY IN OUR TIME *Martin Ebon*	2.50
___ PSYCHOLOGY OF HANDWRITING *Nadya Olyanova*	5.00

The books listed above can be obtained from your book dealer or directly from
Melvin Powers. When ordering, please remit 50¢ per book postage & handling.
Send for our free illustrated catalog of self-improvement books.

Melvin Powers
12015 Sherman Road, No. Hollywood, California 91605